The Conwy Valley
& The Lands Of History

K. Mortimer Hart ARICS MRTPI

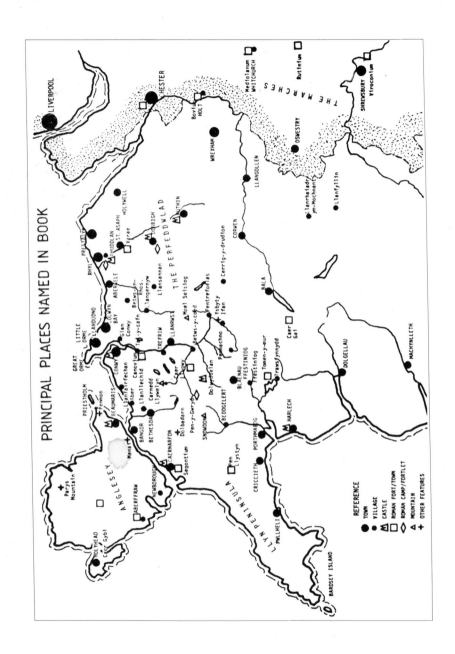

PRINCIPAL PLACES NAMED IN BOOK

REFERENCE

- ● TOWN
- • VILLAGE
- ☐ CASTLE
- ⬚ ROMAN FORT/TOWN
- ◇ ROMAN CAMP/FORTLET
- △ MOUNTAIN
- ✛ OTHER FEATURES

Previous page: Pont Rhyd-y-gynnen ("Roman Bridge" see p130)

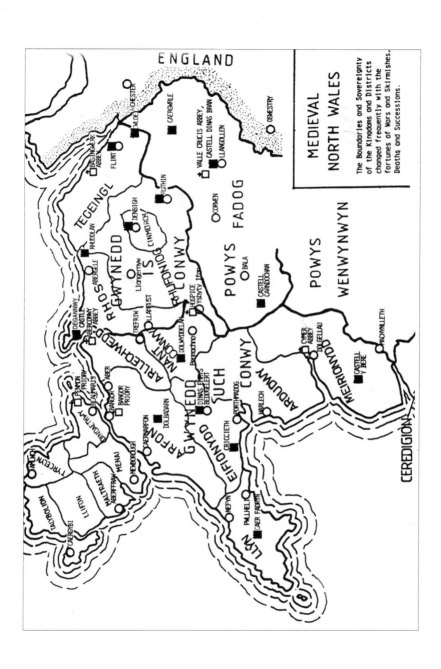

MEDIEVAL
NORTH WALES

The Boundaries and Sovereignty
of the Kingdoms and Districts
changed frequently with the
fortunes of Wars and Skirmishes,
Deaths and Successions.

ENGLAND

CHESTER
FLINT
CAERGWRLE
VALLE CRUCIS ABBEY,
CASTELL DINAS BRAN
LLANGOLLEN
OSWESTRY
BASINGWERK ABBEY
TEGEINGL
RHUDDLAN
DENBIGH
RUTHIN
CORWEN
CINMERCH
POWYS FADOG
ABERGELE
RHOS
GWYNEDD
IS
Llangernyw
CONWY
RHUFONIOG
BALA
POWYS
CASTELL CARNDOCHAN
DEGANWWY CASTELL
ABERCONWY ABBEY
TREFRIW
LLANRWST
HOSPICE YSBYTY IFAN
ARLLECHWEDD
NANT CONWY
DOLWYDDELAN
Bermotho
POWYS WENWYNWYN
CYMER ABBEY
DOLGELLAU
MOCHNLLETH
ABER
BEAUMARIS
PENMON PRIORY
GWYNEDD
UCH
CONWY
ARDUDWY
CASTELL Y BERE
MEIRIONNYDD
BANGOR PRIORY
DINAS EMRYS BEDDGELERT
DOLBADARN
DINORWIG
CAERNARFON
PENMORFA
CRICCIETH
EIFIONYDD
PORTHMADOG
HARLECH
MENAI
ABERFFRAW
MALTRAETH
NEFYN
LLEYN
PWLHELI
LLIFON
TALYBOLION
CAERGYBI
TYRCELYN
CAER FALARN
CEREDIGION

Published by

Ashbourne Hall, Cokayne Ave
Ashbourne, Derbyshire DE6 1EJ England
Tel: (01335) 347349 Fax: (01335) 347303
e-mail: landmark@clara.net
web site: www.landmarkpublishing.co.uk

2nd edition

ISBN 1 84306 114 7

Publisher's note: Although the University of Wales' Gazetter of Place Names is
followed in this book, that authority uses "Degannwy". Local convention still
uses "Deganwy", which is followed here.

Printed by Gutenberg Press, Malta

Design & reproduction by Simon Hartshorne

Text updated by Eryl Orwain

Cover captions:

Front cover: Tŷ Mawr, near Penmachno, now in the hands of the National Trust
Back cover top: The Inn, Ro-wen
Back cover middle: Tŷ Mawr
Back cover bottom: The Cromlech above the road over Bwlch-y-ddeufaen

Contents

Author's Note

It would be possible to write ten volumes the size of this, and only touch upon the history of the Conwy Valley area, its places and its people, so that it has been necessary to make a somewhat random choice of what to include, and what to omit, and some might wish the choice to have differed in this or that respect.

Of what has been included, every effort has been made to ensure that it is correct, and very little has not been derived from more than one source. Where some uncertainty exists, this has been indicated, but in dealing with history, as is here done to substantial extent, opinions exist and differ, and new information comes to light which changes beliefs which were previously firmly held. Some such matters give rise to controversy, but I have not for that reason avoided them, for such controversy can often add to the interest of the subject, or lead to more certain knowledge being produced.

Names are often a problem, spelling differing from age to age. The policy here has been to adopt that spelling which appears to have been the original, and to keep to that in all references made, as Caer Rhun, now more commonly Caerhun, but in earlier times Caer Hen.

Where old pack trails are involved, there is no doubt that they crossed and crisscrossed in such a way that alternative routes could be followed, perhaps according to weather, or war, or political or religious fields of influence. This generation has a multitude of lanes and tracks, and since the population of this area has in the past exceeded that which lives here now, it is not surprising that many paths and routes were used, and it is most unlikely that we have yet found all the roads which the early Celts constructed (for they built many), or those improved or laid down by the Romans — they must, for example, have had roads from Canovium to the copper mines and look-out posts on the Great Orme and to Caer Leion.

Modern research has shown that the early Celts did not live in caves or huts of mud. The Romans did not just pass through, or live reclusive lives within the tiny confines of their forts; they lived here for 300 years, and they had their wives and their families, and they enjoyed a social life with the Celts, who were their cultural equals and with whom they intermarried, and who held offices of public administration and command. They had their farms and their homes, their stables and their chariots. Those who passed along their roads were not all military and trading convoys, but included families and retinues from Chester and other towns, making their way to the coastal villas of Cardigan Bay for holidays, who stayed overnight at local hostelries and villas just the same as those on holiday do today.

The post Roman and Medieval Welsh of Gwynedd were not barbaric tribes of no account, but were educated Celtic/Roman stock, who did not suffer as did the people of England the full impact of invasion by pagans and barbarians from the north of Europe.[1] They had and kept a history of high civilisation going back much further than that of the invasive Normans, who sought their military submission but were glad to accept the hands of their sons and daughters in marriage. They were here in great numbers, and they used and maintained the roads and tracks, largely the same as those of the Romans, the earlier Celts, and maybe those of the even earlier Iberians.

In other parts, where timber did not grow on the scale which it reached here, and where the Celtic crafts of working that material were not so high, building in those far-off days was carried out in stone, or bricks, or other materials which do not decay. Here some fine buildings were built in stone, as those of Caer Rhun, the huge round-houses of the hills, Maenan Abbey and many others, but when disused, collapsed; the stone was robbed, to build the miles and miles of walls to keep the sheep in bounds, to build new houses and farms, so that, as at Maenan Abbey, where the stone was used to repair Caernarfon Castle, even the foundations were dug up and taken. But other fine buildings were of timber, as in more recent times have been those of America's deep south; when they grow old, perhaps collapse, timber rots, or makes good winter fires, or can be salvaged for another job, so that in time no more remains by which to judge. Whole towns in that way disappear.

In ancient genealogy it is not always easy to be sure who was the son of a father, largely because sons were usually sent to be brought up in the houses of peers or those of higher rank at such an early age that they were often identified more with those who fostered them than with their parents, and not infrequently acquired loyalty to their fostering families which exceeded those to their own. Beli, for example, was most probably a son of Einion ab Owain ab Einion (but he is often regarded as being the eldest son of Rhun ap Maelgwn) and therefore Rhun's cousin twice removed. It matters little in that case, for all were of the direct stock of Cunedda 'Wledig, and it was the generations of Beli who ruled in Gwynedd to the time of Llewelyn the Last, and by part female lines via Gwladus Ddu, daughter of Llywelyn Fawr, who married Ralph de Mortimer, and via Susanna, daughter of throne of England[2] and redeemed the bardic prophecy.[3]

But I shall have made errors, and if a reader knows of some, I shall be most pleased to hear, if only to discourse on differing sources of information — many a reader will know more than I of this or that.

I wish most sincerely to thank all those who have, knowingly or unknowingly, provided the essential parts of the jigsaw to make up the picture here presented, including those who over a period of many centuries have committed their thoughts and their knowledge to words, in books, in letters, on monuments, in some cases even in advertisements.

Particularly I thank those whose modern research has given us much clearer understanding of the people who were here before the Romans came, and formed the main part of the forebears of the Welsh who took over as the Romans gradually departed, a process which took place not suddenly, but smoothly over a period of two centuries or so.

Perhaps those to whom Wales is home will bear with me if I just explain for our friends and visitors that "ap" between two names means "son of', and to some extent still is Welsh usage in place of surnames. Likewise "ferch" or "v" signifies daughter of. In Scotland and in Ireland they used "Mc", "Mac", "Ua" and "0", and the Normans used "fitz", derived from "fils". In England the Nordic/Scandinavian influence produced "sun" and "son".

K. Mortimer Hart

1. *A history of the English Church. A.D.M. Spence 1900.*
2. *See family tree page 249. 3. See page 252.*

The Conwy Valley is a place of beauty; the name and the description are synonymous. It is a place of history, a history which went back thousands of years before the Romans came, or the Celts before them. In its widest terms it must include the valleys of its tributaries, the Lledr, the Machno and the Llugwy, and many a smaller stream, which we shall visit.

Minerals have been worked, wars have been fought, roads and railways have been built; the land has been farmed, and it has been pillaged and burnt; forests have grown and been destroyed, and new forests planted. Dyffryn Conwy, to give it its Welsh name, has suffered the depredations of progress — yet despite all this, and despite the smallness of its scale, it has overall remained unchanged throughout the centuries.

Whether he were to land again in the valley of the Conwy itself, or of one of its tributaries, a centurion of Rome, or a Prince of Gwynedd, would not be lost. A stone-age man from the axe factory behind Tal-y-fan would look out over the land from his high abode and recognise all he saw, though he might wonder at the disappearance of so many of the trees that he knew, for it was said in earlier times that a squirrel could swing from branch to branch over the length and breadth of the Valley without once touching the ground.

Unlike the belt of the coastal towns, through which the new Expressway road approaches, there is in the Valley areas no such mass of development that even the contours of the land are lost to sight. The valleys have escaped the vast mineral waste heaps of southern Wales, and the great slate heaps of so much of Gwynedd. There are still more cattle than cars, more sheep than people, and green grass and heather prevail.

Coming through the urban sprawl, after Colwyn Bay the coastal road from the east passes through Nant Semper. The Romans came to Britain in A.D.43, and within two years they were at Chester. It was to be another sixteen years before they advanced as far as this, and when they did, Sempronius, second in command to Suetonius Paulinus, the Governor of Britain, tried to proceed too rapidly through the land of the Ordovices, and here in this little pass he

was killed. The Celts in the fort of Dinerth on Bryn Euryn on the north, and other forces on the slopes to the south, swept down on the foreign invaders, and wiped out the whole of the force. Many another ambush of troops and travellers is said to have occurred in this once forbidding place, where now two roads and rail compete for space.

Top inset: The Pin Mill, Bodnant. Bottom inset: Roman Trirem on Conwy

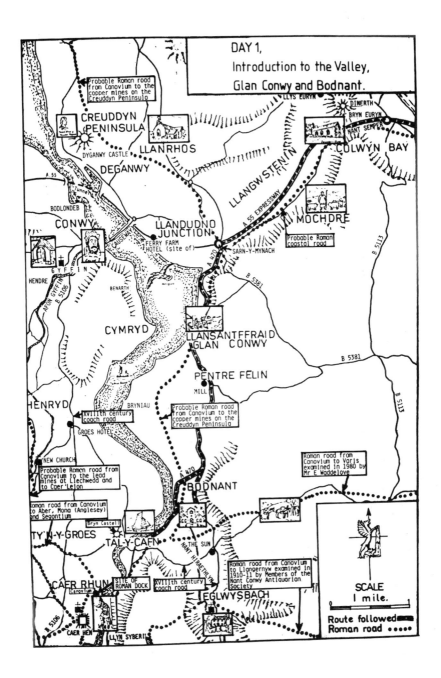

DAY 1,
Introduction to the Valley,
Glan Conwy and Bodnant.

This is not yet part of the Conwy Valley, but it would be unfortunate to ignore the northern slopes of Bryn Euryn where there are now estates of houses, but where eight hundred years ago or rather less was built Llys Euryn, the mansion of Ednyfed Fychan, Seneschal of Gwynedd in the days of Llywelyn Fawr, Prince of all of Wales. Of both of these much will arise in travels through the Conwy Valley, and from Ednyfed Fychan was descended in direct male line one Henry Tudur, who was to be victor at Bosworth Field, and become the King of England — but also, as Sir John Wynn of Gwydir wrote of one who he claimed as an ancestor, *"Iorwerth was the father of Llywelyn the Great, and ancestor (through the female line) of the Royal Family of Tudur"*. Ednyfed's house was large by any standards, though not much remains. More stood in the early part of this last century, when the outlook was still in part as it had been in Llywelyn's time, a vista to the coasts of Anglesey, the Isle of Man and Lancashire, with a foreground of marsh and pasture and the Great Orme and the Little Orme. From the ruins of Edwardian days, when the walls were still a dozen feet above the ground in parts, it appears that to the south it had a frontage of 140 feet at least, some 43 metres, and in the western part of that, which may or may not have been a major part of the whole, there was a hall some 66 feet long and 35 feet wide, with a great fireplace which had been restored for use in the nineteenth century; though the house was then in use it had been divided into two or more dwellings and many parts of the original had been demolished.

This is part of the ancient township and parish of Dinerth, in the Rhos Cantref of old, lands of the Conway family in Tudor times, and Edward Conway, High Sheriff of Denbighshire, a descendant of Ednyfed Fychan by his son Tudur, is known to have been living at Llys Euryn in *1565:* but it was Ednyfed Fychan who was destined to become of importance not just to the Conwy Valley, not even just to Gwynedd, but to Britain and indeed the world when his descendant Henry ousted the last of the Normans from the English throne.

Through Nant Semper the road comes into the area of Llangystennin, named after St Cystennin (St Constantine),[4] son of Elen of Arfon, and of Macsen Wledig who went from these parts to be Emperor of Rome. This way once passed the Conwy River, to sweep to the sea by the Little Orme. In those days, the legends say, to the west lay the great cantref of Gwaelod, the fruitful lands which stretched from the Conwy river to Priestholm (Puffin Island), all that is now the Great Orme, the Conwy Sands, the Dutchman's Bank and the Lafan Sands, and more perhaps between. Here, we are told, at one time lived Helig ap Glanawg,[5] whose palace lay between the Great Orme and Penmaenmawr, but all his land was submerged in a great inundation of the sea in the sixth century. If that be true — and many insist it is — then it must give rise to the question why Suetonius Paulinus took his great army across the Carneddau mountains, and not across the plain. Most likely the legend is true but the dates are not, and the inundation occurred before Paulinus came.

An area of great history, Llangystennin is not in the valleys to which this

Cistercian Monk

book is directed. Of its lushness in the past, in the valley bottom much is now lost, buried beneath the rubbish of the twentieth century, the discard of a wasteful age, which now itself is hidden beneath factories and offices and roads. Here also are estates of houses, gas works, cemetery and railway, the road of the past, and now the great modern highway.

Here is Mochdre — 'moch dre', the place of the pigs. A hundred years before Conwy Castle was built, in the days when Deganwy [6] Castle on the Creuddyn Peninsula to the north of here had for seven hundred years at least stood supreme on the eastern side of the river estuary, Cistercian monks built a convent on the western side. First they came from Strata Florida in mid-west Wales to Rhedynog-felin near Caernarfon in 1186 or thereabouts, but that, it seems, was not to their liking, for within a year or so they were on the banks of the Conwy, almost opposite Deganwy castle. There they settled, and having in 1198 been granted a charter and a grant of land from Llywelyn Fawr, they built the first great Aberconwy Abbey. It was here at Mochdre that they kept their pigs, to feed themselves, their visitors and their servants. Some would say otherwise, that it was here that Gwydion and his eleven companions rested a night when they returned through the Cantref of Rhos with the twelve pigs which they had tricked from Pryderi the son of Pwyll of the New Tribes.[7] Here was one of the early Calvinistic Methodist Chapels, but the present building dates but from 1832.

This great new road is the fourth to be built through the coastal belt. The Celts built the first, perhaps in wood. The Romans rebuilt it, no doubt in stone, it is said at the rate of a mile a day. From the time of Edward I it deteriorated until a new toll road was built in the eighteenth century, the road which Telford improved. This most recent road intrudes into the landscape with its concrete and its size as its predecessors did not, but it serves to speed the traffic which before was often delayed.

This monster in a tiny scene has produced one visual gain. The first view of the Conwy Valley and its backcloth of hills when seen from the Telford road was one of note and great magnificence.

This road is on a different line, so that the view as now first seen is one of even greater impact, and beyond Mochdre the eyes are drawn from the drabness of this last century, the walls and the roofs, the tarmac and the concrete, to a glimpse of the Conwy Valley itself, the river just becoming visible; and beyond, the peaks of Tal-y-fan and Drum, of Carnedd Llywelyn and Carnedd Dafydd, like the waves of the sea, but each wave higher than the one before.

The route to the Valley is down a slip-road to a great new roundabout, taking the traveller out of that part of northern Wales, the Perfeddwlad, which the Romans, the English and the Normans in turn occupied from time to time, and into the parts which have never been really conquered, by the Romans,

11

the English, or even the Celts themselves.

Buried now beneath these works, the roundabout to which we have come, lies the Sarn-y-mynach, the Monk's Causeway, built by hand eight hundred years ago by the Aberconwy Monks as passage for themselves and their visitors over the marshes of the Afon Ganol, those same marshes which for countless years had helped to protect the Creuddyn Peninsula, the stone age and Celtic camps of the Great Orme, and the Castles of Deganwy.

Turning south to another, smaller, roundabout, and then going right, the route to follow leaves the stark modernity, to sense the peace to come in the real Conwy Valley. It lies along the gently curving A470 between tree-clad hillside on the left, and low-lying meadows on the right, to emerge to a further example of views in store. Stretching west is the great inner basin of the river, now sadly disfigured at all but the highest tides by *Spartina Anglica*, the grass of estuaries and salt water most foolishly introduced here about the middle of the twentieth-century. For years it spread inexorably, foot by foot, yard by yard, acre by acre, ignored and uncontrolled by all authority, trapping the silt brought down by the river, raising the level of the channel bed, turning silver expanses of estuarial waters into unsightly mudbanks, encroaching on the feeding grounds of the wading birds, and eventually topping the level of the highest tides.

The chance arose with the commencement of construction of approaches to the Conwy Tunnel to remove the eyesore, but it was not taken: instead authorities constructed a great stone bund to enclose a massive area, to be infilled with silt from tunnel construction works and used, it seems, for some development which will no longer provide lush feeding grounds for wading birds, nor broad expanse of water to be gazed upon. So are well known scenes wantonly or uncaringly defaced. And now the cycle starts again outside the bund — the grass is there.

These unfortunate events have not as yet destroyed all view, and one can cross the road to the convenient layby, where the old road remained when the new was made, to lean on the roadside wall, as many have done before, and many will do again. To the west, across the waters are the massive walls of Conwy, castle and town, rising from the river, part hidden by bridges and works of an industrial age — but one may still imagine the awe with which they were viewed by any who in a bygone age proposed attack. All else around was wild countryside, marsh and river, long before there stretched out the causeway which Telford built, which now carries both road and rail.

This Afon Conwy has provided a formidable obstacle to travel throughout the ages. It slowed Suetonius Paulinus in his advance to Anglesey twenty centuries ago. It holds up progress of the North Wales Expressway road at this time, necessitating the construction of one of the major tunnelling works of any age and place. It stopped the advance of the Normans into Wales for two centuries and more.

In historical terms, bridges over the Conwy are modern at any points north of Llanrwst, eleven miles from the sea, where Pont Fawr has stood for 370 years, and bridges were there before. Till the end of the century before last, crossing of the river here had been by ferry. Its location was described by a writer of 1912 as follows —

> The coaches used to stay at the Ferry Farm Hotel, and the passengers and mail were transferred to boats. The "Old Ferry", where the ferryman lived was 50 yards higher up the river, and remained in existence until 1896, when it was removed by the Railway Company to make room for the new large signal box west of the Junction Station. The landing place at Conwy was a slip by the quay.[8]

The ferry was, therefore, over three-quarters of a mile north-west of the lay-by.

It was a very old ferry, dating from the days of the Abbey and before. In the days of Edward II it was a Royal Ferry, and an order was issued to the people of Conwy under which the boat was to be repaired, the inhabitants to pay eight marks a year towards the cost. In later times it passed into the hands of the Marl Estates. The Ferry Farm Hotel was demolished in 1898, and a token was then found, bearing the date 1788, for the payment of the ferry toll by carters for the Parys Mines Company of Anglesey.

That was not remarkable, for that company issued some 250 tons of penny tokens and about 50 tons of halfpenny tokens, as well as farthings between 1787 and 1793. There were 458 major types and nearly 2,000 types in all. While their mines were on Anglesey, their foundries were at Holywell in

The old ferry crossing the river Conwy

Flintshire, and there was much passage of men and goods between. But Parys Mountain, as it has been called for many generations, affected the Conwy Valley from the earliest times. The Iberians and the Celts mined copper there, as they did at the Great Orme, and the Phoenicians from what we now call Lebanon came there to trade. Coming to Anglesey they came to the Orme, and then to the Conwy river for lead and silver, maybe for cloth as well, and pearls.

Later Paulinus came, the Roman Governor of whom more will be heard, and in a later day Agricola, perhaps in part attracted by the fabled wealth of those Celtic mines.

It was Robert Parys in the time of Henry IV, Chamberlain of North Wales, who again exploited the copper near Amlwch in Anglesey, who gave his name to the Mountain, which was to prove so fickle in its yields that in the days of James I it would contribute greatly to the financial problems of Sir John Wynn of Gwydir.

It was not until March 2nd, 1768, that the Mountain really yielded to prospectors. The local manager had been instructed to close the mine, but in a final effort he instructed his men to split up into gangs, to prospect away from the area he had been appointed to work. On that day one of the gangs found solid copper ore at a depth of only seven feet, half a mile west of the earlier workings. The great era of the Parys Mines Company (Lord Uxbridge and the Rev. Edward Hughes) was about to start, and the Mona Mine Company (Lord Uxbridge on his own) was soon to follow. They were to employ 2,000 men in later days, and to make the fortunes of many men in Gwynedd and the Conwy Valley. It was the successors of Lord Uxbridge who were within the next half century to become the Marquesses of Anglesey.

Many are the stories of disasters which overtook the ferry and those who travelled in it. One with claim to truth is of an occasion in the seventeenth century when there was a fair at Conwy. Eighty people were crossing from the Creuddyn side to the fair when the ferry capsized, no doubt from overloading. One girl alone survived, Anne Thomas of the Creuddyn; she was on her way to meet her lover, Sion Humphries of Llanfairfechan, who had his own misfortune on the way. He fell down the cliff at Penmaenmawr, but also survived. They later married, and she was in due course buried at Llanfairfechan on April 14th, 1744, where it is recorded that she was 116 years old; she seems to have had a charmed life. The story is that her husband survived her, and died on December 10th, 1749, but there must be considerable doubt if it was the same husband, unless perhaps he was much younger than she.

Even that disaster did not lead to the construction of a bridge, which would, of course, not only have been a major task for those days, but would also have interfered with the thriving navigation of the tidal reaches of the river. Those were the days when bridges were of arched construction, inflexible masterpieces of stone or brick, not really suited to span a capricious tidal river, or the major fault which lies below — a problem overcome when iron and steel provided other ways to build a bridge, by Telford first with chains and a suspended road, by Stephenson later with his tubes of which one end is firmly anchored, but the other moves on massive steel rollers. The matter came to a head on Christmas Day, 1806, in the times when the whole coach used to be taken across the estuary by ferry. The regular ferrymen were collecting their Christmas Boxes, and the ferry was in the charge of four relief men. The Irish Mail coach from London still used the Chester route, and came this way, although twenty-six years earlier Lawrence's express coach had started coming via Pentrefoelas and Llanrwst, then along the west bank of the Conwy, so avoiding the ferry crossing, and three years earlier had started to avoid the coast route altogether by using the new road through Betws-y-coed.

When the Mail Coach arrived at the river, the water was so rough that several passengers refused to embark on the ferry, and remained at the Ferry Farm Hotel, but the rest set off to make the crossing. When they were half way across they were caught by a squall. It may be that the regular ferrymen could have coped with the situation, but as it was there was panic, and the whole lot turned over. The coach, the horses, eight passengers, the coachman, the guard, a boy and four ferrymen were tipped into the river. One passenger swam ashore, another clung to the Mail Trunk, and was rescued, the rest were drowned. The bodies of those who were found were buried in Llanrhos churchyard in the Creuddyn.

Even so, it was to be many years before Thomas Telford, a man whose name means much in northern Wales, was instructed to improve the road from Chester to Bangor, and more years still before, on July 1st, 1826, when that master engineer was in his 69th year, his great suspension bridge over the river at Conwy was opened for use. It carried the traffic of the nineteenth and twentieth centuries on its 326 feet of span until 1959, and still is there to be walked across.

Faced with a difficult task, to cross an estuary which, of placid beauty most of the time, was a place of great terror when storms and squalls came in from the sea, he chose to construct his bridge from a small rocky island, Yr Ynys, near the Conwy side. From there it spanned to the base of the castle, where he cut through the rock up into the town. Between the eastern bank and the island he constructed a causeway some 550 yards long and nearly 100 yards wide, which is there today.

From the lay-by where we stand there are views across the Conwy to Benarth Woods, and upstream towards the Carneddau, and when full tide coincides with onfall of night, here may be seen reflections and sunsets to be remembered with nostalgia for many a year.

Introduction of *Spartina* has not been responsible for all the silting of this eastern side of the river. It has been going on since Telford built his causeway and changed the current flows, and Glan Conwy, to which we are coming, has been its victim. Now most obvious for modern houses and flats in alien materials, it was once a very thriving port. In Georgian times, and long before, to less extent in times more recent, ships plied from here to Liverpool, to Chester, Anglesey and Ireland, sometimes to Bristol and places far away, and river boats plied the Conwy to Llanrwst.

Somewhere not far from here, *"apud castrum Deganno nomine, juxta litus immensi mare"*[9], about the year 500, Saint Bride (St Ffraid) landed from Ireland with her two companions, Luge and Athea: maybe it was at the rock by which they later built a chapel, which became Trwyn Capel.[10] Off there in later times the ships would lie, to be loaded and unloaded by gang planks to the rock. Others would lie offshore to load to or from the river wherries and small sloops and lesser craft which plied to Tal-y-cafn, Trefriw and Llanrwst. It was also off there that, when the local people were suffering a famine of vegetables and meat, St Bride cast rushes into the water which immediately turned into fish, which the people caught and ate. Glan Conwy is named after her, for its full name is Llansanffraid Glan Conwy, the church or enclosure of St Bride alongside the Conwy. In spite of its first appearance, it is a place at which to stop.

The energetic may walk, the less able may travel by car, up the steep hill which leaves the main road alongside the village fish and chip shop. The road continues, with the Church Hall on the right, to wind up between houses to the top, the road which was for centuries the village's main link with the upper reaches of the Conwy Valley, and with the moors of Denbighshire, before there were built the toll roads of the eighteenth century. From time to time it is worth stopping to look out over the Valley, towards the mountains, to Conwy, to Anglesey, and over the open sea. If the mountains are covered with snow, the view is particularly spectacular.

Glan Conwy may not now be a place of great beauty, and well one may wonder why in these days of planning control, modern development on a coastal hillside cannot compare with the old towns of the Mediterranean shores, or the fishing villages of Cornwall and Yorkshire, but it has a history closely linked to that of the Valley, which it served before Conwy existed. To see it now it is hard to think of it as it formerly was, agog with hustle and bustle when the packet came in from Ireland, or a cargo vessel from Chester, or from Liverpool, or from far across the ocean. It would echo to the hammers of shipbuilders, for its boatyards thrived for centuries. Several ships built here were operating late into the 19th century, maybe early 20th, among which were the schooner *Wavecrest* of 90 tons, the sloop *William Orme* of 80 tons, the *Providence*, launched in 1799, and the *Seven Brothers*. Others were built at Tal-y-cafn, the *Union*, 1789, the *Phoebe*, 1844, and the *Elizabeth*, 1847, being among them. Some had their masts adapted so that they could be lowered to pass under the Conwy bridge after Telford's road was built, and re-assembled on the other side on the passage out to sea or up the river.

The sounds of the shipbuilders, the mariners and the shoremen, the teamsters with their drays and wagons, would have mingled with the cries of the gulls whose descendants are here today, with the sound of horses' hooves, and the gay prattle of the fishwives at Trwyn Capel. But all that has gone, and many a house and shop, warehouse and boatyard, chandler's and hostlery, must have disappeared even before the railway was built to sever village from water, and took the trade which the boats had once monopolised.

When first there was a school at Llansanffraid may not be certain, but education came to these parts in general for the less well off in the early eighteenth century. In Conwy there was a school by 1675, and in 1698 Edward Cley was appointed there to read prayers at a salary of 10s.6d. a year.[11] By 1720 the Rev. Lancelot Bulkeley had by legacy of £60 provided for the teaching and maintaining of six poor children, two each from the parishes of Llangelynnin, Caerhun and Llanbedr-y-cennin on the western side of the Conwy. Lancelot Bulkeley was not only the Rector of Llangelynnin, but was also Vicar of Caerhun and Rector of Llanbedr-y-cennin, and he left another £60 to the first of those parishes, the income to go to the Rector provided he ensured the education of the children "to teach them Welsh for ever". In 1753 the Rev. John Pugh, curate of Llangelynnin was appointed to be schoolmaster at Conwy at a salary of £5 a year to teach Conwy boys. In Gyffin beneath the walls of Conwy the S.P.C.K. opened a school in 1770, but before that Griffith Jones' circulating schools had been established throughout the County of Caernarfon.

One who appears to have benefited early from local schooling was John Jones who was born in Llansanffraid Glan Conwy in 1790. After his initial education he went, at the age of twelve as apprentice to printers in Liverpool, and there later he set up his own printing works. It was then that he met the young William Rees, who had been born at Llansannan in 1802, and they started the first successful Welsh newspaper, *Yr Amserau.*

The first edition came out on August 23rd, 1843, and it was published fortnightly. William Rees was the editor until the paper was amalgamated with *Baner Cymru* in 1849, but John Jones had been superseded by John Lloyd as publisher when Lloyd's family purchased the paper in 1848. After 1859 the paper was printed and published by Gees of Denbigh as *Baner ac Amserau Cymru,* and after a chequered history ceased publication in the mid-1990s.

John Evans was born here in 1814 and attended a local school before 1824. In that year he went to another school in Abergele, and then to Wrexham, where he was still a pupil in 1830. In the intervening years, perhaps only in holidays, he was back in Llansanffraid, for he was working in his uncle's shop in 1826. Before he left Wrexham, before he was 16, he had a book published by John Jones of the Venedotian Press at Llanrwst, *Hanes yr Iddewon,* so he must have benefited well from his education. He afterwards published many books, some in Wrexham, some in Denbigh, but many in Llanrwst by the Venedotian Press. Among these were *Geiriadur Saesneg-Cymraeg* (an English-Welsh Dictionary containing a glossary of herb names) and translations into

Llansanffraid Glan Conwy Church

Welsh of *Paradise Lost* and *The Life of Dick Turpin*. He started preaching when he was 26 and was ordained as a Calvinistic Methodist Minister when he was 39. He must have been the first Preacher for the Bryn Ebenezer Welsh Calvinistic Methodist Chapel built in 1844, and was still the accredited Preacher in 1851. He was an adjudicator at Eisteddfodau and an active Temperance worker, notwithstanding which he found time to be very successful in business, so that when he died in 1875 aged 61 he not only owned his uncle's former shop, but also another shop, a sawmill, a nail factory and a flour mill all in the Llansanffraid area. He married twice. A great number of letters by him appeared in *Baner ac Amserau Cymru* under the pen name of *Adda Jones*.

There are still, within the village, corners to explore which have survived from the past — an old warehouse alongside the main road, houses opposite and others up little lanes, old walls — but the church was altered almost beyond recognition in 1829. Like so many churches in this area, its size had been increased long ago by adding a second nave to the original. In 1839 John Welch removed the arcade and turned the building into a single naved church "through the munificence of Ven. Hugh Chambres Jones". In his alterations, which must have amounted almost to rebuilding, he incorporated two windows which are believed to date from about 1500 and which show St John the Baptist and St Catherine. The earlier parish or township church in pre-Reformation times was the church of Dinerth in the Cwmwd of Uwch Dulas in Rhos Cantref, but there has not been a church or parish of Dinerth for the last two centuries. In those days this part of the Cwmwd had just its chapel of St Ffraid down by the waterside at Trwyn Capel.

The days of the river boats and the sloops have gone and will not return. No more will sea-going ships come here. But Glan Conwy has a beautiful setting, and an equally beautiful outlook, and in time the new development will maybe mellow, as has that of the past which when new was itself conspicuous — but the *Spartina* must be stopped from spreading on the foreshore. Before we leave we will look once more at the view of the river, from alongside Riverbank Motors, the car sales premises on the west of the road.

Leaving the village, were it not for the traffic we should almost be leaving the century behind. The A470 road curls over the hill between trees on one side and rolling fields on the other, then descends into the valley of the little river Cenarth. It and its small tributaries rise close by in the hills to the east, yet it has flowed enough throughout the centuries to provide power for two mills, Felin Uchaf and Felin Isaf, of which the latter works today. It can be

Sloop 'Elize' ~ c. 1775

visited and inspected, to see the grain ground to flour between relentless stones, ever turned by the massive water wheel.

At the end of the eighteenth century one of the mills was owned by Cadwaladr Williams. His son John, who was born in 1801, became a physician, having been apprenticed to his brother, who was a physician and apothecary at Abergele. John's real interest was natural history, and by various means he managed to spend time at Kew Gardens and Ashbridge, notwithstanding which he obtained his doctor's degree at Dublin, and started practice at Corwen. He must have been keen on travelling, for at the age of 48 he joined the Californian gold rush, but came back a few years later to practise at Froncysyllte. His main interest is that in 1830 he published a book on the natural history of the Conwy Valley under the title of *Faunula Grustensis — Being an Outline of the Natural Contents of the Parish of Llanrwst*, which was printed and published by John Jones, then in Little Bridge Street, Llanrwst.

Flour from these mills would be among the cargoes shipped to Cheshire and Lancashire, with fruit from the Valley, timber and slates, lead and leather, in the vessels that sailed from Glan Conwy. There may even have been iron from the furnace at Bodnant and nails from John Evans' factory.

John Cary's map of North Wales dated 1787 shows nothing but a track south from this village, Pentre-felin, the Mill Village. At least after the construction of a turnpike road for coaches via Denbigh to Conwy in the 1750s, by way of Eglwys-bach, the ferry at Tal-y-cafn had been made fit for regular use by coaches, but even by 1829 the road from Llansanffraid Glan Conwy south to Tal-y-cafn was not recorded on maps as a turnpike, although in 1777 a turnpike trust had been given a remit to construct a toll road the whole way from Glan Conwy to Llanrwst. In 1787 nothing had been done, but John Evan's map of 1795 shows that the length from Tal-y-cafn to Llanrwst had been completed.

There must, however, have been a road of some sort between Pentre-felin and Eglwys-bach, and when coaches were diverted from Conwy Ferry to Tal-y-cafn Ferry because of rough weather, they must have gone that way. There was also a track from Pentre-felin up to the moors and the roads to St Asaph and Rhuddlan, towns of cathedral and castle respectively in the old province of Is Gwynedd, Lower Gwynedd, the Perfeddwlad or Middle Country, because the old hazardous ford of Cymryd across the Conwy was here, at which the Mercians from England were defeated and destroyed by the men of Gwynedd in the year 881.

But for centuries the river was the main highway through the Valley. The traffic to St Asaph and Llansannan would be infrequent, and these roads were unmade, old grass tracks where over many years some stone had been put down to fill in mires and puddles. They were each the "green road", from which derived the name by which Pentre-felin is commonly known, Ffordd Las.

But maybe Ffordd Las was a green road as in England, the route by which the drovers took their cattle from Arfon, and from Anglesey to swim the Menai Strait, along the verdant pastures from Aber to the Sychnant Pass, to swim across the Conwy at Cymryd, to pass through Pentre-felin on the way to Abergele and to Wrexham for the markets of the ever-growing English towns.

The next place to be visited is Bodnant, and the route by which to get

Two views across the river from Glan Conwy
Above: Conwy's castle and railway bridge
Below: Towards the mountains

there is the old Eglwys-bach road, following at first the present A470, winding up and over the hill to the south from Pentre-felin. Gardeners will know not only of the name,[12] but will also see in Pentre-felin and on the roadside the several signposts to Nursery Gardens beside or near it. All are worth a visit.

Beyond the brow of the hill, the road divides, the left hand branch, the old road, being that which we shall take. The newer road, now the main road, down the hill between the trees, was constucted sometime in the latter part of the 19th century. A short way beyond the junction, on the left of the old road, is a large car park for those who wish to visit the famous gardens.

In 1841 there was a track from here which went down by way of a series of hairpin bends to the west, through a small valley to Furnace Mill, and a track along the Valley floor to Tal-y-cafn on the line of the present trunk road, but that winding route was closed when Bodnant House was built, and the new road was formed between the trees, which we saw before. The mill remains within the Bodnant Gardens, but no longer works. It dates from Tudor times at least, and until well into the nineteenth century it provided the various power requirements for a blast furnace, producing iron for the needs of the Valley and of even greater areas. The adjacent farm is still the Furnace Farm, and the bridge on the main trunk road, only recently by-passed, is still the Furnace Bridge. After its use to power the furnace, the mill was converted for milling flour, but that use passed away in time.

There is a building known as the Pin Mill within the Bodnant Gardens, but that has no connection with the Furnace Mill. It was built in Woodchester in 1730 as a gazebo, then later it was used there as a pin mill. It was moved to Bodnant brick by brick as a kind of summer house as recently as 1938.

Three generations of the Lords of Aberconwy, and three generations of the Head Gardener family of Puddle, have been involved in the development of these famous gardens, but it was before their time, in 1875, that Henry Davies Pochin and his landscape architect, Milner, planned the layout of the 69 acres, and George Ellis and his five assistant gardeners began the task of turning the plans into reality. George Ellis and his brother Henry had been trained as gardeners in London. Of Henry we know no more, but George became Head Gardener to Lord Byron at Kirkby Mallory, and it was from there that he came to Bodnant. He was here for many years, and brought up a family of two daughters and four sons, of whom one went to Alberta. Very sadly his wife died at the age of 41, and was buried in Eglwys-bach churchyard on July 7th, 1881, and one of his sons was killed in a railway accident. He lived at Bodnant Lodge, one of the many houses and cottages built by Henry Pochin in the Bodnant and Eglwys-bach area, most of which have his initials above the front door — H.D.P.[13]

In 1895 Henry Pochin died, and his daughter carried on where he left off, developing the gardens until she handed over to her son. In 1911 her husband became the first Baron Aberconway. The second Baron continued the

Cormerant

development, collecting plants throughout his life from all over the world. He was for many years President of the Royal Horticultural Society, as was later his son, who still lives here part of the time. In 1949 the second Baron gave the gardens to the National Trust, and now the present Baron [now deceased] oversees control on behalf of the Trust and the Royal Horticultural Society. In this he is assisted by the Head Gardener, Mr Martin Puddle, who succeeded his father, Charles Puddle [now deceased], who had followed his father, F.C. Puddle, who came here in 1920.

A guide to the gardens is available at the entrance. It takes some time to explore all from the formal gardens by the house to the Furnace Mill, through the Dell to the Mausoleum and back to the greenhouses, where all kinds of trees and shrubs may be bought, mostly container grown. Some will be found to bear witness to their development in these gardens by the generations of the Aberconways and the Puddles or their predecessors, Gurney (1910 to 1920) and Sanderson who succeeded George Ellis — such names as Viburnum Bodnantense. Henry Pochin chose his location well, for here grow plants of a tenderness that would not survive in the colder climes of most of these islands, but even so in the severe winters of the decade before last there have been some losses, and the onslaught of the gales of a few years ago has left its toll.

Continuing our journey, we will not proceed further at this time in the direction of Eglwys-bach, but will instead return by the way we came to the junction where we left the main trunk road, there to turn left and down the hill, between trees and woodlands, to emerge alongside the Conwy River near Furnace Farm.

Here the road widens and there is a lay-by. From that, or better still from the fence on the other side of the road, if the tide is high there will be reflections, of Bryn Cwn, or Bryn Castell at Tal-y-cafn and Pen-y-gaer, the Celtic fort, and of the majestic Carneddau beyond. If the tide is low, there are likely to be waders and cormorants, perhaps a heron — sea birds and fresh water birds of many kinds, for the rich silt provides food in abundance for them all, as it has done throughout the ages, and as it did for the mussels [14] of the Celts and Romans, the Princes of Gwynedd and the Tudors.

The view from here is never the same when seen again, for it changes with the light, with the tide and with the season, but throughout many generations, resting farmers, sweating furnacemen, weary travellers, from the days of our grandparents, of the middle ages, of the times of the Romans and the earlier Celts, must have stood near here to marvel at the enchantment of all around.

Here perhaps stood Suetonius Paulinus to survey the river and the menacing hills beyond, shrouded in the mists from which the hordes of the Ordovices were to pour and drive his mighty army back to the Conwy River when first he tried to cross, on a late spring day in A.D.61. The troops of Agricola were to stop again on their more friendly expedition of A.D.78. Both these armies passed, but the Marcher Lords and Henry III, then Edward I, all faced the same forbidding mountains, of whom none was to pass again, and stay against the wishes of the Welsh but Edward, twelve hundred years after that mighty Roman army.

4. *Variously Cwstenin, Custennin, Cwstennin, — an alternative dedication to a Cornish saint which it is sometimes suggested appears to be improbable.*

5. *See page 231.*

6. *The name originally seems to have been Gannoc, then it became Deganwy, and is now most normally Deganwy — part of the area is, of course, still called Gannock.*

7. *The Legend of Math, King of Gwynedd. Perhaps the New Tribes were the Romans, for it was they who first brought pigs to Britain. See "The Mabinogion".*

8. *W. Bezant Lowe, 'The Heart of Northern Wales, 1912.*

9. *Life of Modwenna, Irish Saint (authorship unknown).*

10. *Chapel Point.*

11. *Conwy Parish Records show that "the wife of Richard Smith schoolmaster at Conway the 20th August was interred 1669".*

12. *For many years American cruise liners have anchored in Llandudno Bay to allow passengers to visit Bodnant.*

13. *Source, Mrs Davies, wife of the Rector of Llansannan, grand-daughter of George Ellis.*

14. *The river mussel, 'Unio Margaritiferus'. The importance of the mussels was not only that they were a table delicacy, but also that they provided pink pearls of exceptional quality. Conwy Pearls are mentioned by Spencer in 'The Fairy Queen'.*

Day 2, Part 1 - Tal-y-cafn
& Eglwys-bach

Today we start at Tal-y-cafn Bridge, on which we will first stop and look and listen, as it says at the nearby level crossing gates "Stopiwch, Gwrandewch, Edrychwch". Over the tidal reaches to the north, across the shimmering waters if the tide is up, lie the slopes of Bryniau and of Bodnant, a tree-clad background to a view unchanging over the years, yet never the same at twice of viewing. On those waters, as far as this place and some beyond, came the great open trading ships of the Phoenicians and the galleys of war and peace of the Romans. Later in the dark ages of Post-Roman England came the ships of passage and trade of the Brythonic[15] nations which plied the Celtic Sea,[16] from Scotland and Ireland, Cornwall and Brittany, even from the Mediterranean before the Arabs captured Gibraltar and closed the shipping routes. This was an important place in years gone by.

We are within the fluctuating bounds of one of the oldest trading routes in western Europe. Long before the Roman Empire was born, before even the days of the Greeks and the Celts, on the summits of the hills to the west of the Valley, high above what we now call Penmaenmawr, were the stone axe factories of Graig Lwyd. Four and a half thousand years ago and more men sat, in winter huddled in rings around fires to fend off the worst of the icy blasts, in groups of dozens, hundreds or thousands in all, labouring to rough-shape the local stone favoured throughout the then known western world for axes and all the needful tools of peace and war. Yet more laboured to bring from the mountainside the raw material for their craft, and from the shore the hard round stones to use as hammers, while others gathered firewood from the nearby forests covering the hills. Some even worked on the hillside itself. There would be others, men foraging for food, women and children preparing meals and carrying out the normal chores of life in groups of huts not far away, for in these hills they were born, and they lived and died, and they buried their dead in the cairns and mounds, the carneddau some of which remain to be seen today.

Not far away, in the Bwlch-y-ddeufaen, lay the road, the track for men and packhorses,[17] the

Top inset: Plas Llan Eglwys-bach. Bottom inse: House at Eglwys-bach

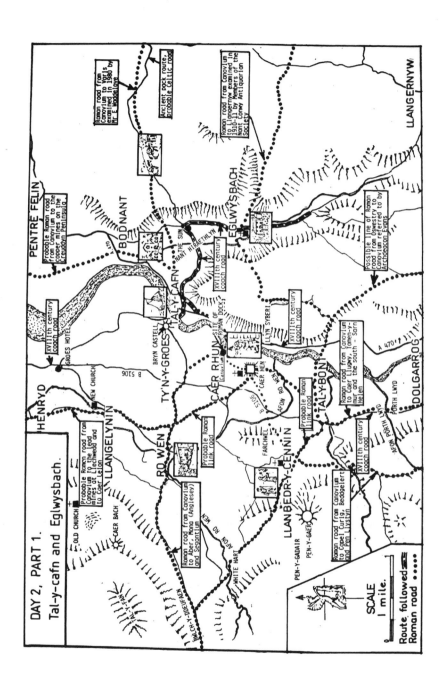

route for mystics and for the later traders from what we now call Parys Mountain, the copper mines of Anglesey, to cross the Conwy, on through the northern parts of Wales to the lands of Britain, to the eastern coast, to Bridlington. From there they sailed in ships to Europe, to the ports on the Amber Road which led through the heart of the continent to the lands of the Mediterranean.

The tools and weaponheads from the factories of Graig Lwyd went on their way unsharpened, for no doubt on such long and arduous journeys they would have lost all edge, and the rough-shaped, unfinished heads have been found at Avebury and Windmill Hill and on the Essex Coast, and in places throughout Europe.

These traders passed this way, taking the wares of the west to the east, to Europe, to the rising civilisations of the south, and on their return bringing amber and gold, trinkets and finery, and messages of wars, of births and deaths, rejoicings and disasters. They were the bankers and newscasters as well as the carriers.

They would cross the river some twelve hundred yards south of where we stand, where the Romans two and a half thousand years later were to cross, and rebuild Caerhun.[18]

When the Celts came (some five hundred years before the Romans) — the great civilisation of central Europe which spread to the furthest shores of Britain, of Ireland and of France — they settled, as they did wherever they went. Wales absorbed them, as it did all who before and after came as foe, but chose to stay. They kept sheep, and they wove cloth which was prized by the rich of Greece and later Rome, for the best of cloaks, for mats, for furnishings. Unlike the Iberians, who came before them, who were plainly dressed in well-made clothes of utilitarian kind, the Celts wore brightly patterned trews and plaids in tartan wool, and fine spun blouses, and their women's best-wear would pass for fashion in any age. They mined, and they made fine jewellery from gold and silver and bronze, with Conwy pearls, and these and their cloths joined copper and lead, and maybe silver, as the wares of trade, along this age-old route when the storms of winter, and the raids of pirates, made the routes by sea unsafe.

The pack trains continued throughout the centuries, their wares changing, but along the self-same route down from the Bwlch-y-ddeufaen (the pass of the two stones) through Ro-wen, over the hills and down here to the river and on to the east.

In A.D.61 the Romans came under Gaius Suetonius Paulinus, who had taken an army across the Atlas Mountains — perhaps the greatest of the Roman generals. Governor of Britain from A.D.59 to A.D.62, he was later,

Above: One of several guide stones on the route over Bwlch y Ddeufaen
Below: The Cromlech above the road over Bwlch y Ddeufaen

in A.D.69, to be Consul of Rome and one of Otho's generals in the wars against Vitellius.

He did not come along the pack trail, but instead from Chester via the coast. He set out with a mighty host, the XIVth and the XXth Legions and a fleet, with engineers, artisans, followers and suppliers, in all some 25,000 men. When they came to the Conwy estuary, they turned south to find a crossing. What a sight it must have been when that great army appeared over Bryniau and Bodnant hill. The scene of course was different, a landscape of rough, uncultivated ground, covered largely with scrub and bushes of various sizes, and trees all dotted thickly in among.

What came was not a cheerful, resplendent and victorious force, but rather a bedraggled, tired, frustrated horde, harried all the way by organised bands of Celts too wise to engage in open battle on the coastal plains, but instead content to draw the Romans on.[19] From time to time they would ambush and destroy a part of the advancing force, as they had done with the cohort at Bryn Euryn, which had come too far ahead. When chance arose of land through which pursuit by cavalry could not be carried out, they would unleash a hail of arrows from among the scrub, and kill a score or more of men, perhaps some beasts as well. That way the Roman force was slowed and kept in fear, and its numbers inexorably reduced. The army did not advance in a column of ten or twenty abreast, with measured pace — it could not across a boulder-strewn terrain, through bushes, scrub and trees. It shambled on as best it could, clearing a track for the wagons that brought supplies, for the catapaults and other engines of war.

It did not arrive unheralded to the Celts, who had followed its progress all the way from Chester — the noise it made must have been heard ten miles away. From van to rear it extended for nearly that distance when on the move, and it went like a looper caterpillar — the first troops moved off at dawn at an ordinary marching pace, to find a site for a camp for the following night, and the rest of the force came on behind, so that if possible no part of it was too far from good support if the Celts decided to attack. When they found a site, they set to work to dig a trench and bank to form defences within which all could rest at night, and as the following army came the workforce was increased. The first were already building the night's defences before the last left the previous camp and cleared it up so that if retreat became necessary there was no fort to provide a cover for the Celts. Of course this meant that in retreat an army had to rebuild its camp for overnight where just a day or two before it had destroyed a camp.

And so this force came down to Caerhun, to the ford and the Celtic fort

The Conwy estuary from Tal-y-cafn

— but the fort had been destroyed, and though its plateau provided some start for the Roman camp, its area was far too small. The German and Belgian forces, for that they were, tired, disgruntled, far from their native land, and it must have seemed almost as far from the relative comfort of their English forts and camps, had first to cross the river by the ford, plagued no doubt by objects floated down upon them by the Celts. Next they had to dig, and parties had to forage for timber for a palisade, knowing that at any time a straggler would be picked off with an arrow or a spear. There would be little comfort in seeing the mountains which they knew they would be forced to cross, into land to them uncharted and unknown.

The army did, at second attempt, cross the Carneddau mountains, with its great machines of war, catapaults and seige engines, the farmers' and the engineers' wagons and equipment, with all its food and clothes and arms, chariots and carts, men and horses and oxen, but the cost of the crossing was terrible.

The first attempt was in thick mist or fog, and the Celts and the Iberians kept sallying out of the woodlands and the bush which covered the slopes up to 1,000 feet or more, picking off and slaughtering the scouting parties and any who were lost, bogged down or left behind, or those intent on heaving and levering a wagon up the slope, or rescuing one which had got stuck. The wagons and the war machines rolled backwards down the slopes when a beast was hit by a spear or a dislodged stone, crushing the men who tried to hold them back as well as any in their path, running into others following behind. The animals panicked. Men and wagons fell over unseen cliffs, got bogged down in the many swamps; men and beasts collapsed and died of sheer exhaustion. The day wore on, and Paulinus realised he would not get over before the fall of night, nor even to an up-land plain where all could camp. His troops would be at the mercy of the native troops, who knew the land, so he ordered all to be brought back to the Caerhun base. The men were wet, exhausted and dispirited, and their losses in getting back perhaps exceeded those on the upward way.

The desperate effort of a few days later was of more success. The army crossed to the Menai shores, but again the losses were horrific in terms of men, machines, stores and animals. Those who remained of the mighty force that had set out from Chester then had to cross the tidal Strait, where they fought some Celts on the Anglesey shore. One cannot help but feel some sympathy for those hard driven Roman troops, but their troubles had hardly begun. Word came that the Iceni under Boadicea had risen in the east, and Paulinus withdrew to London with the greatest speed. Again he crossed the Carneddau, but without the great machines of war, with-out baggage and supplies, which were left behind to the mercy of the Celts — and it is likely that the wounded were also left, for it is said that the men on foot covered the journey in less than 6 days by way of Chester and Wroxeter, some 270 miles. The cavalry went on before, and were there in only four.

The Ordovices let them go, crossing the river here again in haste, unharried on their way — why should they risk loss in attacks on an army in full retreat, when Boadicea was poised to destroy it in the east?

Paulinus claimed in his despatches that he had inflicted great losses on the Ordivices and the Celts of Anglesey — that he had wiped out the Druids and their followers. But generals in retreat have always made such claims, and it is of note that Paulinus stripped Chester and Wroxeter of horses and of men, but still arrived at London with but a single legion. We do not know what happened to his navy, but between leaving Chester and arriving back at London he lost 12,000 men or more, and it was to be fifteen to seventeen years before another Roman army was to venture to come this way.[20] When it did, in the times of Sextus Julius Frontinus and Agricola as Governors it was on a friendly basis, the Ordovices keeping their forts, such as the 11 acre Craig y Dinas above Penmaenmawr, the

Romans manning theirs. Agricola's men came to help suppress a small uprising, but stayed to deal with the Gaugani, Irish incursors into Anglesey. The Romans were then to stay, although after A.D. 140 in reducing numbers, for 300 years or more, accepted and absorbed like the Celts before them and the Normans in the next millennium.

With no doubt some changes in line here and there, they were to improve and use the route from Segontium (Caernarfon), through Deva (Chester) and Eboricum (York) to Bridlington. They were to pave it with neat fitting stones on sound foundations, and with wheel tracks of dressed boulders so well that more than 500 years later the forces of Cadwallon, Prince of Gwynedd, were to advance along it to meet the men of Penda, King of Mercia, and on to destroy the mighty army of Edwin, King of Northumbria, in a battle near Doncaster that ended the Northumbrian onslaught on the rest of Britain. Yet later were the forces of the Princes of Gwynedd to advance victoriously to the banks of the Forth, to crush once more the power of Northumbria.

Just south of here, south also of the line of their great road, the Romans rebuilt, this time in stone, the camp Caerhun, to grow to be the town Canovium, and from there to the south they improved a road over the mountains by Llyn Cowlyd, to the Llugwy Valley and Bryn Gefeiliau, and on to Tomen-y-mur [21] and the south, and built a second through the Valley to Bryn Gefeiliau [22] and on to Beddgelert and Cardigan Bay; to the east they built another by way of Llangernyw and Denbigh;[23] there is no doubt also that they must have had a road to the north, for there would have been a proper link between the fort and community of Canovium, and the copper mines and look-out posts on the Creuddyn Peninsula at the Great Orme. It is likely also that they had yet another road to the north, west of the river, to the lead mines at Henryd and the look-out posts at Caer Leion and Caer Bach. W.J. Hemp, F.S.A., who carried out a lot of research in the early 1920s, was of the opinion that they had also a road to the south on the east side of the Conwy, and that coupled with the research of Archdeacon Evans [24] suggests that there may have been a road east of the Conwy by way of Caer Oleu, Llanrwst and Capel Garmon to Pentrefoelas and on to Viroconium. The Legio XX Valeria Victrix was stationed there in Agricola's time and it was a detachment of that Legion which he sent to North Wales with Ostorius, which went on to Anglesey, and garrisoned Caerhun and Segontium.

How many of these roads were built by the Romans, how many were Celtic roads which the Romans used, and how many were Celtic roads which they improved, may always remain a matter for conjecture, although careful research might yield answers, for the Celts very largely used timber for the surfaces of their roads,[25] allowing greater speed and less wear and tear on the shoes of their horses and oxen, and on the wheels of their chariots and wagons (it is not long since many of the streets of London and other great cities were paved with wood — some may still remain).

Along all those roads the soldiers marched and rode, their wagons and their chariots rolled, mingled with the trading pack trains and the Celtic-Roman and Iberian travellers, till the last of the legions were called away, and two centuries later the last Roman soldiers left with the armies from Wales that were to capture Gaul, and even Rome itself. The old pack trail continued withal through the dark ages of England, when it served not to take through that troubled land the wares of Wales, but in reverse carried the wares and stock of the Perfeddwlad to the great sea-trading routes of the Celtic nations. In those days the Brythons of Scotland, Ireland, Cornwall and Brittany, and the Celtic-Romans of Strathclyde and Wales, plied the western seas, away from the coasts of the almost lawless England of the Post-Roman era. In medieval times it again became the route into England, and the long-wagons and later coaches used this way and crossed the treacherous Bwlch-y-ddeufaen, which still appeared as a usable by-road (but not a toll road) on Henry Teesdale's maps of the 1820s.

But those old pack routes, the later Roman roads, were not the only trading routes through Tal-y-cafn. The river played an important part up

Llyn Syberi

to the coming of the railway in 1863. Unfortunately there were rocks in the river a furlong south of where we stand on Tal-y-cafn bridge, sometimes referred to as a reef, and known as Yr Arw[26] — the roughness — no doubt a good description of a rocky part in a generally sandy riverbed. In more recent centuries, no doubt as the river changed its course silting up one side and eroding the other, these presented a significant obstacle to river shipping, to the extent that much of the trade upstream in medieval times and later was by river boats which loaded onto and from seagoing ships here, below the rocks, or at Glan Conwy, or later Conwy.

Records of Watkin Owen, who was agent to the Gwydir Estate, refer to such shipments in the 1680s. Nevertheless we shall learn in our travels of seagoing ships which did navigate through Tal-y-cafn. Watkin Owen was the first Agent of that Estate, appointed when Mary Wynn, only 13 years of age, succeeded to the inheritance in 1674. His records for 1685 showed that there were a number of boats of between 2 and 12 tons regularly sailing up the river as far as Llanrwst. We shall also learn later of seagoing ships that sailed as far as Trefriw, so evidently the effect of the reef was to limit the passage to the fortnightly spring tides.

As the size of ships grew, and the trades of the Valley increased, especially in timber and slate, the problem of Yr Arw became greater, and in 1797 there was a meeting to discuss blasting it away. It seems, however, to have been between five and ten years before the work was done. The customs records show that boats which were relatively large by the standards of their times went to Trefriw after it was carried out, on into the late 1800s.

There is known to have been a dock and settlement here at Tal-y-cafn in Roman times and in later centuries. *The Union* was built here in 1789, the *Marchwell, Phoebe* and *Elizabeth* in 1820, 1844 and 1847 respectively, but they were few of many. The existence of a foundry at Furnace and the presence of oaks in great abundance supports the possibility that there was a permanent boatyard (maybe more than one) in medieval, Tudor and later times. The former sailmaking industry of Llanrwst reinforces that theory. It is of interest that the boat building continued long after the navigation of the river was so severely limited by Telford's causeway and bridge at Conwy.

There are few relics of houses or other buildings, but Tal-y-cafn may have been quite a hub of trade for many generations. Maps as late as those of Teesdale (1829) show concentrations of buildings greater than at many places that are small towns today: photographs taken before the present bridge was built, but after the railway, show much that is no longer there. The river has changed its course, except between the rocks below where we are standing, washing away all in one place, covering all with silt in another. The constant raids of foes throughout the ages, including the avaricious Normans, contributed to the start and continuation far into the middle ages, and even beyond, of the construction of buildings in wood, so that whole communities could, and did, vanish into the soil or into the waters, with social and other changes, with the wars and pillaging, tides and floods, and later the building of the toll roads, the railway and the present bridge. But here for long had been a mart, for some years relegated to a twice yearly sheep fair, but then revived and restored to its former weekly status. However it closed in the mid 1990s.

Through the early ages of the pack routes, and through Roman times and for long after, the crossing of the river was by ford, upstream from where we are, but not, perhaps, as far away as camp and fort. By the time of Edward I there was a ferry, and in his reign it was known as the passage of La Taverne, a Royal ferry. On October 6th, 1685, Watkin Owen recorded *"Tal-y-cafn Ferry in use, more than one ferryman employed"*, which suggests that there may have been some interruption in the service, though for how long we do not know. It was not until 1897 that the ferry was replaced by the present bridge.

When the railway came, thirty years before the bridge, Tal-y-cafn had its station, and its goods yard serving much of the Valley both sides of the river, but the rail track has been reduced from double to single, and all that remains of the goods yard is one roadside warehouse. Not so long ago a small steam tank engine would leave the sheds at Llandudno Junction every day on scheduled time, to puff first to Glan Conwy, then to Tal-y-cafn, to Dolgarrog and Llanrwst, to each goods yard in turn all the way to Blaenau Ffestiniog, to shunt around as needed the wagons and the trucks. As night drew near it would puff proudly down the track all the way to the Junction yards, to set off again next day on the same important mission.

The name Tal-y-cafn, the high hill, is derived from the knoll on the western side, from which the Iberians looked out over the river for invaders from the sea, and on which the Celts, and perhaps others before them, had a fortified camp. No doubt from here the worried guards looked fearfully on the Roman army as it wound its cumbersome way from Deganwy. In their days the Romans used it as a fortified look-out post, as they did the larger camps at Caer Oleu and Llanbedr-y-cennin which we shall come across at a later time. The Welsh in turn, in the dark ages of England and of the raids by Scots and Danes, and in the days of the Normans, no doubt looked out from here for invaders from the east or north. Now none but a sheep is likely to appear to stare to north or south.

From here the road to Eglwys-bach leads east, up the hill opposite the

Tal-y-cafn Hotel. It dates only from the time of the ferries, but became the turnpike road of 1759, to Conwy from Chester by way of Denbigh, Llansannan and Llangernyw — a route which avoided the dangers of the Rhuddlan marshes, Penmaen-Rhos[27] and the Conwy ferry inherent in the coastal turnpike of 1756. It was even practicable to avoid the much greater dangers of Penmaenmawr and Pen-y-clip[28] by going over the Bwlch-y-ddeufaen on the old pack-horse route, as the army of Cromwell did on its way to Caernarfon a century before.

Two hundred yards or so up the hill this road merges with the older road from the Caerhun ford, which comes in from the south, and by which we shall later return. Over the crest of the hill, the road goes down into Nant Hiraethlyn, the "valley of the waters of longing", a name which so well introduces the tranquil beauty of the lands ahead.

Beyond the Hiraethlyn river there is a crossroads by The Sun, which no longer provides hostelry for weary travellers as it and earlier buildings did of old. To the left the road leads back to Bodnant. Ahead it goes meandering up a steep and narrow cwm to the moors of old, the "rhosydd" which gave their name to the Rhos Cantref, and to such enchanting-sounding places as Betws-yn-Rhos, Llanelian-yn-Rhos, and Llanrhos itself in the Creuddyn Peninsula. This was the road of the stone-age men, the Iberians

Tal-y-cafn bridge which replaced an ancient ferry

and the Celts, and of many who came between; and again in later times it became a turnpike road in the days of the coaches; but it is now no more than a narrow lane. If we were to follow it, we should arrive in time at Chester.

The Roman road from Segontium (Caernarfon) to Deva (Chester) is referred to in the Itinerary of Antonine, Iter XI, dated about the end of the second century. In that the distances are given from Segontium to Canovium (Caerhun), 24 miles, Canovium to Varis 18 miles, and Varis to Deva 32 miles. The distances are, of course, in Roman miles. It appears also in the First Iter of Richard of Cirencester.[29] In 1980 a Mr Edmund Waddelove traced the route from Caerhun to St Asaph, which he, like others, assumed to be Varis. As regards that part which lies within the Conwy Valley, he found that it lay north of this present road, west and north of the house Penrhyd, and did not rejoin the line of the road we are on for about two miles. It is strange that the Romans abandoned such a length of the older track, but that it was re-adopted in later times. His view was that the ford was by the rocks at Tal-y-cafn, but the waters are deep and fast at that point, so it is much more likely that it was a distance to the south, the lane which runs from Penrhyd to join the A470 by the telephone box being the route of the old road, the newer short-cut to the ferry only having been adopted at a much later time. That older route would lead directly to a ford by the Roman dock on the Caerhun side, adjacent to which a causeway ten feet wide leading to the water's edge was traced in 1929.

The Nant Conwy Antiquarian Society in 1911 was convinced that the major Roman road was that to Llansannan, the Sarn-y-ceisbwl (see note 23), and that Varis was Denbigh, not St Asaph. That Society suggested that there was a ford across the Conwy south of the Afon Roe at Farchwel, necessitating also a ford across the lesser river.

Modern research and excavations are leading to suggestions that Varis was neither Denbigh nor St Asaph, but was Prestatyn. It seems evident that much information may yet come to light about the extent of settlement and development in these parts in Roman times — that it will be found to be more intensive than has hitherto been assumed — for St Asaph and Denbigh were both settlements and camps as well as Prestatyn — they were not alternatives to each other. The probability must be that two roads existed from Caerhun towards the east, the more northerly being that which we have followed, going on through Betws-yn-Rhos, and the more southerly through Eglwys-bach and Llansannan.

From The Sun the road to the right was the main turnpike route, that of the coaches of the Georgian and Victorian eras to Denbigh and to Chester until the effects of Telford's bridge at Conwy began to tell, and later the train became the means of travel. It leads first to Eglwys-bach, past small groups of modern bungalows, so neat and tidy, into the village from which the tithes for many years provided income for the almshouses of Llanrwst.

But should the name be Eglwys-bach or Eglwysfach? Originally it was neither, the parish having been Erethlyn, the brook or river now Hiraethlyn being then spelt likewise, but formerly having been the Afon Asa. It was at the end of the seventeenth century that Edward Lhuyd, who toured and recorded the north of Wales, quoted the name of Eglwysfach. Sir Edward Anwyl, who was Professor of Welsh at University College, Aberystwyth, at the start of this century, attributed Eglwys-bach to "*the power of 's' to harden a spirant that follows*". There are those who today will tell you that Eglwys-bach is just a slovenly form created by those who care nothing about mutated feminines, while others say that the reference is to the "dear little church", which in colloquial Welsh is Eglwys Bach. Map makers have indiscriminately chosen this or that, and those who paint the roadside signs have likewise taken their pick. Cary's and Evans' maps of 1780 to 1805 used Eglwysfach, the Ordnance Survey of 1841 used Eglwys-bach, while that of 1911 used Eglwys-fach. The Census of 1801 referred to Eglwys Fach in the Cwmwd of Uwch Dulas, Cantref of Rhos. The Religious Census of 1851 likewise used Eglwys-fach. The Conwy Parish Records show Eglwys-fach as early as 1718 and as late as 1782. Eglwys-bach or Eglwys-fach, it matters not, but it provides food for many a friendly argument in the village pub which would be lost if the name went back to Erethlyn.

Beyond a small estate of houses in the much criticised Georgian style, time has stood still. These little houses fittingly introduce a gem of a village street,[30] where in the past the coach from Denbigh would trundle along, to meet a chaise, or a wagon harnessing an extra team for the hills ahead.

Why is this village ignored in guidebooks? Perhaps because its church dates only from 1782, when it was built to replace one of long before, on the profits, perhaps, brought by the turnpike road and the coaches. In an area where so many churches are so very old, this is comparatively modern, and does not contain the remains of any of great and lasting fame — and, moreover, it is in an oft-despised neo-Gothic style; but if modern buildings were half so well designed, then modern architects and planners might have some claim to judgement — it is a very attractive little church. That the coaches brought prosperity is shown by the increase in parish population from 894 in 1801 to 1157 in 1851.

In 1684 there was built the fine house Plas-y-llan, by Sir John Wynn knight and baronet, who was the son of Henry, tenth son of the first Sir John Wynn of Gwydir. He in most unlikely manner inherited the Gwydir baronetcy, but not the estate. That had passed to Mary, 13-year-old daughter of the fourth baronet in 1674. Of all Sir John Wynn's sons there was not another male heir, and even the son of this Sir John of Plas-y-llan was to die childless so that the baronetcy was extinguished. That Mary was married when she was 17, on July 30th, 1678, at Westminster to Robert Bertie, Baron Willoughby de Eresby, so that the lands which were separated from the title passed to him. He became the Duke of Ancaster, and the Ancaster Estates have remained great landowners in this Valley area until today.

At the entrance to the village is a garage, formerly the village blacksmith's shop, which was a hive of industry in the days of the Denbigh coaches, but dates from long before those times, and must have served the team of many a long wagon and traveller's horse, for it reputedly operated first in 1628. Today it is run by John and Hefin Jones, father and son, of whom John has been famous in the world of wrought ironwork, one time, I believe, champion smith of the United Kingdom.

Is it possible that there was a village here in Roman times? The Nant Conwy Antiquarian Society in 1911 found that their road from Canovium came into the area of the village alongside the present blacksmith's shop, but that it then turned sharply south as far as the centre of the village, before turning sharply east again, to go up through the valley past Coed Pen-y-bryn and over the top to reach, eventually, Llangernyw — quite a different route from that followed a dozen and more centuries later by the Turnpike Road for the Denbigh coaches, which continued through the village and on up the valley of the Hiraethlyn river. The two right angled turns might suggest some obstacle in the direct line, but it is much more likely that they developed at a later time, perhaps when the turnpike road was constructed.

Between the Conwy Valley and Eglwys-bach the Roman road climbed over the hilltop beside Llyn Syberi. From that part of the road there would have been a track suitable for small troops of soldiers going to and from the Celtic camp on Garreg Oleu, Caer Oleu;[31] there have been finds of Roman material there, to indicate that they used it, as the Celts had done, as a look-out post, no doubt for the protection of Canovium.

There on those rocks, overlooking the Conwy Valley, is one of the finest vantage points of all, behind Plas Maenan Hotel, Cadair Ifan Goch (the Chair of Red Evan), which is on National Trust land. This can be reached easily by a footpath from Maenan School, where we shall be later. Ifan Goch was the giant who lived in the Conwy Valley, who used to stand with his left foot on the mountains on the west of the river, and his right foot on Cadair Ifan Goch, in order to wash his hands in the river. We do not know why he never stood the other way round.

But all that is further up the valley, off a track which perhaps went on to Llanrwst, and is quite a long way from where we are, at Eglwys-bach.

The village's most famous son lies buried at Glanadda Cemetery at Bangor; Owen Roberts was born here on January 17th 1793, at Cefn-y-coed, and was educated at Llanrwst Grammar School before going to medical schools at Edinburgh and, like John Williams of Pentre-felin, at Dublin. His interest was public health, and he served as Medical Officer of Health at Chester, and in the Llanrwst, Caernarfon and Bangor districts, where, no doubt, he would have had a private practice or a hospital job. He made a study of cholera, became an authority on it, and wrote books on its prevention as well as treatment. He was one of the people behind the establishment of the C & A Hospital at Bangor and Denbigh Psychiatric Hospital [both hospitals no longer exist].

A great supporter of the chapels, in particular the Wesleyan Methodists, was Absalom Roberts, born at Trefriw, but who lived in this village much of his life. A shoemaker by trade, he was a poet as well as preacher, who wandered around a great deal, but still found time to marry twice and have twelve daughters and two sons. He was buried at Llanrwst, having died two years before Owen Roberts.

Another cobbler who made a name for himself was Owen Williams, who lived here from 1877 to 1956, chapel worker, author and musician.

John Evans was born at Ty Du on September 18th, 1840. Educated at the local National School he worked on his father's farm before entering the Ministry. By the time he was 17 he was becoming well known for his preaching, and more people would be crowded outdoors around the chapel windows than could be accommodated inside. He served on many circuits in both England and Wales, and was always renowned for his oratory. He died in 1897.

From 1830 to 1833 the village school was kept by John Williams, who was born at Llanddoged and came under the patronage of the Bodysgallen family, but upset them by radical views expressed in his poetry. Subsequently he also became a Minister and published books on religious subjects. He died in 1856.

The village may not have claim to historic fame, but each year now for one day it comes into its own, for then it is home to Eglwys-bach Show, one of the two great shows of the Conwy Valley. To it come from far and wide, from England as well as Wales, countryfolk and townspeople, farmers and businessmen, their wives and their families, and with them come

sheep and cattle, pigs and horses and goats, farm machinery, garden produce and flowers, and riders and artists, those with a ware to sell or a
point of view to air. Here may be seen the finest Shire Horses in the land,
Jacob's Sheep and Welsh Black Cattle. In the nearby school are paintings
and drawings by artists known and unknown, local and not so local, amateur and professional, competing for sale on equal terms, or just displayed
for show. There are riding and jumping competitions of many a
kind,something for all, young, old and in between.

The roads beyond the village are as ancient, almost, as time itself. They
wind up unbelievable slopes to the moors, to Llangernyw and Llansannan,
to Maenan and Llanddoged and Llanrwst, old pack trails which in time
became toll roads, but are the by-roads of this modern age. They lead to
Pennant Ereithlyn, from the early fifteenth century the family home of the
Hollands, who married and intermarried with the notable families of
Caernarfon and Denbigh shires, and provided sheriffs and bards throughout the centuries, but still no man or woman of lasting fame. Nevertheless
they were one of the families descended, it is generally believed, from the
Conways of Llys Euryn, and thereby from Ednyfed Fychan through his son
Tudur. The first recorded member of the family at Pennant Ereithlyn was
one Howell in the early part of the fifteenth century; he was the son of
Robin Holland who was with Owain Glyndwr in the fight for independence between 1400 and 1410 — and yet it was Owain Glyndwr who
burnt down the ancestral home Llys Euryn in 1409.[32]

How hard the dray horses of the past must have pulled, and those with
riders on their backs must have panted and blown long before the heights
were reached. The teams that drew the long wagons, the coaches and the
chaises must have found the ten mile stint from Conwy to Llangernyw a
very hard day's work. With no such burden, with a car as transport, the
modern traveller may explore and enjoy the peace of Nant Hiraethlyn and
the hills around, but we will return to the modern road, the toll road in
the Valley which we left at Tal-y-cafn.

*Above: These houses stand on the paddock where beasts were kept
prior to swimming the river at low tide at Tal-y-cafn
Below: Trees hiding a bailey at Tal-y-cafn*

15. *Chamber's Twentieth Century Dictionary — 'Brython — a Celt of the group to which Welsh, Cornish and Breton belong — distinguished from the Goidel'.*

16. *Celtic Sea — the seas from the Firth of Clyde to the Bay of Biscay.*

17. *The tarpan, the ancestor of the British mountain ponies, was possibly introduced into Britain fairly early in the stone age, and the larger Arab horses no doubt came later, perhaps with the Phoenicians.*

18. *Caer Hen, the Old Fort, hence Caerhun, but also later Caerhun, after Rhun ap Maelgwn — see later.*

19. *This was the tactic which had forced Caesar to withdraw from Britain 100 years before — see later.*

20. *History books traditionally credit Paulinus with a laudable purpose in his campaign, and with great success, but everything about those years has been so unclear from the few records which exist that there is still not even certainty as to who was governor of Britain at a particular time, let alone what was done and achieved.*

    The main historian of the time was Publius (or Gaius) Cornelius Tacitus, who was son-in-law to Agricola, and as such had been a friend of Paulinus, for Gnaeus Julius Agricola had been a young officer with Paulinus when he was Governor of Britain — the date of which seems fairly certain at A.D.59 to A.D.62. Agricola himself became Governor, but historians argue whether that was in A.D. 76 to A.D.83 or A.D. 78 to A.D.84; they even argue about who was governor in the ensuing three decades — decades covered by the writings of the same Publius Tacitus.

    It was between A.D.110 and A.D.112 that Tacitus wrote about the North Wales campaign, when Agricola had been dead for eighteen years and Paulinus for much longer. He was therefore writing of events which had taken place fifty years earlier. Modern historians have re-examined his works and their background, and other information and conclude that Paulinus did not come for any such laudable purpose as destroying murderous bloodthirsty Druids (who were in fact neither bloodthirsty nor murderous), nor even on the instructions of the Senate to acquire the wealth of the North Wales mines. He came, they now tell us, purely for personal aggrandisement, to gather for himself glory to vie with that of his great rival, Corbulo, who had just reconquered Armenia. Instead, they conclude that he was lucky to escape with some part of his army, and with his life. See more on this matter in the final chapter, 'Farewell'.

21. *The Romans had a fort and settlement in the Lluguy Valley, near Bryn-y-Gefeiliau Farm, which for want of knowledge of its Roman name is commonly called either Caer Lluguy, or Bryn Gefeiliau. Tomen-y-mur was a settlement of considerable size and importance south of the present Blaenau Ffestiniog. The building of both Caerhun and Tomen-y-mur may have started in the time of the Governor Sextus Julius Frontinus, prior to Agricola.*

22. *The map on page 54 of the Atlas of Caernarfonshire published by the Gwynedd Rural Council in 1977 shows a possible fort at Betws-y-coed as well as that at Bryn Gefeiliau. Very limited excavations were carried out on a possible site for*

such a fort north of the Log Cabin in 1974-75 without result, but the possibility of such a camp or settlement is still real because of the importance of the nearby lead mines.

23. *The road to Denbigh was traced in 1911 by the Nant Conwy Antiquarian Society, and some suggest that the Roman Varis was Denbigh, not, as is generally assumed, St Asaph. The existence of the route had been known for a long time under the name of Sarn-y-kasbwll, which was probably a corruption of Sarn-y-ceisbwl, the Bailiffs Walk.*

24. *Archdeacon Evans will be referred to again later — he wrote a History of Pentrefoelas which was never published. He actually suggested that the road went to Oswestry, but it seems more likely that it went to Viroconium (Wroxeter, near Shrewsbury).*

25. *Caesar's 'Invasion of Britain'.*

26. *Garw, roughness, mutates to Arw. There is a copse some 800 yards south-west of Tal-y-cafn Bridge known as Coed yr Arw, which must justify speculation that the reef may have been upstream of the Ferry.*

27. *Penmaen-Rhos is the high headland east of Old Colwyn.*

28. *Pen-y-clip is the headland between Penmaenmawr and Llanfairfechan.*

29. *Richard of Cirencester, 1335-1401. Wrote "Speculum Historiale de Gestus Regum Angliae 446-1066". He recorded Canovium as existing after the middle of the fifth century.*

30. *What a pity that the electricity poles have been installed so unfeelingly in prominent positions. Such monstrosities can be erected and remain, but a man who puts up a flagpole to display the Welsh Ddraig Goch is made to take it down.*

31. *Perhaps this was the route used by the Romans between Wroxeter, Llanrwst and Canovium to which Archdeacon Evans referred in his history of Pentrefoelas, in which case it would have been a road.*

32. *See page 10.*

To have travelled south on the Valley floor from Tal-y-cafn in the times of George II would have been well nigh impossible, for it was, as it had been for as long as mankind remembered, a land of undrained marsh and mist, thickets and copses on the higher grounds, and not a road but a few ill-kept farm tracks. It was a land where strangers would not be welcome.

But later in that century came the toll road linking the farm tracks, and the lands were drained; next came the time when the days of the car demanded good surface to the road, and now is the age when the road is being widened and straightened, and made to look like almost any other main road in any land. Alongside is the railway, which for more than a century has been a bar to flooding on the grand scale of the past.

River and road and rail, in that order the highways of trade and travel, with road again the king, lie one alongside another through the length of the Valley. In part all three are close, and there from a lay-by it is often possible to see some of the flocks of shelducks for which this Valley provides grazing and nesting for part of every year.

The scenery, varied and attractive, with the mountains in the background, is marred to small degree by the industrial complex of Dolgarrog beyond the river, and by the great pipelines down the hillside which look from this side of the river for all the world like a mountain railway.

We come to Maenan, of which all that now remains here in the Valley floor is a small community of houses formed by the conversion of a nineteenth-century farm and farm buildings, and a large house of similar

date which is now an hotel. But Maenan is more than that. For two and a half centuries it was the focal point of the Valley, and its influence was to last much longer still.

It was Edward I who, of the Norman kings, first succeeded in overrunning the whole of North Wales, after Llywelyn the Last had been murdered near Builth, reputedly by Edmund Mortimer, [33] son of his own cousin. W. Bezant Lowe in *The Heart of North-*

Top inset: Bridge Street — Llanrwst. Bottom inset: A quiet corner in Llanrwst

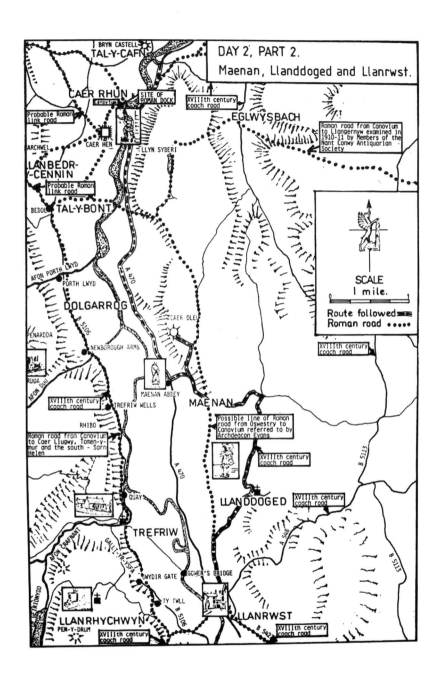

ern Wales quoted the following translation from "The Register of Chronicles of the Abbey of Aberconwy" —

> "In the year of Our Lord 1282, on the 11th September, Llywelyn ap Griffith ap Llywelyn ap Iorwerth Droyndon, Prince of North Wales, through treachery, was captured by night and killed by Edmund Mortimer, and was beheaded near Builth. His head was sent to London, and fixed above the Tower..."

The report was compiled by a group of Norman and English Bishops and Lords.

The dispirited Welsh armies surrendered at Dolwyddelan Castle. Moreover some Welsh traitors had not handed over the new Prince, Dafydd, who, as Lowe's translation goes —

> "In the following year... was taken prisoner, about the time of the Nativity of St John the Baptist, and was led to Rhuddlan... led to... Shrewsbury, and there, by the judgement of the Barons of England, he was dragged to the gallows by horses, secondly hanged, thirdly beheaded, because he despised the peace of the king..."

What typical hypocrisy by an invader, to regard those who seek to defend their country as rebels — Tacitus called them such — the Normans treated them as such. But the report does not end there, for, in reference to a man who was known as a devout Christian, it proceeds —

> "fourthly was disembowelled and his bowels burnt because he was the enemy of the Catholic Faith, and of the Church, and slayer of the Just, fifthly his body was divided into four parts [34] and was suspended in the four divisions of the Kingdom of England, because he was a disturber of the peace of the Kingdom, sixthly his head was sent to London, and fixed above the Tower, alongside the head of his brother Llywelyn, in order that other traitors might be terrified by his example, and as a sign that the King is just, and the exterminator of traitors. This judgement was pronounced on the 4th of October, and on the same day fully carried out.

What an interesting indication of the barbaric character of the Normans. It was the same Edward who in 1290 expelled all Jews from England and confiscated their property. But such barbarity, while it might for a time quell resistance, in the long term had an opposite effect. The Welsh rose again many times, until at last two centuries later the bardic prophecy of revenge [35] came true, and Henry Tudur defeated Richard III at Bosworth and took over the throne of England.

But the immediate effects on the Conwy Valley were great. Edward knew that of all the lands in Wales, Gwynedd would never willingly yield, and to keep it suppressed he built walled towns at Conwy and Caernarfon, and castles there and at Harlech, and rebuilt Dolwyddelan. To build at Conwy, he needed to remove the Cistercian Abbey, for which he had to get Papal dispensation, for though the Llywelyns were dead, their charters held good against the conquering king. The dispensation obtained,[36] he gave the monks a new site at Maenan, and money and materials to build a new, perhaps greater, abbey. The site was nearer to the rich lands given to them by their erstwhile benefactor, Llywelyn Fawr. It was also nearer to the mother foundation, Strata Florida, in Cardiganshire, itself endowed the previous century by the great Lord Rhys — he had himself no direct connection with this Valley, but is of interest to all of Wales, and to England, for his daughter Gwenllian married Ednyfed Fychan of Bryn Euryn and Nant Conwy, and with him founded the Tudur dynasty, which produced Henry Tudur and the later kings and queens of Britain. In 1177 he held the first gathering of Bards at Cardigan, which may be regarded as the first Eisteddfod. It was also he who sent the sons of Nest to conquer Ireland.[37]

The monks had one complaint. Maenan was on the east side of the River Conwy, in the Perfeddwlad, and not in the heartlands of Gwynedd. It was in the lands into which the Normans and the English had to some degree infiltrated, not the untamed homelands of the Celtic Welsh. It was outside the area which Edward himself was prepared to recognise as the Princedom of Wales. To overcome this, Maenan was declared to be part of the new-formed County of Caernarfonshire, and that it remained until local government boundaries were disrupted in 1974.

Since there was no road in the Valley, nor even, it seems, a pack track on this side of the river, the monks brought their materials here in boats, and probably made much use of them to move around. Their only other means of travel would have been to climb the steep hills to the hazardous roads of the Denbigh Moors, through the lands of the English and Norman lords, or to cross the river to Trefriw, and along the roads and tracks from there. To move anything of bulk, the river would be the way. It was, no doubt, on boat along the river that they brought from Conwy the great coffin of their patron, Llywelyn Fawr, and those of others which they shifted with them.

For two and a half centuries the abbey was to grow, to dominate the Valley and all its life, only to be dissolved in 1536 by decree of Henry VIII. Most rapidly the building was demolished, and more completely than many another abbey of much smaller size. Even the stones of the foundations were dug up and taken away, sold, no doubt, by the Prys family of whom we shall learn, maybe to their own personal profit. Much of the stone was carried off by Henry VIII's officials to repair Caernarfon Castle, for which it would again be carried by water. The Tudor-supporting Wynns were still building Gwydir Castle, about three miles upstream, and many of the timbers were used there. Some materials remained here at Maenan, and part of the building was evidently incorporated in a newer structure.

The coffin of Llywelyn Fawr, who had died on April 11th, 1240, and had been buried at Conwy with Gruffydd ap Cynan and Llywelyn ap Maelgwn, is reputed to have lain here after its removal,[38] in a stone lined chamber within the abbey.

When the abbey was dissolved the great stone coffin which had rested in that chamber was sent from here to St Grwst church in Llanrwst, being taken once more by water, together with other items of which we shall learn when we visit that church. No body has been in the coffin since its arrival there, and it is not known if or how it was lost. No doubt it could have been on the journey from the abbey, overboard into the river by mishap. It could perhaps have been at a much earlier time, when the former abbey at Conwy was raped in September, 1245, when —

"On the Monday next before Michaelmas in the afternoon... it was pillaged by soldiers of King Henry III, who...

like greedy and needy men, indulged in plunder, and spread fire and rapine through the country on the other side of the water, and amongst other profane proceedings, they irreverently pillaged a convent of the Cistercians, called Aberconway, of all its property, and even of the chalices and books, and burnt the buildings belonging to it."

Those words were written on September 24th, 1245, only a few days after the event, by a courtier in the King's camp, to a friend in England.[39] As he proceeded to say, at the time —

"His Majesty the King, with his army... encamped at Gannock for the purpose of fortifying a castle which is now built in a most strong position there; and we are dwelling round it in tents, employed in watching, fasting and praying, and amidst cold and nakedness. In watchings through fear of the Welsh suddenly attacking us by night; in fastings because of a

Gwydir Castle & Peacock

deficiency of provisions, the halfpenny loaf being now risen to five pence; in prayings that we may return safe and scot free home; and we are oppressed by cold and nakedness, because our houses are of canvas, and we are without winter clothing."

How typical that description is of the sufferings of soldiers in wars of any age. There is little doubt that they would be much out of love with the Welsh leaders, including Llywelyn Fawr who had died only five years earlier. His coffin was heavy, but why should its contents escape the rapine? If it did not, would the monks have been likely to broadcast the news that they had failed to guard the body of the national hero entrusted to their care? The Royal Commission on Ancient Monuments expressed the view in 1914 that the coffin dated from 100 years later than Llywelyn's death. That seems very unlikely, but it might date from 43 or so years later. If so the original coffin may not have been heavy, and may have disappeared with the body. The headstone then or later found its way to Gyffin.

When we come to Pentrefoelas we shall learn of the "Levelinus Inscribed Stone", believed to have stood on "Y Foelas", a mound in that parish. While it is usually said that the stone marked the resting place of Llywelyn ap Seisyll,[40] who was killed in a battle nearby, Mr E.W.B. Nicholson, Bodley Librarian in 1909, suggested that the barely legible inscription related to Llywelyn ap Gruffydd, Llywelyn the Last, who is known to have been buried by Cistercian monks, at Abbey Cwm Hir in Radnorshire. There could be another explanation, that the body buried there was that of Llywelyn Fawr, when it disappeared from Conwy or Maenan, and the stone coffin at Llanrwst could be a substitute then prepared by the monks about 1283.

Very little is really known about the Abbey. It seems probable that it was here that the young Prince Edward, later Edward II, received the oaths of allegiance of the Bishop of Bangor and the local clergy. The Abbey manuscripts disappeared, probably spirited away by the last abbot, hidden, and then lost. The last abbot was Richard ap Rhys, brother of Robert ap Rhys of Plas Iolyn, and uncle of Elis Prys,[41] the Red Doctor, whose name crops up frequently in history of northern Wales in the times of Henry VIII and Elizabeth. He was uncle to the wife of William Salesbury, whose name will also occur again. After the dissolution Richard was given a pension of £20 a year and the living of Cerrigydrudion, not far from Plas Iolyn. Any one of those would have been capable of spiriting the records away, and any could have had the opportunity.

Richard ap Rhys seems to have been elected abbot only in the year of dissolution in succession to Abbot Sieffre Johns, who had been elected about 1528 to succeed an older brother of Richard. The election of Richard is interesting in view of Elis Prys' position (see below). The other monks seem to have dispersed, though some may have stayed locally as teachers, perhaps at Gwydir School established by the Wynns. The land and buildings passed into the hands of the Crown, probably under the custodianship of Dr Elis Prys of Plas Iolyn, the Red Doctor, Visitor of Monasteries for North Wales, then perhaps by lease to John Gwyn, fifth son of John Wynn ap Maredudd of Gwydir (who had set up Gwydir school). John Gwyn died in 1574, and in his will left £40 a year out of the Maenan estate to maintain three Fellows and six Scholars at St John's College, Cambridge. This was later reduced to just three Scholars in 1650, and that remained a charge on the estate until the early nineteenth century, although many of the subsequent generations had tried to get it set aside by courts.

By 1598 Robert Wynn of Foelas (Pentrefoelas) was Steward of the estate of the Abbey of Aberconway for Queen Elizabeth, and the estate was probably leased. A very large Dutch style house was built, with extensive formal gardens, of which there used to be a portrayal in oils on wood painted in the eighteenth century, which may still exist somewhere.[42] This may be the same house of which one Richard Symonds recorded in 1645 —

> "the roofe of the chamber over the parlour was the roofe of the chapel of Conwey Abbey."

Thomas Myddelton, of the Myddeltons of Chirk and Denbigh, was living there in 1599, and he may have erected the new house. The power of commerce was already being felt, for Thomas Myddelton was apprenticed to a London grocer, and worked up to become a freeman of the Grocers' Company in 1582, advancing after that so rapidly in wealth and status that he was lending money, in conjunction with his friend John Williams, goldsmith (more will arise about him later) on the grand scale, including a number of advances of as much as £500 at a time to John Wynn of Gwydir.

The family owned it until 1654, or maybe until 1662, after which it passed into the hands of another branch of the Wynn family. In 1736 the heiress to that family's estates was married from here to John Wynn of Boduan (a different family). Their son Thomas became the first Lord Newborough, and that family owned the property until early in the twentieth century. They pulled down the old house, and built the present one, together with the farmhouse and the farmbuildings (now a house) on the opposite side of the main road, between 1848 and 1852.

In the last decades of the eighteenth century the site was split by the Turnpike road, and more recently there has been development of a caravan site alongside the house, which is now an hotel. Now the old winding turnpike road has been made into a broad modern highway. Unlike so many other monasteries, little now remains after all these changes and depredations.

What is known about the buildings comes mainly from excavations in the 20th century, which gave some indication from the different nature of the soil used to fill the trenches when the foundations were taken away. There was under the former house a long vaulted brick cellar with a gothic arch at the end, bricked up, but it was destroyed at the time of the re-building in the 19th century. Two large underground rooms at the back of the present building now seem to be all that remains of this once proud and powerful monastery. The rood screen at Llanrwst church is formed of carvings taken from the abbey. Available information points to a very large establishment, extending far under the present caravan site, the hotel, the farmhouse and the farmbuildings, and to the west of the present road.

One of the abbots of Maenan was Geoffrey Kyffin, whose grand-nephew, David Kyffin, was rector of Llanddoged in the latter part of the sixteenth century. David Kyffin had, soon after the dissolution of the Abbey, become the owner of part of the Abbey estates on which stood a house known as Maenan Hall. Of what size it was we do not know, but the Kyffin family was old established, and had been tenants of the land for a long time. David married Margaret, daughter of Maredudd ap Ieuan of Dolwyddelan and sister of John Wynn ap Maredudd who started the re-building of Gwydir Castle. Their son Maurice Kyffin rebuilt Maenan Hall about that same time or a little later (sometime during the reign of Elizabeth).

The lanes and byways up the hill opposite the hotel are meandering and narrow. Their number and complexity, and the age of some of the buildings still there, suggest that there was a significant community at the time of the Abbey, of which many buildings, being of wood, will have disappeared without trace. The building of Maenan Mill still exists, as does the old smithy, where the ancient arts are still practised alongside modern brazing and welding. But the lanes are more distinguished now for the views which they provide, across the Valley and to the mountains.

From Maenan went Thomas Hughes to Colwyn. It was in 1865 that he attended a sale of part of the Erskine Estate in that village and bought a plot of land there on which he built a house and shop. His business grew as Colwyn grew. He was closely involved in the growth of Methodism there, but his main service for the town was that in 1890 or thereabouts he persuaded his fellow businessmen that they should buy Llyn Cowlyd, a lake away to the west of the Conwy Valley, to secure a proper water supply. The lake was eventually purchased and developed for that purpose in co-operation with the adjacent Borough of Conwy, and it supplies those towns still. The lake and the site of the Llyn Cowlyd Railway will be visited later in this tour.

To get to Caer Oleu it is necessary to walk, parking the car near Maenan Post Office and proceeding north, the footpath being shown on the Ordnance Survey Map. The earthworks are variously named Pen-y-castell, Garreg Oleu or Caer Oleu. They are situated about a quarter of a mile south-south-east of Plas Maenan Hotel, but are not properly accessible from there. It was the site of castles or forts from Iberian times or before, right up until the medieval period, being almost certainly used by the Romans as a look-out post. It is most remarkable for the views of the Valley.

Continuing on our way, at Bryn Glas we shall join the old toll road from Eglwys-bach to Llanrwst, now partly an almost impassable lane. To the right is the old village of Llanddoged, which has little to show of its age except some of its farmhouses. Its church is on an ancient site, but was rebuilt in 1838 by the rector at a cost of £495. It is a listed building. It was rebuilt on the old foundations with two aisles separated by an arcade of

Llanrwst Parish church showing the Gwydir Chapel

square wooden columns. It is said (mainly on the authority of the Topographical Dictionary of Wales, 1833) that the second aisle was added to the original church after the Reformation, a survival in that case of the double-aisle plan into post-Catholic times. There are tablets to the Kyffins of Maenan, David Kyffin having been rector. No man of very great fame lived here from the time of Saint Doget. But the satirical poet and playwright Elis Roberts was here in the eighteenth century, and John Williams, Baptist Minister and author was born here during that same century, but spent most of his life at Aberduar.

Between 1780 and 1819 Moses Evans, clockmaker worked here, but also, it seems, at Llanrwst and Llangernyw. Timepieces exist bearing that name and those three addresses dated from 1751 to 1830, and since it is improbable that the earliest known clock was the first he made, or that the last known was his last, it seems likely that Moses Evans was two people, maybe father and son. Be that as it may, over a period of eighty years a very great number of "cottage clocks" were made under that name, that of 1751 bearing the address of Llangernyw, many between 1780 and 1808 bearing that of Llanddoged, with the last known of 1830 bearing the address of Llanrwst. The term "cottage clock" relates to five feet to six feet high pendulum clocks of very simple design, operating for 30 hours on one winding, using the same weight as a rule for both timekeeping and striking. Their simple mechanism allowed them to work under adverse conditions, and since they did not require high rooms and were relatively cheap, they were very popular in the homes of the rather less wealthy. The case was usually made in elm or oak, of which there was much in this area, with good furniture and coffin craftsmen to work it.

Here was born Evan Jones in 1793, but in 1815 he left the area, never to return. He was to become known as a preacher and as a writer, and he published several small books under the name of Gwrwst ab Bleddyn Flaidd.

Beside the road into the village is Saint Doged's well, which still spouts forth clear, fresh water. In the past the waters were famous as a cure for sore eyes, but with modern pollution it might be unwise to try the remedy now.

The old name of the parish seems to have been Doeg, since there is in Llanrwst church an old brass commemorating a former rector of this village, "Griffith Lloyd, Rector Doegensis".

Passing on from Llanddoged we come to Llanrwst, market town and traditional capital of the Valleys, burnt and sacked, rebuilt, only to be sacked again and rebuilt. On the borders of the princedoms of the early days, between Yorkist and Lancastrian in the Wars of the Roses, it had been a sort of no-man's land, fiercely independent, so that there was a saying "England, Wales and Llanrwst".

There was a great battle here in 954 when Dyfnwal and Rhodri, the sons of Hywel Dda, Prince of Deheubarth (south-west Wales), attacked the north. The site of the battle was possibly about 700 feet up on the slopes of Gallt-y-foel, about three miles south of the town. Twelve years earlier Idwal Foel, prince of Gwynedd, had been killed in a battle against the English. Under Welsh law he should have been succeeded by his sons. Instead the throne was seized by Hywel Dda, Prince of Deheubarth and overlord of much of the rest of Wales. When in 950 the powerful Hywel Dda died, the sons of Idwal set out to reclaim their rights. They attacked the south and at Nant Carno in 951 they defeated a South Wales army, a year after Hywel's death. Thus it was that three years' later Dyfnwal and Rhodri ap Hywel attacked the north in retaliation only to be defeated. Having successfully disposed of the southern threat, the decendants of Idwal Foel fell upon each other. In 986 Maredudd ab Owain of Deheubarth, grandson of Hywel Dda, invaded Gwynedd, supressed the line of Idwal Foel and united Gwynedd and Deheubarth once again.

At the start of the fifteenth century the town supported Owain Glyndwr in the great uprising, and as a result it was so devastated by the forces of the king that it was said that grass grew in the market place and deer fed in the churchyard for many a year.

In the Wars of the Roses the town espoused the Lancastrian cause, and followers of Dafydd ap Siencyn rampaged through the king's territories in Denbighshire, and burnt and pillaged the town of Denbigh itself. The king later retaliated by sending a strong force under the Earl of Pembroke to recover his estates, and to punish the people of the Conwy Valley. Large parts of the area were laid waste, and Llanrwst itself was sacked in 1468. Of Dafydd ap Siencyn we will learn more later.

The town's importance dates from far, far back, no doubt because the river was navigable, and the tidal reaches used to extend this far. There was a bridge here at a very early date, the first south of the river mouth, and to here came roads from several directions. In the 1770s the toll road from London via Shrewsbury was reconstructed through Pentrefoelas, Nebo, Llanrwst and on to Conwy at the instigation, it is said, of a Shrewsbury innkeeper, Robert Lawrence, who immediately started running a coach service from London to Holyhead. Twenty-five years or so later another toll road was constructed on the east side of the river to Tal-y-cafn, and maps of a few years after that show toll roads from Denbigh via Llangernyw, and from Beddgelert via Capel Curig. But those roads and others had been pack trails since the days of the Romans, and probably earlier.

The age of the town is a matter for conjecture. There is a tradition that the Romans had some sort of harbour here, but whether it was for river boats alone we do not know. The river has no doubt changed its course since then, and washed away, or covered with silt, any works which they may have constructed. However, the belief would be consistent with the fact that lead was mined on the other side of the river, and with the routes of other known Roman roads and tracks, some of which we shall later explore.

At the time of the great battle of 954 it was an established community known as Gwrgwst. It features throughout the history of North Wales.

After the Welshman Henry Tudur took over the throne of England and ended the Norman dynasties, it seems to have been consistently monarchist in its support — not surprising, since the Tudor family, although of Anglesey, had its origins in Rhos, Creuddyn and Nant Conwy, generations before Llywelyn Fawr appointed Ednyfed ap Cynwrig as Seneschal of Gwynedd. Much later, there is a tale, now known to be untrue that in the Civil War, when King Charles was being pursued by Cromwell, the townspeople supplied him with a boat to escape to Conwy.[44]

By that time Pont Fawr, the present bridge, had been erected under the direction of Sir Richard Wynn to replace one declared in 1626 to be unsafe. The bridge was paid for by the people of Denbighshire and Caernarfonshire in equal proportions, and is said to have been designed by Inigo Jones, who was certainly a visitor to the area from time to time, and is apochryphally said to have been born near here — not, as some would say, in London. He is said to have been christened Ynyr Jones, but to have thought that Inigo was more appropriate for a career in London. However there is no evidence to support this claim. The day it was opened, just ten years later, the centre arch collapsed. The central locking stones had been put in upside down, an error which was attributed to the addiction of the workmen to mead (which was probably part of their wages, as was local custom). The men engaged to rebuild it were, according to repute, condemned to drink only buttermilk until the job was finished. The bridge is still sometimes known as the Buttermilk Bridge. Due to the rows which have always occurred when vehicles meet at the top, it has also acquired the name of Pont-y-rhegi — the swearing bridge. In 1702 the centre arch collapsed under the stress of a great flood, and the structure which carries the loads of today was then erected. There may be truth in the suggestion that the western arch suffered a similar fate in 1676.

Until 1962 there stood in the market square of the town, named Ancaster Square after the Earls of that name who own still much land in the area, a town hall.[45] That fell victim more to the demands of highway engineers, to clear the way for modern traffic, than to the disrepair from which it was said to suffer. With its departure went much of the real character of the town. It had in it a "birdcage" clock, constructed in the middle of the eighteenth century by one John Owen. The clock is still in existence, all in repairable order, at the Welsh Folk Museum at St Fagans, but it is not assembled.[46] The clock face, but not the internal workings has been installed in the recently built clock tower in the town square.

That is unfortunate, because Llanrwst has a history of clockmaking, and John Owen was a member of one of its most famous horologist families. While some towns, and many larger villages, had their clockmakers in the eighteenth and nineteenth centuries, Llanrwst was quite an important centre for the industry. The first Watkin Owen was here at the turn of the seventeenth/eighteenth centuries; was he, perhaps, a son or nephew of the Watkin Owen who in 1680 and earlier years was the agent for the Gwydir Estates, who wrote about the boats on the river, and about Tal-y-cafn Ferry? By the middle of the eighteenth century there were the son, the John Owen who built the town hall clock, and Moses Evans of whom we heard at Llanddoged. The Owens' shop in Denbigh Street was in the later years of the business known as Greenwich House.

The Llanrwst of those days was a very go-ahead town, and had some of the fashionable names for shops — London House for ladies' wear and linen, which is now an ironmongery and hardware store, where there was until into the late nineteen seventies one of those delights of small boys, an overhead wire cash conveyor between the counters and the desk, along which the cash and the bill were shot with magical force, to come back quite shortly with the change and the receipt: did it, as others did, go with unbounded ingenuity to the upper floor? Paris House in Station Road, now pulled down and rebuilt, but up for sale, sold ladies' gowns. In Bridge Street The Old Library now sells antiques. Manchester House, the specialists for cotton goods, is now C. L. Jones, hardware and builders' merchants. The Pharmacy in Market Square has now gone and in Station Road, Birmingham House no longer sells shining brass.

Harp House in Denbigh Street now sells fruit and vegetables, but the town was once famous for its harps and harpists. The craft of making them died out with the development of the cheaper piano, easier to play, and with plenty of printed scores of the popular tunes of the day. In 1586 one William Camden, the English antiquary and historian, in his *Britannia,* a survey of the British Isles, said "This town, small and ill-built, is famous for harpmakers and had a good corn market". Published first in Latin, it was translated and published in English in 1610. But he was writing two centuries before the hey-day of the town and the days of one of the most famous of all its harpmakers, John Richard, who was born at the King's Head [47] in 1711, and lived until 1789. At one time he was employed by Queen Charlotte, and two of his harps are at the Welsh Folk Museum, St Fagans. In the same century came Rowland Griffith, who died in the town's Almshouses, and we shall learn more of him when we visit there. In the churchyard are tombstones to David Roberts "Merchant and Harper", who died in 1779, and Thomas Parry "Harper of this Town", who died in 1791. Another famous son (a poet) was Robert Williams (Trebor Mai), who died in 1877. More may be read of Conwy Valley harpists in *Seiri Cerdd Nanconwy* by R.M. Williams, published by Gwasg Carreg Gwalch.

The town was much involved with the wool trade, and there were dyers and mercers as well as those who handled and sold the raw wool and fleeces. In 1656 John Davies, Mercer, of Llanrwst was issuing his own copper one farthing tokens bearing the arms of the Mercers' Company, the weight of which were nearly a gram each. In 1686 there were Thomas Davies and Robert Davies, also mercers, who clearly may have been sons of John Davies.

Tanning was a thriving industry, a natural offshoot of the wool and dairy industries, which prospered from the middle ages until the last tannery closed in 1979. The tanners were evidently an unruly lot, who thought nothing of hanging their drying skins in all kinds of places, on trees, even in the churchyard. Locally tanned leather was made-up here. In 1686 Hugh Jones was a glove maker and Robert Jones was a saddle maker (there were as many as three saddlers within living memory). These and other traders were evidently significant employers, for they used to supply labour on a casual basis for Watkin Owen of Gwydir Estate.

There was printing, of which we shall learn more at another time, and brewing and caskmaking — casks and slats for the making of barrels were exported to Ireland — no doubt Dublin— in ships from Llansanffraid Glan Conwy. There was manufacture of carts and wheels, clogs and boots, furniture and sails.

Sailmaking was no doubt a relic of the days when ships were built here, as at Trefriw and Tal-y-cafn, and of course Glan Conwy. Seagoing boats could ply the river as far as here from Roman times until the twentieth century. Records in the Registers of the Customs House refer to a ship *The Hopewell,* belonging to Conwy, being built in the Parish of Llanrwst in 1756, 35 feet long, 12 feet wide and 25 tons burthen. The builder may have been Robert Roberts, Shipwright of Llanrwst Parish, whose illegitimate son John was buried at Conwy on 14th February, 1751. That may seem very small to us, but it was half as big again as the *Peter,* recorded by Watkin Owen of Gwydir as plying between Tal-y-cafn and Chester in 1686, and twice as big as another ship referred to as sailing between Tal-y-cafn and Liverpool. It was well over twice the size of the river boats normally working only on the Conwy. Ships were, of course, of tonnages that seem to us incredibly small, even those trading at the great ports. The Day Book of Richard Neale, a customs officer at Pill on the Somerset Avon, listing all the vessels entering and leaving the then leading port of Bristol between 26th May and 23rd June 1763 (two dates at random) shows that the ships engaged in trade between that port and Ireland and the Continent were mainly between 20 tons and 30 tons burthen, and the great ocean-going ship the *King Frederic* of Liverpool was only 200 tons. The slave trading ships of the time operating from Bristol and Liverpool were of 35 to 80 tons, with a few up to 200 tons. In 1685 at least two boats of 12 to 13 tons had been working the river regularly between Glan Conwy and Llanrwst, but one of them was holed and sunk at Yr Arw in that year. Evidently the silting of the river was beginning to show its effect on the sizes of ships which could use it, so that by the time *The Hopewell* was launched such boats could only pass with care, probably only at the highest tides. The nineteenth century had produced a similar phenomenon at Trefriw, so that it is unlikely that the steamers which went there as late as 1939 could now do so.[48] With such changes in the river in the last 200 to 300 years, it is believable that conditions for navigation in Roman times may have been very different, and that quite large ships may have been able to sail to Llanrwst.

Very fine furniture was made here, particularly in the seventeenth and eighteenth centuries when there was plenty of good local oak and elm, and to this day Llanrwst canopied and plain Welsh dressers will fetch high prices on the market. The skill of the local cabinet makers was without doubt one of the reasons for the early growth of clockmaking in and after the arrival on the scene of the first Watkin Owen about the beginning of the 1700s — according to Bob Owen (Croesor) he was mentioned in a legal document of 1702. That he was making clocks in the town about 1700 was accepted as fact by the authority G.H. Baillie forty years and more ago in his great masterpiece *Watchmakers and Clockmakers of the World*. In Volume 2 of that horologists' bible, compiled by Brian Loomes in 1976, the year 1702 is quoted as the date of a Watkin Owen clock which he had traced. Watkin was followed by his son John who made the birdcage clock for the Town Hall, then by his grandson Watkin and his great-grandson, also Watkin.

The third Watkin is regarded as one of the best clockmakers the world has known, but he was also the maker of very fine watches, including fusee alarm watches in chased and pierced cases. At the other extreme he made simple, reliable cottage clocks. He is generally credited with having invented arched brass dials for clocks with the moving dial for moon phases, which he incorporated in his longcase clocks. His favourite text associated with such dials was *He appointed the moon for seasons*. He usually made the cases for his watches, but one has a case made by the famous London silversmith Hester Bateman, hallmarked London 1789.

The last of the family seem to have been David and William, younger brothers of the third Watkin. Their last recorded clock is one by William dated 1835, after which the family is said to have disappeared from the town. Most of the time they were all in Denbigh Street, where in 1842 there was also a Griffith Owen, but apparently he had no connection with the older established, more famous family. He was in business with his son Humphrey Owen until 1902. There are also in existence timepieces bearing the names of Thomas Owen (undated) and John Owen (1875) in the same street, but they may have been retailers who had their names put on clocks which they purchased elsewhere. John and William Jones whose names appear on many clocks and watches may also largely only have been retailers, though they are credited with having made some of their own: W. Thomas probably traded in the same way, but George Jackson, who had a shop in the town in 1805, made his own clocks in

Old Denbigh Street, Llanrwst

Dolgellau. Rowland Griffiths was in Denbigh Street in 1835, and Richard P. Hughes in 1887; at various times in that same century there were Robert, Matthew and Owen Williams, Matthew appearing also at Penmachno in 1874. Between 1820 and 1890 there were also C. Roberts and Robert and John Roberts. From 1856 to 1876 Theophilus Davies was in Little Bridge Street (now Station Road).

That total of 23 makers and dealers (excluding Moses Evans, whether that be one or two people) over a period of about 200 years is itself an indication of the commercial wealth and importance of the town. The clockmakers regarded themselves as quite important people, and they wore top hats and black tail coats, in the same way as butchers wore what we now call straw boaters. W. Humphries Jones who wrote of this town in *My Yesteryears — From Farm to Pharmacy* recorded visits to Griffith Owen's shop opposite the Metropolitan Bank in Denbigh Street. He described him as a tall man of handsome appearance who donned a silk hat and frock coat when going out. An elder in the Methodist Church, he well maintained his status.

The town became a centre for the carriage of passengers and goods. The inns and the livery stables, and the warehouses prospered. In 1780 Robert Lawrence's express coach from London to Holyhead started to come by the new Turnpike Road, by way of Shrewsbury through Corwen, and on to Conwy and Bangor, doing the whole journey in the record time of 39 hours. The ponderous carts and the long-wagons had used the earlier tracks, but now as well as the coaches there came the elegant and faster chaises, and later the phaetons. There were also coaches and carriers' wagons, and private carriages, to and from Chester and Denbigh, Abergele, Llansannan and Beddgelert or Caernarfon, and in a later time direct from Bangor. A passenger on one of the coaches at the time commented on the number of small boats carrying goods on the river, and there was a small canal or dock behind Ancaster Square where hides and wool and other wares were loaded, and coal and other goods from afar came in. By the end of the eighteenth century Llanrwst was a very busy place indeed.

Pernant (Bob Owen mentioned before), when a young man, was engaged in clearing the area alongside the old "canal", and found there a plaque with schedules of charges for the mooring of river boats, and also a timetable for a steamboat, which could perhaps have been the flat bottomed boat known to have plied from Llandudno in the latter part of 19th century and the early part of the 20th century. He regretted not having kept it.

Those trades have gone, and ships no longer ply the Conwy. The name

Steam Packet Lane has gone from the alley by London House which led to canal and wharf. Few can now remember the last river boat below the churchyard wall, or the occasional passenger boat by Tu-hwnt-i'r-bont. The town now depends much on its thriving cattle market. There is a tourist industry, but an unprosperous town will not attract. There is some light industry, but if the town decays, none will stay to work therein. The professional offices depend likewise on the other prosperity of the town. But officialdom can be blind, and also stubborn.

Today we will just look round some of the corners, into nooks and crannies, because we shall return another day, when we have visited other parts of the valleys, and have discovered some more of history, in which the town and the valleys are quite inseparable.

We will start in the market square, for that has been there since the town began. As it now appears, it dates from the end of the fifteenth century, when it was rebuilt, no doubt a bit at a time, after the devastations of the Wars of the Roses. But to say that is rather like putting a date on the schoolboy's pocket knife after two new handles and four new blades. In its shape and form it does so date, and some of the buildings are of that kind of age. Recent alterations to *The Pharmacy* led to the uncovering of old timber-framed con-struction and reed-based plaster work, a small part of which has been left open for inspection, protected behind glass. That building is an integral part of the corner shop, *Contessa,* and of *The Old Library* in Bridge Street, and the floors overlap and interlock: the Bridge Street frontage was altered in 1909 for road widening works, and that facade was destroyed: the whole internal structure of those two is now supported on steel girders dating from that time. The *Pen-y-bryn* and adjacent *Hand,* and part of the *Eagles Hotel,* must be of the same era, as (just outside the Square) must be the *Cornuco-pia* and *Pen-y-bont* Hotels in Bridge Street, and the *Hen Aelwyd Café* in Denbigh Street. *Hen Aelwyd,* the Old Home, or Old Hearth, is reputed to have been a farm long ago, but it was quite normal to have a farm in the midst of shops and offices. It probably sold milk and cream, butter and eggs. At the other end of the time scale, McColl's was rebuilt a few years ago, after a spectacular fire destroyed much of the old Gwydir House.

Through all the ages the main form of the Square, of Bridge Street and the western end of Denbigh Street and part of Little Bridge Street and Willow Street, have remained the same, but the eastern end of Denbigh Street has been changed out of all recognition by the destruction not many years ago of the lovely old row of shops and houses opposite Jones and Bebb. There has, of course, been the demolition of the old Town Hall, and Steam Packet Lane seems no longer to be regarded as a public high-way, but the little lane off the south west corner of The Square still leads

Above: Gwydir Uchaf Chapel
Below: The Gwydir Chapel Llanrwst Church
& the effigy of Hywel Coetmor

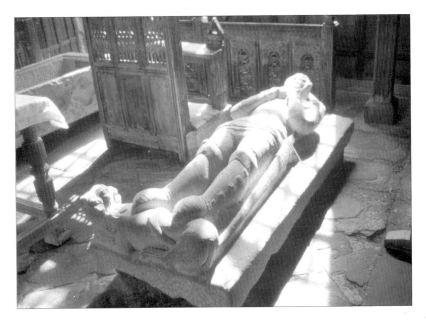

Above: The Almshouses, Llanrwst
Below: The Almshouses from the churchgate, Llanrwsrt

to St Grwst's Church and the Gwydir Chapel, past the old almshouses, which we shall visit on our return. True, the almshouses were built only in 1610, but the church was mostly rebuilt about 1470 to replace that which was destroyed in 1468.

The original church or chapel was on another site, now Cae Llan whereon council houses have been built, and the present site was given in the eleventh century by Rhun, son of Nefydd Hardd, in expiation for a murder committed by his father. Nefydd Hardd was the founder of one of the fifteen great tribes or families of Gwynedd. The chapel at Cae Llan is reputed to have dated from the fifth century, which would be entirely consistent with the existence of a Roman town or settlement which continued into the latter days of the Empire. However, in that event the chapel cannot originally have been dedicated to Gwrwst ap Gwaith, as is generally assumed, because he did not live until the seventh century — he came eight generations, approximately 250 years, after Coel.[49] Coel was a contemporary of Macsen Wledig, Maximus Magnus (who went from these parts to become Emperor of Rome in the year A.D. 383) and, as indicated on pages 10 and 11, was a powerful Celtic commander of a Roman district.

There are therefore two possibilities. The first is that the original dedication was to a different Gwrwst, possibly Gwrwst ap Ceneu, who did live in the fifth century — he was a grandson of Coel. The less likely answer is that the chapel was originally dedicated differently, and was rededicated to Gwrwst ap Gwaith at some later date. It seems unlikely that the chapel dated only from the seventh century if the Romans were here.

A thatched church was built on the site which Rhun ap Nefydd Hardd had given. That was partly destroyed by fire at the time of the sacking of the town in the Owain Glyndŵr uprising, and was completely destroyed later in the fifthteenth century by the Earl of Pembroke's men when the Yorkists retaliated for the burning of Denbigh.

The rebuilding was started in 1470, but how long it took to complete is a matter for conjecture, for the beautiful carved rood screen came from Maenan Abbey after the dissolution 66 years later. We will leave fuller examination of the church until our next visit, but will just look now at the grave slab of Griffith Lloyd, one time schoolmaster in the town, later a lecturer, and finally rector. He died in 1719, and maybe he was responsible for the education of the first Watkin Owen, master clockmaker, pioneer of Llanrwst's great clockmaking industry, and perhaps even other members of that family. Adjoining the east side of the churchyard was formerly the schoolroom and a hospital.

Off another corner of Ancaster Square, adjacent to Bridge Street, is a small pedestrian lane, Tan-y-graig, which leads to Watling Street. The

Above: St Grwst Church by the river's bank
Below: Sheltered housing development, Llanrwst

houses on the right have been restored by the District Council, which has also developed an extremely attractive sheltered housing estate which won a well deserved design award — but of more importance than these is the isolated restored house facing down the lane towards the Square. There when a boy lived Bob Owen, "Pernant", but before his time it was the town gaol.

There is plenty to occupy us here for the rest of the day, to visit the Encounter Wildlife Museum, off School Bank Road, swim in the modern Baths, go fishing, or explore the Gorsedd Stones and the recreation ground with its attractive riverside walks. The stones, regrettably, have no claim to antiquity, having been erected for the National Eisteddfod when it was held here in 1951. There is a local eisteddfod held each year in June, and the National Eisteddfod was held here in 1989.

We may be here at the time of the Llanrwst Show, which rivals that at Eglwys-bach in size and variety. There is a walk down Station Road and into the Station Yard, there to turn off to pass first between factories, then over open fields to the Gower Bridge and on to Trefriw. The original bridge was erected by one John Gower, Rector of Trefriw, in the 19th century, shortly after the coming of the railway, to link that then growing Spa with the railway station. That bridge was washed away in a flood fifty years or so ago, and the present bridge was erected, financed very largely, it is said, by a Llanrwst cinema owner who was losing patrons from Trefriw. There is no longer toll or house, and only pedestrians can use this replacement bridge. In June there is a fishing contest in the town; in July a vintage car rally, a gala and sheep dog trials take place on different days.

Just across the river, by Pont Fawr, is the National Trust property, Tu-hwnt-i'r-bont — which just means "beyond the bridge". In summer it is open as a craft shop, and coffee and tea rooms. In the winter it is closed, because now it gets flooded. It was first a farmhouse in the fifteenth century, when maybe there was not even a bridge at this particular point, only a ford and ferry. It became a Court House in the sixteenth century, and it must surely not have been subject to flooding at that time, which, like the fall-off in shipping, confirms that there have been radical changes in the river due to silting in the past 400 years.

Just outside the town, on the Betws-y-coed road, the A470, beyond the Meadow Vale Garage, is a house of equal age, Cae'r Berllan. The title deeds to Cwmlanerch, rather nearer to Betws-y-coed on the western side of the river go back to Wyrion Eden, which itself dates from the twelfth century. That was a concessionary landholding granted to all the descendants of Iorwerth ap Gwrpan, who was grandfather of Ednyfed Fychan — they were to hold their lands free from taxes and liability to service, except military service in time of war. It was granted in recognition of service of Ednyfed's father, Cynrig, to Llywelyn Fawr, so maybe he was Seneschal before his son Ednyfed.

This little town, through which the juggernauts of today pound their way, shaking to the foundations the buildings of the past, is steeped in the history of Gwynedd and of Wales, of which we shall learn more in our travels. Most who pass this way, save those to whom it is home or market, race madly through in headlong rush to the sea, the resorts of the west coast or the north, or to Snowdonia. They know not what they miss. There is a choice of hotels and houses, farms and camping sites for overnight.

Standing stones at Llanrwst celebrating the Eisteddfod

The Market Place, Llanrwst

33. *See family tree, page 171.*
34. *The four parts of his body were, in fact, sold by auction to the highest bidders.*
35. *See page 252.*
36. *Papal Bull of Pope Nicholas dated August 22nd, 1283.*
37. *See page 120.*
38. *The body of Llywelyn Fawr was reputedly moved to Maenan (see page 51) but the others were left at Conwy. See page 234 for headstone.*
39. *Matthew Paris' English History. 66*
40. *See page 250.*
41. *The idea that he was brother of Elis Prys, so often quoted, is erroneous.*
42. *In 1912 it was in the possession of the Hon. F. G. Wynne of Glynllifon.*
43. *See page 249.*
44. *A boat could slip quietly down the river without arousing the attention of any of the Wynns of Gwydir, whose loyalty to the king was doubtful.*
45. *The town hall built in 1661 was severely damaged by fire in the early 1800s and had to be substantially rebuilt, so that the building demolished in recent years was mainly only a century and a half old.*
46. *Authority, Ambrose Mason, late of the Pharmacy.*
47. *Now the British Legion Club.*
48. *At the time of writing a motor launch has been commissioned which it is hoped will be able to go to Trefriw.*
49. *His full line of descent was Gwrwst ap Gwaith ab Elffin ab Urien ap Cunfarch ap Meirchien ap Gwrwst ap Cenau ap Coel, which would make him approximately contemporary with Yspwys ap Yspwys — see page 249.*

Day 3 - Nebo, Capel Garmon & Betws-y-coed

The main road to the south from Llanrwst is now the A470, leading direct to Betws-y-coed, but it was not always so. It is a relatively modern road which does not appear on Henry Teesdale's map of 1829, or on Cary's map of 1809, or on earlier maps by John Evans and others. Before the Shrewsbury turnpike road of 1777, from Llanrwst through

Pentrefoelas, the only roads were by way of Capel Garmon, the road to Ysbyty Ifan and beyond, and at a later date the road on the west side of the river by way of Gwydir to Betws-y-coed. It is the turnpike road which we will follow. Along this, after 1777, travelled many an Irish Member of Parliament on his way to Westminster, in Lawrence's coach or hired gig or chaise, and many an Irish Governor and civil servant of the past. From then to 1803 all of those, and the wagons and the wagonettes from the Holyhead Irish Packet, and most who came on horseback, came this way if they did not wish to chance the hazards of the coastal road to Chester, at Penmaen-Rhos and across the Rhuddlan marshes.[50] Of those a writer[51] in 1797 said —

> "...the mode of travelling through Wales has been entirely changed within thirty years. Travellers going between Chester and Holyhead were then obliged to take a guide to conduct them safely over the almost trackless heaths and mountains in Flintshire and Denbighshire."

This road leads from the A470 within the town, just beyond the graveyard where till now stood the ruin of a church. Here on the right is the old toll house, beyond which the road rises gently up between schools[52] and industry, so that as we climb from the town we look down on the Valley, as many a traveller has done before, half shrouded in mist if we have set off early — though not so early, perhaps, as those who caught the coaches, for they most likely started "at five of the clock in the morning". In those days as the hill got steeper the coachman and the guard would have cried "first class passengers stay in their seats, second class passengers get off and push". Those second class passengers must have

Top inset: White Horse Inn, Capel Garmon. Bottom inset: St Michael's Church, Betws-y-coed

pushed long and hard on the road from Bangor to Nebo.

As we climb further, out of the top of the mist will appear on the right the beautiful panorama of Eryri and the Carneddau, Snowdonia; Eryri, the home of the eagles, but the eagles have all gone long ago, slaughtered by man with his bows and arrows and his guns. Near the top of the hill we may pick out Snowdon itself, Carnedd Dafydd and Carnedd Llywelyn,[54] and the other high peaks known well to climbers and historians alike. In winter, with snow, the scale is magnified, and the view is reminiscent of the Far Pavilions from Kashmir.

Nebo no longer has a post office and shop, and little else than a few houses, yet it has been occupied since the Bronze Age, if not before. In 1832 the population in the area could still justify the building of an Independent Congregational Chapel to accommodate 292, and in 1851 average attendances were 305 souls on Sundays. The old hilltop trail of ages past from Ysbyty Ifan to Creuddyn and the Conwy ferry came this way, over the high moors east of Maenan. The Rev. John Evans, born in 1815, after being curate of Llanbedr-y-cennin, became curate of Pentrefoelas and in due course archdeacon of Meirionnydd. In 1854 he wrote some articles about Pentrefoelas and Ysbyty Ifan, and concluded that the Romans had a route for troops, presumably with some vehicles, from Oswestry[55] to Caerhun, passing through Pentrefoelas and Llanrwst. It could have passed through Capel Garmon, but the direct route across the top would have been more in accord with Roman patterns. He did not refer to Nebo, but in his days that name did not appear on maps — the place was then just "nowhere", despite the rural population.

In 1810 a bronze spear was found. Until about 1850 there still stood not far away Maen Pebyll, a large stone surrounded by a circle of smaller ones, but the large one was blasted away at that time, and only the pieces remain to be seen.

On the fringes of the moors which surround Moel Seisiog, are some 16,000 roadless acres of peat and crags and bog, a thousand feet above the sea; Nebo was always a bleak and forbidding place to live. But that people did live here in the very distant past we know, for on the slopes of Moel Seisiog itself, at a height of some 1,500 feet, there was still in 1912 a ruined cairn which had been used as a base for a peat stack. Within a short distance were the foundations of two hut dwellings of 17 feet and 12 feet internal diameter respectively. Some 60 feet away was what was left of another dwelling 12 feet diameter inside. It seems that in the eighteenth century there were other cairns and huts whose stones were taken about 1803 to build walls and other structures following the Enclosure Acts, and ancient bones were then dug up. We may never know how much was then destroyed. One cairn in par-

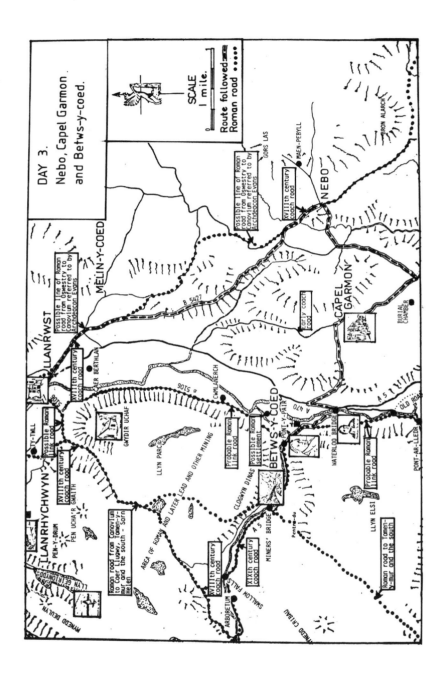

ticular there used to be, Garnedd Wen near the farmhouse Bryn Cyplau.

In more recent times, if not in the Bronze Age, the packmen passed; in later times long-wagons, then the coaches and the chaises and the wagons, till winter came, and the snows and the gales. Then Nebo was on its own, the only link with the outer world being the road to the Valley which we shall follow.

In such winter weather, all would go by way of the lower road, through Capel Garmon, where woods and valleys gave cover for robbers and high-waymen, where in earlier times the bandit gangs of Ysbyty Ifan would lay in wait, and many a traveller met his end.

At the far end of the village is the road we want, half hidden on the right, leading down to Capel Garmon. We must take care to turn left at the first T-junction, and right at the next, or we shall travel in a circle, or find ourselves at Pentrefoelas. Before the village a signpost directs the passer-by to the famous Capel Garmon Burial Chamber, a megalithic cham-bered tomb with a false portal. Beaker pottery was found here, and it seems that it must have continued in use into the Bronze Age. It is re-garded as one of the finest examples of a passage grave in the British Isles. At 3,700 years old, dating from the same times as the spear and cromlech at Nebo, it is still more than half a thousand years less old than the axe factory at Graig Lwyd, and yet was over a thousand years old when the Celts arrived, and near two thousand when the Romans came — such is the scale of history in the area in which we travel.

Leaving here we come into Capel Garmon village, where once was found a Roman-Celtic fire dog: of domestic type, it was a relic of the times when the Romans had their forts at Caer Llugwy and Caerhun, mines at Llanrhychwyn and possible settlement at Llanrwst, when there was peace-ful co-existence, when soldiers, traders, scribes and discharged legionaries lived in the surrounding areas. Perhaps there was a village here in those days, as there was in the middle ages. The church was built in 1863, and the only signs of antiquity are the seventeenth-century communion table and font. There was a church before, which in 1774 was reported to be "a very ancient building and greatly decayed in the foundation walls and roof ". That building had been built by Dafydd Anwyl ab Ieuan, sometime rector of Llanbedrog and chaplain to the Earl of Warwick, in the sixteenth century. After that report it was rebuilt in 1789, but the replacement only lasted until 1863, when the present church was erected. The dedication suggests a much older foundation, possibly fifth or sixth century.

Through the village, which still has a chapel[56], an inn and a school, we turn left down a winding hill to join once again the modern A470, then left again.

Above & opposite page: The burial chamber at Capel Garmon

The Betws-y-coed to which we come is that of the last three centuries, for it has developed since the construction of the Capel Curig Turnpike road. That road crossed the Conwy River by a great stone bridge of single span[57] which now carries the traffic of today on the road to Blaenau Ffestiniog and the south, the A470. In Welsh "Pont yr Afanc", formerly "Pont Llyn Afanc", the bridge of the monster, or the bridge of the lake of the monster, over the pool where the monster used to live, it has been wrongly translated into English as the Beaver Bridge. But the monster does not live there now, for it was pulled out of the pool many years ago by two oxen, and taken to a lake far away in the mountains, from which it has not escaped. From 1803 to 1821 the bridge carried the westbound traffic which came down the steep new hill cut by the Trust in the slopes of Dinas Mawr, so steep that its dangers compelled Telford, when reconstructing the Holyhead road from Shrewsbury to the Ferry, to abandon it. He cut a more spectacular road in the face of the hill, and built his massive cast iron bridge, the Waterloo Bridge; it is so named because the casting of the ironwork was commenced and largely completed in the year of the battle.

Before the turnpike trust constructed this road from Pentrefoelas, and Pont yr Afanc, the way from the east to Betws-y-coed had been quite different. From Denbigh or from Shrewsbury or Corwen the route had been by Rhydlydan, a village north-east of Ysbyty Ifan now almost forgotten, from there to Ysbyty Ifan itself, and thence to Penmachno Mill and down to Pont-ar-Ledr on the western side of the Conwy River, to come into Betws-y-coed by way of the old road, known now as the Old Toll Road, behind the Waterloo Hotel and the Little Chef restaurant. It was a very pretty route indeed, but tortuous and difficult for men and horses. We shall look at it in various stages when we come to the Lledr, Machno and Upper Conwy Valleys.

It was Parliament which, dissatisfied with the state of the roads on this important route, and the working of the several turnpike trusts, appointed Thomas Telford a decade after the Pont yr Afanc was built to make a survey and submit a report on the whole Holyhead road from Shrewsbury to that port. For this part here, in the Conwy and the Llugwy Valleys it voted £20,000 towards the cost of works in the year 1815, and in 1817 and 1818 added to it another £30,000. In 1818 the work began, and was completed by 1821. The Capel Curig Turnpike Trust, like others on the route, was superseded by the Shrewsbury-Bangor-Ferry Turnpike Trust.

Before we join his road we shall come to a waterfall, cascading down the sheer face of rock upon our left, to disappear, it seems, into the very bowels of the earth, which in any other place would be of note. Across the road a small path used to lead down, and people could climb to the river's bank to see at closer hand the great cast-iron bridge, and to read upon its side the clear cast letters *"This Arch was constructed in the same year the battle of Waterloo was fought"*: the path has disappeared. The span is 108 feet, and it stands as it was built, in part supported by concrete beams cast within itself not many years ago to take the weight of modern traffic.

But Telford's road was remarkable for more than just this bridge. Across the Menai Strait he built his famous suspension bridge, and in these parts in another scheme he built that which spans the tides at Conwy. For those he is best known, but his real genius is in the enduring fitness of his works in general for the traffic of today, and in the skill and ingenuity by which he built his mail-coach road through the mountains of Gwynedd without exceeding a gradient of 1 in 22. When horses strained with heavy loads, and speed was of high importance for the Royal Mail, this was an achievement of no small import. How pleased must have been the second class passengers. His cuttings in rock, his embankments and retaining walls, endure after 115 years of horses, and 95 years of cars and lorries.

The road straight on leads to Pentrefoelas, and on to Shrewsbury; by another route it leads to Dolwyddelan, Blaenau Ffestiniog and the south. To the right is Betws-y-coed, the "oratory in the

Thomas Telford

wood", where the holy men on their way to Bardsey, the Island of the Twenty Thousand Saints, would stay to proclaim the Word of God, while laymen on their pilgrimage would rest and pray, and hear the Word.

Where was the oratory, or the chapel? Was it where now stands St Michael's Church, within the present village, or was it near Bryn Gefeiliau, where stood the Roman Camp of Caer Llugwy,[58] four miles out on the Bangor Road? Perhaps the answer is that it was neither.

It was about AD 80 that the Romans built first a wood-fenced camp on the Llugwy banks, which they were later to develop into a stone-built fort, only to withdraw any great force of garrison by the year 150. They stayed, however, in these parts until near 400, and some who settled remained after the last of the legions had left with the armies of Gwynedd to capture Rome, or returned with Elen, the widow of the deposed Emperor. A hundred years before the end of the Roman occupation, long even before the times of Macsen and Elen, the Romans accepted Christianity, most particularly in these parts of Wales, and it is likely that the

Waterloo Bridge

chapel would have been established where the people were, and where some protection existed against pagan raids.

Whether or not the original chapel was where St Michael's Church now stands, there was certainly a church here before the present building, to find which we turn along a road on the east side of the railway, going north. Now a cul-de-sac, leading to the golf course, it was at one time the main village road, before it was severed for the building of the railway.

Although mainly built in the fourteenth century, when the parish was listed in the Records of Caernarfon as "Bettus and Comlannerch", the church has been altered over the years, the last major works being in 1843, when the north transept was added and a balcony was removed.

Here lie the remains of Gruffydd, son of Dafydd Goch, (David the Red). His home was at Fedw Deg, 800 feet up on the slopes of Iwerddon south of the River Lledr, 2^1/2 miles away. He was the grandson of Prince Dafydd who had taken over the command of the Welsh forces against Edward I after his brother, Llywelyn, had been murdered at Builth. It will be re-called that Dafydd was betrayed, and taken to Shrewsbury, where he was subjected to the utmost barbarity as a so-called traitor, despite which this grandson, Gruffydd, served with the Black Prince in France with some distinction, possibly at Poitiers. This Gruffydd is sometimes confused with Gruffydd ap Hywel, who was present with the Black Prince at Crecy in 1346, 11 years later, by which time Gruffydd ap Dafydd Goch was prob-ably dead. Gruffydd was a heavy man, and the bearers had very great dif-ficulty bringing his coffin all the way from Fedw Deg. There is in the church a carved effigy of him in full armour, with the inscription *"HicJacet Grufyd ap Dafyd Goch agnu dei miserere me"*. He was the father of Hywel Coetmor, who lies buried in Llanrwst Church, who was captain of a hun-dred men at Agincourt, and who owned the Gwydir estates. It was his son Dafydd who sold those lands to the Wynn family.

There are two lychgates, the northern one having been built about 1756, when it was conveniently placed for the pack trail through the village which originally came from Conwy and Llanrwst, via Gwydir, to cross the Llugwy by a ford. From there it came past the church and on into the Lledr Valley. Later Pont-y-pair was built, and in due course Telford's road came through on the line of the present A5, by-passing the length between the Royal Oak and the present railway bridge. Finally it was severed for the railway, and in 1868 a new lychgate was erected at the southern end of the churchyard. Legible tombstones in the churchyard date from 1696, but are not as old as some within the church.

It is something of a mystery why Betws came to be located where it is. Archdeacon Evans maintained that the Romans had a road from Oswestry[59]

to Pentrefoelas, and thence to Llanrwst and Canovium, and if that is correct, then no doubt they had another road down the Conwy Valley from
Pentrefoelas to Caer Llugwy, through Betws. It seems quite likely that, as
some authorities think, they had a camp or settlement here as well as that
at Caer Llugwy, but there is still no direct evidence that they had any
confluence of roads nearer than Pentre-du, nearly a mile away to the west.
A settlement here may just have been because it was an attractive place to
live. That is not unlikely, for the mines at Llanrhychwyn and in the Llugwy
Valley would have required the presence of a considerable number of
administrative staff of many kinds from managers to scribes.

Whatever the reason, by 1749 Betws had a population of 200 which
increased in the following half century, so that in 1801, before there was
a coach road from the west, it had 88 houses and a population of 359. It
was to be two years before the Capel Curig Turnpike Trust would link
Lord Penrhyn's road from Bangor to Tŷ Hyll with Lawrence's road from
Pentrefoelas to Shrewsbury, and establish a coach road through Betws
from Holyhead to London. Lawrence's coaches at once used the new road,
but the first mail coach did not come this way until 7th September, 1808,
nearly two years after the ferry disaster at Conwy.

No doubt there had from before Roman times been a track for pack
horses and riders, from Ysbyty Ifan through Betws, to Capel Curig and
over the mountains to Llanllechid and Llandegai, and another down the
Lledr Valley from Dolwyddelan and on through the Conwy Valley to
Gwydir, Llanrwst and Trefriw.

The coming of the coaches, and of course the private chaises, even
before Telford completed his greatly improved road, led to rapid development and by 1851 the resident population was 478. Those who passed
through remarked on the beauty of the place, and artists came, and honeymoon couples, fishermen and visitors of all kinds. There was some setback to the new-found prosperity when in 1826 Telford, commissioned
to improve the road from Chester to Bangor, built the suspension bridge
at Conwy and made relatively safe the roads round Penmaen-Rhos,
Penmaenbach and Pen-y-clip. As a writer of the latter part of the century
before last said, just after some work had been done to the earlier road —

> Before this safe commodious turnpike road was made, to which the
> kingdom of Ireland contributed liberally, travellers were obliged to
> wait till the tide went out, that they might cross the sands under
> Penmaenbach; or otherwise to ride some miles over a bank of loose
> gravel, formed by the tide, and ascend Sychnant, then a steep rugged
> precipice, to go to Conwy...[60]

Thomas Telford's report of some 20 years later indicates that "this safe commodious turnpike road" was itself no more than seven feet wide in parts, and other writers indicated that there was no wall on the seaward side.

The coastal road in the early nineteenth century must have been very frightful, steep and dangerous, and the Betws-y-coed road much more attractive; but with Telford's new works there was a coastal road of very different character which sufficed well into the days of the motorcar, into the early 1930s. Twenty years after his road and bridge were completed, the Chester and Holyhead Railway Company constructed a line along the North Wales coast, and across Anglesey to Holyhead, completing the rail link from London to Holyhead and the Irish Ferry. The London coach traffic through Betws-y-coed was finished.

Betws and Llanrwst suffered, and not to be outdone and left off the map, the people of Llanrwst and the rest of the Valley set up such demand that in 1860 work was started on a railway line from the marshes at Llandudno Junction. The original Conwy and Llanrwst Railway Company planned its line via Glan Conwy and Tal-y-cafn only as far as Llanrwst. In 1867 that Company was absorbed by the London and North Western Railway Company, and in the next year the line was completed and extended to Betws-y-coed. In 1872 the Company obtained powers to construct a light railway from Betws-y-coed to Blaenau Ffestiniog, to take advantage of the highly lucrative slate trade of Dolwyddelan and Blaenau. The line took five years to construct, the main time being that taken to construct the Dolwyddelan Tunnel, 2 miles 328 yards long. Part way through construction it was decided to adapt the scheme to take standard gauge rolling stock, but the tunnel could not be widened throughout, and some bridges could not be altered, which always limited the size of engines and other stock which could be used. Two years after its completion, passenger trains were introduced.

The railway brought back to Betws-y-coed the trippers and the holiday makers, and gave it prosperity such as it had never known before. The Royal Oak Hotel was rebuilt and enlarged, other hotels developed, and Betws thrived. Artists came in even greater numbers, amateur and professional, to follow in the footsteps of David Cox, who had died before the railway came. Born in 1783, died in 1859, he specialised in water colours. Among his claims to fame was that he found a cheap form of wrapping paper made in Dundee which he liked for his sweeping washes— it was later marketed in the art world as Cox's Paper. It was he who in 1847 painted the sign for the Royal Oak Hotel which was used for the new hotel when it was built in 1861, but is now preserved inside the building. When in 1890 the proprietress of the hotel was declared bankrupt, the sign was listed as one of her assets at a value of £1,000, and thirty years later *Wonderful Britain* reported that £5,000 had been refused for it — both, of course, were large figures in their days. Another artist was the unfortunate James Whittaker, who fell backwards into the river when studying a view he proposed to paint, and was drowned. Among others less famed, but whose works fetch good prices now in sales, were David Bates, Alfred Fontville and Benjamin W. Leader.

But we are standing at the church, and have let our thoughts wander. The railway has far less traffic than in the past — no goods except the waste from Trawsfynydd power station — and part of the station and goods yard have been converted into a Railway Museum — its entrance is almost opposite where we are standing. Here are coaches and wagons and railway memorabilia to delight small boys of any age, and a small light railway to give the family a ride.

Behind us is a suspension bridge across the Conwy River. It will sway if any march across it in united step, but it has done so since the day that it was finished. Maybe it should have a notice at the ends like that at its much larger, more famous, relation, the Clifton Suspension Bridge, that companies of troops must march out of step. But it is not likely that any such troops will have marched across, though its predecessor, a pontoon bridge, was built by sappers in the First World War. This bridge is still called the Sappers' Bridge, even though it is a replacement constructed after the pontoon bridge was washed away by floods in 1928; it bears an inscription *"David Powell and Co. Ltd., Engineers, Westminster, 1930"*.

Beyond the bridge, across the river, a narrow path leads to the A470 near where we joined it from Capel Garmon. If we go that way, and turn left along the trunk road, we shall come to Rhyd-y-creuau, the Drapers' Field Centre for Field Studies.

Returning to the church, we may still from within the yard of the Railway Museum cross the railway by the old station footbridge, over which many an artist must in great anticipation have carried easel and paints on alighting from a crowded train, and many a fisherman carried his rods.

In those days this now sad, deserted station was a cheerful, busy place. It had three platforms and one for parcels, and there were two goods depots, one for north and one for south on opposite sides of the tracks. There were cattle pens and the present Log Cabin was the shed for the carters' lurries and covered wagons. The cottages behind were then all occupied by employees of the railway, "The Company" of which they were all so proud. When the trains came in, they came in pairs, one from the north and one from the south, with much ritual exchanging of the "keys" without which no driver could or would proceed along the single tracks. Then there would be much hustle and bustle, with porters in treasured uniforms, some helping passengers with their baggage, and finding that which travelled in the "guard's van". There were parcels to be offloaded, and mail too, then others to be loaded on before the train could go along its way. There were ticket collectors at each gate, and the stationmaster would be there to see that all was well, ready with top hat and tails to don in haste if an unexpected passenger of rank appeared from train or horse-drawn carriage. The waiting room had a fire, and hot tea and coffee, buns and pies were there for those who wanted sustenance before or after travel. There was a newspaper stall in the station yard, and a shop for the repair of boots and shoes. Not much time would ever pass without sound of the signal-box bell.

But none of this caused any slowing down of work in the two goods yards, where what was handled could cover all the needs of life, coal and furniture and food, supplies for the local shops from those the chemist needed to those of the village ironmonger, wines and fruit for the hotels, flowers for their tables, new ploughs for the local farmers, bicycles for presents for the children, the passengers' "luggage in advance" — all came by rail before the days when massive juggernauts belched diesel fumes along the roads to take away the railways' business, as they, of course, in earlier times had taken that of the long-wagon teamsters, the coachmen and, in other parts, the wherrymen and bargees of the navigable waterways.

Facing us there when we cross the railway footbridge is Cae Llan, the church field, of which part has been despoiled as a car park, not reinstated when that other park for vehicles was formed beyond The Log Cabin, on land where perhaps the Romans lived.[61] The station buildings to which we come, before the present café was formed were a model of railway architecture by Owen Gethin Jones of Penmachno, a remarkable man of many talents, master mason, designer, artist and writer. Across the church field, beyond the A5, is the new church of St Mary, itself now more than a hundred years old. Built in 1873 to meet the needs of the great numbers of visitors, as was St Mary's at Llanrwst, it is very beautiful inside. The local origin of the blue stone of which it is built is obvious, but that of the sandstone and serpentine is not. The sandstone came from Ancaster, the seat of the Earls of Ancaster, the local landowners, and the serpentine from their estates in Cornwall. The chiming clock and bells (now electrified) were added in 1907, and the alabaster reredos in 1929.

North past the church are the most prominent features of modern Betws, the shopping emporia, lined along the western side of the trunk road. Here may be bought clothes of local make, garments from the far reaches of Europe and Asia, pottery from Gwynedd and elsewhere, brass from Birmingham and Taiwan, climbing gear, local honey and jams, perfumes

The packman

and scents, boots and shoes, maps and photographs. To them flock now the tourists in their thousands, who in bygone days would have walked the riverside paths and gardens, or taken a trip by wagonette, or sat to enjoy the scenery. Cameras now click where artists stood. But on the road the car rules all, and in very high summer the queues ensnare, and no obvious line for by-pass road appears.

On the right is a bridge across the river, which here flows south, not north — but it is not the river we saw before — that was the Conwy, this is the Llugwy, and it joins the Conwy in the plains below the village. We should have come to the point of meeting had we walked the golf course beyond St Michael's Church.

The bridge is Pont-y-pair, the bridge of the cauldron. Before much water was taken from the Llugwy by authorities, the river in spate here was well so described. The bridge has five arches. Built in the 1500s it is a century older than Pont Fawr at Llanrwst. Its builder was Hywel Saer Maen, "Hol Isear", Howell the Mason, who came from Bala to do the work, and is credited with another bridge which we shall later cross. That such a man should be asked to come from so far away was a sign of the importance, and the difficulty, of the job in hand. His bridge here was perhaps wide enough only for packhorses, for at a later date work was done on one side of the line of road, which seems to have been to make it wider, and not just to effect repairs. This bridge linked the track from Dolwyddelan and Penmachno with that to Gwydir, Llanrwst and Trefriw, and on to Conwy and the coast, avoiding the ford across the Llugwy by where Royal Oak Farm is now, which torrential flows could often make extremely hazardous.

Mill Street, beyond the bridge, is the only part of Betws in which the buildings stand in anything like their original form, though they themselves are in part replacements of others earlier on their sites. The mill ceased to operate before the Second World War, but the wheel still turned in 1940, and remained in position even after that. It has now been altered out of all recognition, with the mill flume filled in where once it flowed through what is now a car park, and then behind the adjacent shop and houses. It raised its protest in recent years, by flooding the foundations of the modern toilets, and refusing to be overcome by pumping.

The iron frame of the old wheel across the river has nothing to do with corn, nor with antiquity. It dates but from the century before last, when

Pont-y-pair Bridge, Betws-y-coed

an enterprising resident set it up for butter production for the demands of the visitors, the churns being operated by the power of water.

In this little corner, or perhaps at the far end of the village on the Old Toll Road, near the smithy, one can still dream of the old Betws, that of the pilgrims on the way to Bardsey, of the days of the Princes of Gwynedd and the marauding armies of Deheubarth, of Powys and of the English kings, and of the times of the Members of Parliament and the government servants who came this way to brave the hazards of the Irish Sea. We can think of the countless generations of the local Welsh, the farmers and the gentry, the shepherds and the packmen who trudged on foot the mountain trails and the valley paths on their errands of work and pleasure, or to come to service at St Michael's, or the church which stood in earlier times. We can imagine the great cortege with the massive coffin of Gruffydd ap Dafydd as it wended its way down the long trail from Fedw Deg which to this day bears his name. In later times on Sundays the people came from all around to the Calvinistic Chapel (1806) and Soar for the Independent Dissenters (1842), which between them attracted over 700 attendances on a Sunday — including visitors, of course.

No doubt the walks along the river banks were enjoyed the same by Roman soldiers from the nearby camp, with their Celtic brides, as by Victorian honeymoon couples and those of today.

The former Pandy Mill, near Betws-y-coed, within the parish of Penmachno (at grid ref 808 533) near the old woollen mill.

50. *For some reason the London coaches and the mail coaches never regularly used the route via Tal-y-cafn, Llansannan, Denbigh and Chester.*
51. *Welch Tours, 1797.*
52. *The first school, on the left, was an agricultural merchant's office, but it is now empty — it was the old Free School which replaced one near St Grwst's church.*
54. *Snowdon 3,558 ft, 1085m; Carnedd Dafydd 3,424 ft, 1044m; Carnedd Llywelyn 3,490 ft. 1064m. OS. Second Series 1:50,000.*
55. *More probably Viroconium, see page 44.*
56. *Capel Mawr, Calvinist, built in 1798, and Bethania Wesleyan Methodist dating from only 1845.*
57. *The span of the arch is 68 ft 4 ins, and the structure is 23 ft 4 ins wide.*
58. *The Roman name of this fort has never been ascertained, and it is variously known as Caer Llugwy, from the River Llugwy, or Bryn Gefeiliau, from the nearby farm.*
59. *See note 24 on page 44.*
60. *Welch Tours, 1797.*
61 *Site excavations in 1974-5 did not reveal positive evidence, but they were on a limited scale. Railway, road and other works may have disturbed much.*

The Afon Llugwy at Pont-y-pair Bridge, Betws-y-coed

Day 4 Part 1 - The Lledr Valley & Dolwyddelan

The medieval history of North Wales is the history of the Welsh Princes. The first trip from Betws-y-coed must therefore be up the Lledr Valley, to the birthplace of that most famous of them all, Llewelyn Fawr, Llewelyn the Great, great-great-grandfather of Gruffydd ap Dafydd whose effigy we found in St Michael's church.

Whilst most of the stone churches of Wales were built by the Normans, and most of the castles built by the Welsh were of earlier dates and built of timber, there were exceptions. The Normans built more castles of timber than of stone, but few remain because the Welsh in the centuries before the conquests of Henry Tudur destroyed and burnt them, just as the Normans before the days of Edward 1 destroyed those of the Welsh which the Welsh did not destroy themselves. Dolwyddelan was one of the exceptions, a Welsh castle built of stone, taken over and extended by the Normans. Originally built of timber about 1170 by Iorwerth Drwyndwn, Lord of Nant Conwy, a few years before the birth of Ednyfed Fychan [62] (Henry Tudur's ancestor) it was altered at various times in the following century to have a stone keep and stone walls. It was here or in the keep of the nearby former motte and bailey, if the castle had not been completed, that Llywelyn was born in 1173.

We could travel up the valley by rail, which is a pretty and enjoyable run; instead we will go by car, leaving Betws-y-coed by way of the famous Waterloo Bridge, then turning right on the A470 to cross the Beaver Bridge, back to the western bank of the Conwy. The Conwy gives way to the Lledr on our left, and we travel through a narrow deep valley, with rocky tree-clad slopes on our right, and wooded glades and narrow river meadows on our left. There winds the river, the Lledr, bubbling down its erratic channel, shimmering on rocks and boulders, or lying limpid in occasional pool — or if heavy rain has fallen, it will roar along in impatient torrent, white and angry, taking all before it.

The present road on the north side of the river replaces that which served the valley in the days gone by, a road of much less directness on the southern side of the river, but even that does not appear on John

Top inset: The arms of Llywelyn ab Iorwerth. Bottom inset: Dolwyddelan Castle

Evans' maps of the 1790s. It was in reality a series of disjointed tracks to get to which now we should cross the Afon Lledr by the Pont-ar-Ledr, known also as the Roman Bridge, as are so many of the older bridges in this area.

John Evans was not of the Conwy Valley, but he was a Welshman, though he was born just over the Welsh borders at Llanymynech in Shropshire, in 1723. He lived in that village, just south of Oswestry, all his life. He prepared two maps of North Wales the first was in nine sheets to a scale of approximately one mile to an inch, and it was published in 1795. The second was to a scale of about three miles to an inch, and was published after his death in 1797. The maps were extraordinarily accurate and detailed for their day. They sold so well that in 1799 his son, who was a surgeon, republished them, and then again republished them in 1802 with revisions and additions.

The old road to the south and east, of the days before Pont-yr-Afanc was constructed, along the western side of the River Conwy, was that which leaves the present A5 alongside the Cotswold Outdoor 'Rock Bottom' shop. It goes past the ancient smithy, now altered and adapted as Betws-y-coed Motors. The bridge across the Lledr, the "Roman Bridge", was built, it seems, by the same Hywel Saer Maen who built the Pont-y-pair, no doubt in one improvement scheme of the roads and tracks from Gwydir to Penmachno and Dolwyddelan in those days in the latter part of the fifteenth century when Maredudd ab Ieuan had taken a lease of Dolwyddelan Castle and lands in the Lledr Valley, had already built or was building Penamnen, and no doubt had his eyes on Gwydir which he bought in 1500.

The bridge has two unequal arches of 35 ft 6 ins and 13 ft 6 ins respectively, no doubt for no better reason or no worse than that such spacing suited Hywel for foundations. Its width is 14 ft 6 ins.

At Craig Lledr the modern road passes under a lovely stone railway viaduct, another masterpiece of that Owen Gethin Jones whose work we saw at Betws-y-coed railway station. Here we must stop, but not alone to see the Gethin's Bridge, for such it is called, but also to explore a track into the mountains. To the south it leads, into National Trust lands, and to Tŷ Mawr Wybrnant, which we could, had we wished have approached another time from Penmachno in the adjacent valley.[63] Here at Tŷ Mawr in the Parish of Penmachno, was born one William Morgan, that much is certain. A stone over the door of the present building used to record (and may still do so) that —

In this house was born William Morgan, D. D., Bishop of St. Asaph, the first translator of the entire Bible into Welsh, born 1541, died Sept. 10th, 1604.

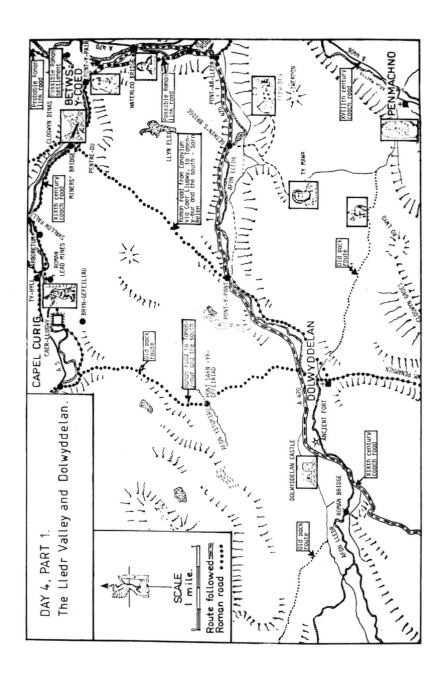

DAY 4, PART 1.
The Lledr Valley and Dolwyddelan.

SCALE 1 mile.

Route followed ____
Roman road •••••

How much of that is true? As to when he was born; he was ordained at Ely on 15th April, 1568, he was then 23 years old, which would fix his date of birth as 1545, not 1541. There was a cupboard upstairs in the house which opened off the fireplace, and it was at one time said that Dr Morgan used to hide there in times of persecution; but there are those who say that the present house only dates from the seventeenth century, being a replacement of that in which Morgan was born. Furthermore, they say, Dr Morgan lived at Welshpool, Llanfyllin, Llandaf and St Asaph, as well as other places in the times of religious persecution. Most of his work on his translation of the Bible was done at Llanfyllin or Llanrhaeadr-ym-Mochnant. How much time, they ask, was he here to need to hide in the cupboard? As regards the first question, it could be, of course, that the great chimney piece of the former house was incorporated in the new, which would have been not at all uncommon. As regards the second, he may have retreated to this part of Wales from his parishes when the persecutions were taking place.

What is clear is that Morgan became an Anglican Bishop, having served as a loyal Anglican clergyman, during the reign of Elizabeth. Protestants such as he, did not of course, face persecution at this time. During his childhood, the Catholic Mary was queen but it is unlikely that there was any forceful persecution of Protestants in such a far flung corner of the kingdom as the upper Conwy valley. References to Morgan living at Llandaf and St Asaph refer to his time as Bishop of thoses places so obviously he would not have suffered from religious persecution.

Pont yr Afanc on the River Conwy

The uncertainties about dates are not important, and do not detract from the facts that he was born here, and that he did translate the Old Testament, largely incorporating with it the translation of the New Testament of William Salesbury, of whom he was likely a friend. The uncertainties do, however, help to show how difficult it is to get accurate datings of the lives of quite eminent people, let alone such as Anne Thomas of Creuddyn, of whom we heard at Glan Conwy. What really matters is that William was the son of John ap Morgan ap Llywelyn and his wife Lowri, and that they must have been people of some culture, as evidently were many who lived hereabouts in those days of trade and prosperity, the great days of wool. He is said to have been educated by a monk, and it is most likely correct, as some say, that as the son of a tenant on the Wynn family estates, he went to Gwydir School set up by the Wynns rather before the time when Maenan Abbey was dissolved. In 1565 he went to Cambridge where in 1568 he graduated as a BA, and in 1571 as an MA. There under his tutor John Immanuel Tremellius he learnt eight languages, including Hebrew, Latin and Greek. In 1578 he became a BD, and in 1583 a DD. After entry into the church in 1568 he held a number of livings before becoming Bishop of Llandaf, and later Bishop of St Asaph. Although he finished his translation of the Bible at either Llanfyllin or Llanrhaeadr-ym-Mochnant, he probably started it while he was at Cambridge.

It was published in 1588 under the title Y *Beibl Cyssegr-Lan*, The Holy Bible. During the time of preparation for printing and publication, Morgan was assisted by Gabriel Goodman, a North-Walean from Ruthin, who at the time was Dean of Westminster, and he stayed with Goodman in London. The cost of both printing and publication was born by John Whitgift, Archbishop of Canterbury, whom Morgan had come to know during the hearing of a law case about the validity of a marriage during Morgan's time at Llanrhaeadr-ym-Mochnant. Of William Salesbury, from whom Morgan took his translation of the New Testament, we shall learn more. The Bible was dedicated to Queen Elizabeth.

Within the Valley, Morgan had his troubles with the Wynn family, because Sir John Wynn claimed that he had at some time accepted a loan and had in return promised Sir John the living of Llanrwst. Both allegations must be discounted, for Sir John was always in debt to John Williams, the Queen's Jeweller and to Thomas Myddelton, and furthermore Morgan was not the kind of man to repay a personal debt with, in effect, church funds.

Back on the road, still we shall climb, both rail and river now on our left, till we reach Pont-y-pant, a little bridge across the river on the left, and so marked on the Ordnance Survey map. Here on the right came into the Valley the Roman road from Caer Llugwy, over the mountains by direct route from Pentre-du at Betws-y-coed.[64] The road of the middle ages lay on the southern side of the river, and it seems likely that the Roman road here crossed over to that line. It went, as does the modern road on the northern side, to Dolwyddelan, the valley becoming wider, with lesser slopes and larger fields.

Dolwyddelan now is greatly changed from that of Roman times, or those which Iorwerth Drwyndwn knew, or even Maredudd ab Ieuan. It now appears a straggling collection of houses dating largely from various times in the last $2^1/2$ centuries, the time of growth and demise of the slate industry. From here went in tremendous numbers, slates to roof the houses of America's deep south, the great houses of the kings of cotton, for they resisted well the tropical heat, not cracking as did many. They roofed the houses of Cheshire, of Lancashire, and of London, where quality was wanted. Of the houses, the farms, the cottages and byres of the earlier middle ages, but little survives — mostly built of wood, they succumbed to the pillaging of the robber gangs of Ysbyty Ifan, and of wars and strife, and some of just old age. A few of stone construction do remain.

It acquired some local importance for cattle, and there was an annual fair held on 20th September. Two centuries ago the name was Dol Wyddelen.

We will at this time just pass through, leaving the line of the Roman road. We come into country of a different kind, ffridd lands, the mountain sheep pastures laboriously enclosed so long ago with mile upon mile of dry stone wall. We must marvel at the work that went into these, the sweat and toil of man and horse to heave and hoist such untold millions of stones, many of quite massive size, to build those walls in relentless lines up hills, down dips, here over rock, there through marsh. Many a stone-age cairn or Celtic camp, or even Roman house or hut, or later deserted farm, was pillaged to build those walls, and many a page of history lost.

We shall pass an area of afforestation, modern planting in larch and pine, and beyond to where even the ffridd lands give way to open desolation — those vast areas known as the cynefin. Even here the walls persist, pushed ever forward over peaks and ridges to define the boundaries of cantrefi[65] and cymydau,[66] and lesser vills or plwyfi.[67] We will go only as far as the road climbs, to beyond 1,250 feet, and then return; if we went further we should leave the areas of the catchments of the Lledr River, and that is not our purpose.

The name cynefin is one of fascination, for which the dictionary will tell you "acquainted, familiar — habitat". Here none but the hardy Welsh sheep can survive, they who are acquainted with, familiar with, the bleak, wild habitat. They are the sheep who know from the teaching of their parents, who learnt from theirs, and on back through the ages, where to graze, where to shelter in the worst of the weather, where to survive in times of drought — how, withal, to live in this inhospitable country. The sheep that are there are the descendants, crossed with other breeds in various ages, of those that have roamed these fastnesses for generation after generation, longer than the families that have farmed these lands, and they may well be descended from the sheep which the Celts domesticated and improved,[68] to provide the wool for the cloth for the markets of Europe.

For as long as records exist, the flocks of sheep have changed hands with the farms, with the land, for new flocks brought in would not survive for a single season.

Perhaps it is no wonder that these placid animals roam the roads. They have, maybe, more right to be there than we who rush along in cars today — roads were not there when the sheep first came — more right, perhaps, than the landowners themselves. Where we are now there was no road a century and a half ago — even the early pack trails went another way. There was, indeed, no road when the men of nearby Blaenau went to the east to fight the Crimean War in 1854. It was well within the lives of their fathers that one Samuel Holland on his way from Liverpool to Llan Ffestiniog to join his father managing the slate mines, had been advised when at Llanrwst not to venture across the path from Dolwyddelan, as his father had suggested, because the moor and peat bogs would be dangerous without a guide —the route by which he was advised to go was through Cwm Penmachno and the carters' track.

It was those returning soldiers who named the road they found on their return, for the country reminded them of where they had fought, and so many had died; they called it the Crimea Pass, a name so often heard of a road which is blocked when snow falls heavily in winter in Northern Wales.

It was on the edges of these lands that the Princes of Wales had their Dolwyddelan castles, and a hundred generations of men before them had a fortified camp between the present road and river. These were well located to protect the pack trails from raiders who might come from north or west; to dominate that most important of the routes, which came in from the south of Wales, from Tomen-y-mur, which the Romans paved, and later Celtic Elen used to such degree that from her it took its name, Sarn Helen. In the days of the Princes it was still the main communication between south and north, and the armies of Ceredigion and Deheubarth marched here against the forces of Gwynedd, and those of Gwynedd set forth to conquer the whole of Wales. That road may still be walked, from

Dolwyddelan across the river and rail, up Cwm Penamnen, over the hill to Rhyd-yr-elen, and on to Tomen-y-mur at Trawsfynydd.

There was also a pack trail in those days on the route from England by way of Chester, and from Rhuddlan, by way of Denbigh and Ysbyty Ifan through Dolwyddelan to Beddgelert, and by way of Pen-y-Gwryd and the Llanberis Pass to Bangor and Caernarfon, for the ferries to Anglesey, to Aberffraw and Caergybi (Holyhead), and the ships across the sea to Ireland. Later that became a road for coaches, but now does not exist, except for those who walk.

The ruin which can be seen to the north of the road is all that remains of the castle of which the first part was built by Iorwerth Drwyndwn when he was granted the commote of Nant Conwy on the death of Owain Gwynedd in 1170. It was at the time when the Norman Barons were conquering Ireland, and many were passing this way to and from the ships of Llŷn and Anglesey. The castle was extended in the following century and became a residence of Llywelyn the Last in the wars with England and the Normans. It held out against the Normans until 1283, when it was surrendered to the armies of Edward I in January after only two months of campaign. The Welsh, of course, had lost heart to fight after the murder of their beloved leader. The fall of Dolwyddelan was to all intents and purposes the end of Welsh resistance to Edward, though Wales was to rise again at a later time.

But it was a hundred years earlier that Llywelyn ab Iorwerth was born here, the only son of Iorwerth Drwyndwn (Edward the Flat Nosed), Lord of Nant Conwy, and Margaret, daughter of Madog ap Meredudd.[69] He was to live for 67 years, quite a long span for those days, and to marry Joan, a daughter of King John of England. He was to rise from the unenviable state of being hustled away from his place of birth as an infant, when his father was killed, for safe upbringing in Powys, the land of his mother. He was to be a signatory of Magna Carta, alternately friend and foe of the kings of England, a great benefactor of the church, and by the time he died, undisputed leader of the Princes of Wales, recognised as such by the Pope and the Kings of France.

He was to leave his mark in another way, perhaps more important in the long run than his conquests, for he introduced the primogeniture system of inheritance into Wales, where before his time a man's estates, his kingdom, were divided between his sons on death. That system had always before caused the splitting up of Wales whenever there died a prince or king who had succeeded in his lifetime in welding all into a nation.

Although he was not to be successful in obtaining the independence of the Church in Wales from the See of Canterbury, there is no doubt that the historical facts of his support of Giraldus (grandson of Nest)[70] in the fights on that score was to have significance in later times.

Not only in his birth, but in his life and after his death, he belonged to the Conwy Valley. He had a house at Trefriw, where he lived from time to time, with his wife Joan, and he built the little church there. He endowed, inter alia, Aberconwy monastery. On his death, as we have heard, he was buried at Conwy, and his coffin at least was later moved, first to Maenan and later to Llanrwst.

When the castle fell to Edward's troops it was re-garrisoned, a constable being appointed in 1284, who was still there in 1290, but the castle was abandoned soon after that. It was re-occupied after 1489 by Maredudd ab Ieuan, who took a lease. In the nineteenth century it was restored by Lord Willoughby de Eresby.

There is nothing very imposing about Dolwyddelan Castle, yet it has more real importance to Wales than those of Conwy or Caernarfon, both of which are of much later origin, and are the work of the Norman invader, Edward I. What remains now may have been largely rebuilt by Edward or his successors, but its origins and its plan are part of the history of Wales rather than its conquest. While it finally fell after a short winter siege, it had held out against the Normans for longer, perhaps, than any other stronghold, and it was surrendered out of despair at Llywelyn's murder, rather than by reason of conquest.

The Welsh people of those later Norman times did not grow much in the way of grains or fruit, except in Anglesey. They rarely built anything of stone, because of raids and skirmishes. They lived a semi-nomadic existence, in that they grazed their flocks of sheep and cattle on the higher ground in the summer (and there grew some crops), but brought all down to the valleys in the winter. Living that way they were able to pack up their possessions and drive their cattle into the remoteness of the mountains when Norman or other force came against them, so that when routed in battle they were rarely defeated; they soon came back to fight again, and harass their enemies. They left behind little that an enemy could pillage or live upon, as Henry III's troops were to find at Deganwy. It was the role of Anglesey as the granary of Wales that earned it the name of Mam Cymru, Mother of Wales. But though nomadic to that degree, they were more cultured than their foreign invaders. What stone buildings they had, disappeared no doubt, as materials for the great enclosure walls of later times. But many were destroyed by Edward I, in the same way as he destroyed Welsh books, pictures and records.

After Maredudd ab Ieuan acquired the lease of the castle in 1489 he built the present church in replacement of one of earlier date. It is dedicated, as was its predecessor to St Gwyddelon, and it stands on the southern side of the river, here crossed by Pont-y-llan, which bears the date 1888. That replaced a previous bridge on the old Penmachno to Beddgelert road, to which we earlier referred, that of the early Irish travellers, of the packmen of the great days of the wool trade, and later of the coaches, a route which was still traceable on the century before last's Ordnance Survey maps, but is now only a way for walking west of Dolwyddelan.

The earlier church is believed to have stood on a hill called Bryn-y-bedd, 300 yards or so south-west of the present building, on the southern side of the river. It would there have been alongside the one-time route to the south, the route of the Roman road beside the Afon Maesgwyn, through Penamnen to Rhyd-yr-elen and the south, the Helen's Way of the later days of the Empire.

At the time when Maredudd built the new church, just before the end of the fifteenth century, the Order of St John of Jerusalem was at its lowest state; its reputation was so bad that action was being taken to curb its freedoms and licences. There was, it seems, no effort to control the robber gangs which roamed the Hospice lands, and the forces of the king had no right of entry. It may have been that which caused Maredudd to buy Gwydir Castle in 1500 so soon after he had built the new house at Penamnen. Whether that be so, the legend is that he chose the site for the new church because he was afraid that he and his family would be ambushed by robber gangs, or even by his enemies, in the older church — the new site, it seems, was more easy to protect.

The church was extended and renovated a hundred years after it was built, by Robert Wynn of Plas Mawr, Conwy, and again in 1850 by another descendant of Maredudd, Lord Willoughby de Eresby. Within are effigies of several of the family of Wynn (the name was derived from Ieuan in Tudor times when the Anglo-Norman fashion for surnames was being followed in Wales). Though the family moved to Gwydir, it did not sever connection with Dolwyddelan, and Penamnen, which Maredudd had built in the Cwm or Valley of that name was still used —though some say that it was Maredudd's brother Hywel ab Ieuan who built it.

Maredudd and his wife Alicia Gwenvera Margreta are buried in the church, and there is a wall monument to them, to John Wynn their son (*Jo Wynn fil Meredith*), and to Maurice Wynn (*Mauritius Wynn fil Jo*) and lana Anna Katerina. The memorial was repainted in 1920 with, it seems, some variations from what was recorded as being on it about 1700. There is also a brass engraving presumably showing Maredudd as "fil Jovanni", highlighting the Roman influence and the origin of the name Ieuan.

Another wall memorial remembers Grace, wife of William Price, died

3rd June, 1727, aged 57. It is curious that there does not appear to be record of her husband's death or burial within the parish. Did he die elsewhere, even at sea, or had he been of the wrong religious persuasion?

The evidence is that by about 1500 there was at least the beginning of an established community, and that people were evidently living and settling on a permanent basis. An award hereabouts of 1541 refers to *"Erw Croft and Lleighweigh yr havot wherein Robert ap Rhys now resides"*. None, however, refers to Dolwyddelan by name, although several refer to Penmachno, which we shall visit in the adjoining valley. Was this perhaps the same Robert ap Rhys ap Meredydd, father of Elis Prys, the Red Doc-

The River Lledr

tor? Rhys ap Meredydd, Rhys Fawr, fought with Henry Tudur at Bosworth, being one of his great supporters, and he lived at Pentrefoelas — we shall learn more of him and his family later.

Yr havot would clearly be the hafod, the summer farm or dwelling in which Robert ap Rhys lived in the summer, and he would almost certainly have had a hendref, now more usually found in the shortened form of hendre; that was a winter dwelling, or more permanent habitation. The hafod would be in the high regions, the hendre down in the valley.

Bryn Moel, a large two storey farmhouse, survives from the 16th century, from the days of Erw Croft and "Lleighweigh". Other houses of that time only remain as ruins or have been completely lost within the 20th century.

In the seventeenth century the demand for slates led to an increase in population, and the number of houses. Before the railway was built, the slates were carried to Trefriw on pack animals and in wagons, which was a mammoth task, so that in addition to the quarrymen and their families, there must have been many engaged in the transportation and in services to the community as a whole. Between 1801 and 1851 the population grew from 492 to 727. In 1879 the railway altered many things, but it also allowed the trade in slates to expand, and the community grew further, as did its prosperity.

Between 1826 and 1835 three chapels were built, one at Blaenau Dolwyddelan beside what was then still a usuable road to Nant Gwynant.

The signs of that prosperity can be seen in the houses, as well as in work carried out to the church. The reredos was added in the seventeenth century, as was the pulpit. But in the last half century the slate industry has died, and the Dolwyddelan we see today is one of commuters and retired folk, of tourism and tourists, threatened with an invasion of a kind very different from those against which the castle was built. As packman and packhorse gave way to coach and wagon, and both gave way to the railway, so now all has to bow to the motor vehicle, the fast car and the juggernaut. For those the demand is for ribbons of race track, where before have been roads. This little road, part a mere track no more than a hundred years ago, and part not even there, has become the artery for modern traffic between the north and the south of the Principality, as did Sarn Helen long before. It has now been widened, straightened and eased in grade, and opened up so that all may speed.

So far as has been traced as yet, in this valley the Romans paved only the roads from Caer Llugwy to Tomen-y-mur, one of which was that later to be known as Sarn Helen after the Romans had left, but the pack-horse tracks which came to here from Beddgelert and the west and Blaenau Ffestiniog and the south, to lead to Penmachno and Ysbyty Ifan and the east are old. Maybe they were there in Roman times, and used by them, for they were not slow to use the ancient routes of trade, but so far there is no sign that they were paved.

A mile to the south-west of the castle is a very old bridge, Pont Sarn-ddu, known again as the Roman Bridge, which has given its name to the railway station. Eight spans of about 6 feet each were bridged by flat stone slabs supported on corbels. Of great age, it carried, according to John Evans' map of 1794, the pack and drovers' trail from the Lledr Valley to Blaenau Ffestiniog, but it is unlikely that its origin was Roman. More likely it is that if any bridge hereabouts is of Roman origin, it is Pont Sarn-Offeiriaid, three large slabs which carried the road between Dolwyddelan and Capel Curig over the sometimes raging Afon Ystumiau a mile or so north of the present village centre.

It is worth noting the river more carefully on the way back to Betws-y-coed. There are few bridges, but all are old. The first is Pont-y-pant near where the Roman road crossed the river, where the modern road hugs the north. A mile beyond is a footbridge to Tan-aeldroch, ancient massive slabs of stone, so large one wonders how such things were handled. But for that matter, how did the men of even more ancient times move the stones of Stonehenge from the quarries of Pembrokeshire? There is the footbridge by Gethin's Bridge by which we crossed to go to William Morgan's house.

The last across the Lledr is the Pont-ar-Ledr. It is possible to walk from there on the southern side of the river to Fedw-deg, or along the earlier road and then to William Morgan's house, or even up the western side of the Fairy Glen. But as one leaves the bridges, wonder increases that they have stood, often without mortar to bind or seal the joints, but have with-stood the torrents of this fitful river through century after century. There are those who hold that this, the last to which we come before the Conwy, replaces one the Romans built on a road which led from Caer Llugwy to Pentrefoelas and the east, a road to which we shall later come in the Machno valley.

So we come again to the Pont yr Afanc, one of the last great bridges of only masons' craft, with a single arch span nearly the length of a tennis court. From here we may walk to the Fairy Glen, so well renowned, along the part which remains of the ill-fated toll road built from the slopes of Dinas Mawr by the Capel Curig Turnpike Trust. Abandoned in less than two decades, it is now a cul-de-sac; but it leads to the Glen, where for countless ages the waters of the Conwy and the Machno have cut themselves a channel through the solid rock. Across the waters, on the south-western side, is the older road, the possible Roman route, from the Betws of the past by way of Pont-ar-Ledr, to the medieval hospice at Ysbyty

Ifan; the travellers who took that road, like those who used the Turnpike road of the Napoleonic times, saw more of the beauty of the Fairy Glen, than those who travel with greater ease and speed on the Telford road. It would be possible to go on to Penmachno by crossing the Pont-ar-Ledr and following that route, but instead this afternoon we will go there by another way.

The Lledr Valley which we have seen is a place of beauty in some of its parts, and a place of desolation in some others, but it is a place of history of the past, and maybe of the coming history of the future, for in the mountains through which it leads may yet develop a mighty hydro-electric pump-storage plant to vie with that of Dinorwic of world-wide fame. The Dolwyddelan of the future may again be unwillingly a step ahead of progress, as it has been many a time in the past between its dormant spells.

62. *Ednyfed Fychan was appointed Seneschal of Gwynedd by Llewelyn Fawr. He lived at Llys Euryn, and was buried at Llandrillo Church, Rhos-on-Sea. See page 10. Iorwerth Drwyndwn was a son of Owain ap Gruffydd, King of Gwynedd, by a second marriage, and therefore half-brother of Dafydd ab Owain, King of Gwynedd.*

63. *The approach from the centre of Penmachno is that which is officially recognised, and is available for vehicular traffic.*

64. *W.J. Hemp, F.S.A., who assisted in the examination of the camp at Caer Llugwy formed the opinion that they had also a road from Capel Curig, via Bryn Gefeiliau, west of Mynydd Cribau, to Dolwyddelan. That would probably be an earlier route, linking with the road by Llyn Cowlyd.*

65. *Hundreds.*

66. *Commotes.*

67. *Parishes.*

68. *It was the crossing of the harsh-woolled native sheep with a soft-woolled variety which produced the wool which became so famous.*

69. *See page 145.*

70. *See page 116.*

A couple of miles from Betws-y-coed, south-east from the Waterloo Bridge, in the direction of Pentrefoelas, the road to Cwm Machno leads off the A5 towards the south-west.

As soon as we leave the main road, on the B4406 we cross the Conwy River, here in the upper reaches of the Fairy Glen, a rocky gorge where the waters tumble down to join the Machno two hundred yards to our right. It is worth stopping along the road to walk back to the bridge to look, both upstream and down, to enjoy a very pretty view in miniature. This road and bridge do not appear on maps before the time of the Capel Curig Turnpike Road, but there may have been a track, a short cut between Penmachno and Capel Garmon not much in use.

Half a mile along this Cwm Machno road is a cross-roads, where for a long time has stood a chapel. The valley road here crosses the old road from Ysbyty Ifan and the east to Betws-y-coed and Dolwyddelan. On the road to the right is an old stone bridge on the route to Betws, but that indeed is modern compared with the arch which spans the gorge a short way down stream. This is called the Roman Bridge, an arch of very great age, and a typical pack-horse bridge. While maybe it is not likely that it is of such age that it provided passage for any cohorts of Roman cavalry or troops of men on foot, it is still possible that in those early days there was a previous bridge.[71] The soldiers of Rome must have travelled this way from Verconium to Caer Llugwy and beyond, and in the later days of the empire and in the centuries that followed there were pilgrimages to Bardsey. In later times again there were those who travelled to Ireland, of whom we will learn more anon; for the moment we will continue our exploration.

Through the small gorge below the bridges flows the Machno, cascading and bubbling in glinting and foaming waves between tightly enclosing walls of rock, the flow reduced now by the piping of part to drive the wheels of the Penmachno Woollen Mills, which we will inspect as we return down the valley later. When there was first a fulling mill may still be uncertain; the present building was erected originally for that purpose a century and a

103

Top inset: Ffynnon Eidda, Migneint. Bottom inset: Stone at Penmachno

half ago, for the roughing and cleansing of cloth; but the hill behind was already Gallt Pandy, [72] and we are in the land of wool, of wool through the centuries, which has dominated all from quite early days, [73] so that Llanrwst fair fixed the price of wool throughout the land for a generation.

From a little further along the lane the Conwy Falls can be seen, far below in the rocky gorge on the right. This is the top end of the Fairy Glen, painted perhaps more often than any other place in the world in Queen Victoria's time. We can stop to admire the scene from the little roadside clearing, as did the travellers to Ireland, the early pilgrims, and the earlier messengers of Rome, and maybe hope, as they did, to see the

The Fairy Glen

Above: The former textile mill, Penmachno
Below: The path to Ty'n y Coed Uchaf by the Afon Machno,
above the former woollen mill at Penmachno

fairies dance from rock to rock, perhaps to actually see one fall in the waters below, which legend says they never do. Sixty-five years ago there was a salmon ladder up the falls, but that has gone, washed away with little trace. In the mid 1990s a salmon tunnel was constructed which enables the fish to access the upper reaches of the Conwy.

The road continues down to Pont-ar-Ledr, and it is easy to imagine the great joy of travelling it on a lovely summer day in the times of horse and coach, but the sheer terror of that same journey on a snowy winter night.

Back at the crossroads on the B4406, the road to the east is the old road from Penmachno to Capel Garmon and Llanrwst, which after a mile and a half crosses the Conwy river on the Pont Rhyd-Lanfair, which bears the date 1780 on its parapet. It is reputed that its builder was Robert Griffiths of Tan-yr-allt in the Lledr Valley, and that he succeeded with the work after two attempts by other men had failed. The span of the bridge is 90 feet, and the carriageway is 18 feet in width. By what means the river was crossed before that time does not seem clear, but the word "rhyd" indicates a ford.

Just before the bridge is a road to the south, the road to Ysbyty Ifan, which after a little over a mile crosses the Afon Eidda by a bridge which, by reason of its similarity to Pont Rhyd-y-dyfrgi further north, appears to date from about 1780. That would suggest that the whole road between Capel Garmon and Ysbyty Ifan may have been reconstructed about that time. Returning to the crossroads by the chapel and the mill, the road to the left is the road through the Machno Valley.

Most likely along all these roads travelled young William Morgan in the mid-1500s, whose home was no more than a couple of miles away, who likely knew Catrin Llwyd who married William Salesbury. And maybe William Salesbury himself and his wife-to-be walked here from Plas Iolyn where she lived with her parents, and later in life would visit her brother, Elis Prys, the Red Doctor. Or perhaps Richard Lloyd came here to enjoy the view, as we have done, or just to pass on his way, or Gruffydd ap Dafydd Goch, whose house, Fedw Deg, was nearer still.

Who were all these people, and when were they here? Of Gruffydd ap Dafydd Goch we heard at Betws-y-coed. He was a great-nephew of Llywelyn the Last, and therefore great-great-grandson of Llywelyn the Great, Llywelyn Fawr. Elis Prys was of another age, son of Robert ap Rhys, who was chaplain to Cardinal Wolsey; Thomas Cromwell appointed him at a very young age as one of the Visitors of Monasteries in North Wales, and he played a prominent part in

Dr Elis Prys

106

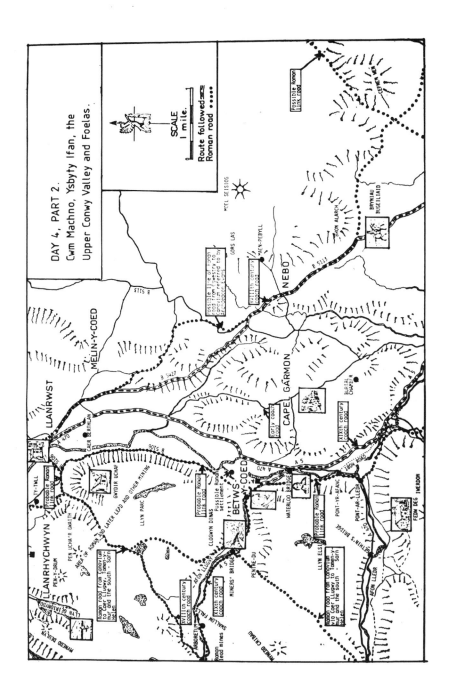

DAY 4, PART 2.
Cwm Machno, Ysbyty Ifan, the
Upper Conwy Valley and Foelas.

SCALE
1 mile.

Route followed
Roman road ••••

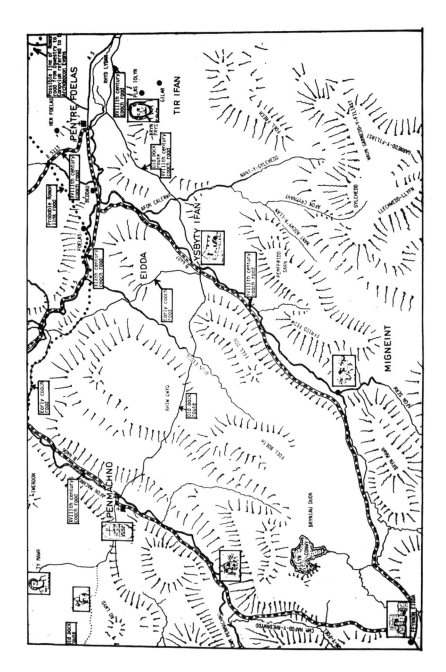

the dissolution of the monasteries although he was not yet 24 at the time. He held many other posts, so many that one wonders how he could have carried out any of his duties in a proper manner. Among these was the office of Member of the Council for the Marches. In 1560 he obtained from Queen Elizabeth the Manor of Tir Ifan, with lands in Ysbyty Ifan and Penmachno. He inherited Plas Iolyn and its lands. His interests, like those of his father, Robert ap Rhys, therefore extended into the valley we are in, as well as that of the Lledr and that in which Ysbyty Ifan lies. We shall find effigies of his father, and of both his grandparents, Rhys ap Meredydd and Lowry, his wife, in Ysbyty Ifan church.

Of William Morgan we have already heard; of his connection and probable association with William Salesbury we will get to know more at Llanrwst. His family were copyholders under the Gwydir estates, here in the Machno Valley, and therefore of some standing. That connection with the estate may account for William's reputed education at Gwydir, where the Wynns had a school, and the pupils were probably taught by monks from Maenan Abbey.

Morgan would have been some twenty years younger than Salesbury, and probably nearer to the age of Catrin, Salesbury's wife. Catrin was one of the numerous children of Robert ap Rhys and his wife Mared, daughter of Rhys Llwyd, from whom for some reason or other she took her name, Catrin Llwyd. In the next century Sir Richard Llwyd (Lloyd) was to be a great loyalist supporter in the Civil War, during the time of Cromwell's Parliament, and on the Restoration.

More or less contemporary with William Morgan would have been Catrin's nephew, Tomos Prys, who was quite a lad, very different from the studious Morgan. Tomos, like all of those whom we recall, was well educated, and gained quite a reputation as a poet. He served in the army in Flanders in 1585-6 with the Earl of Leicester's force which set sail in December and was such a failure through the Earl's incompetence. Tomos survived to serve in Germany, France and Spain, and in 1594 he was in Ireland, after which he became a privateer and a smuggler. He was a friend of William Myddelton of Llansannan, with whom he seems to have shared most, if not all, his expeditions and escapades, and the two of them are said to have been the first to smoke tobacco in public in London. Through all his adventures, he lived to be 70, to be buried on August 23rd, 1634, at Ysbyty Ifan church. He survived his friend Myddelton by 34 years.

The Llwyd family were long and well established in the Machno Valley, and would have been friends of the Morgans and the Salesburys as well as the Pryses. To what extent they were popular locally may be open to question, for in the following quarter century Evan Lloyde who had moved to London and lived at Barnard's Inn (and therefore Anglicised the spelling of his name) was in constant dispute and litigation with a local worthy, Ffoulke Vaughan, and with other local people.

One of the cases which dragged on for years had an amusing origin. Evan Lloyde tried one of his London tricks on Ffoulke Vaughan, granting him a mortgage with possession for a term of four years in return for a loan, of 180 acres of land and two houses in Penmachno; but the land was already let to Evan Lloyde's son Robert and a Hugh ap Morgan. Ffoulke Vaughan exercised his apparent rights, entering into possession of one of the houses and putting a horse out to graze on the land. Robert Lloyde drove it off again, and the feud was on!

It was another member of the same family, Lewis Lloyd, who lived at Hafod-dwyryd who, in about 1740, together with a Richard Anwyl, was responsible for the building in Penmachno of the ten single-roomed almshouses (now two houses). Lewis Lloyd of that address died in 1730, so either he had provided the money for the work and charity before he died, or the assumed dating of 1740 is incorrect. He may have had a son by the same name, but it was the Rev. Evan Ffoulkes who was living at Hafod-dwyryd before 1736, and in 1740.

In 1562, on November 12th, there was a grant completed, from

John ap Cadwaladr[74] of Llanawr, co. Merioneth, gent., to Robert ap Richard ap John ap Madock of Penmaghno, co. Caernarfon, gent., of messuages and lands called Tythyn y meister, Kaer Egloes and y haer managh and all other messuages and glebe lands, late of the chapel or rectory of Penmaghno, to be held of the Crown by knight's service...

The grant goes on at length, but its interest to us is that it introduces yet another family at the time of the Salesburys, the Morgans, Vaughans and Pryses, Llwyds, etc, who were entitled in those days of strict etiquette in such matters, to be called "gentleman". The Penmachno and Ysbyty Ifan area was in those days populous, wealthy and cultured.

The crossroads at which we stand has seen much of history, and we could stay here a long time reminiscing about past centuries, in which the area developed from one of wars to one of literacy, its wealth derived largely from the trades in wool and cloth; but we must go on our way to Penmachno itself, its buildings now largely influenced by development after the spinning and weaving moved from farms and cottages to mills and pandies, and the little masters became the employees of the mill and pandy owners; influenced also by the slate industry, which almost dominated all for some two centuries or more. But its history goes back countless generations, and Penmachno appears on maps of the early middle ages, where places of now much greater fame did not. Before it was Penmachno it was, it seems, Pennant Machno.[75]

The present church was built in 1857 on the former site of two churches which stood side by side, one dedicated to St Enclydwyn and the other to St Tudclyd. The former fell into ruin after the Reformation, the latter was pulled down to make room for the new building. The new church contained a triptych said to be by a sixteenth-century Flemish painter, which is very probable. It is now kept in the Cathedral at Bangor. There was a great deal of connection between Flanders and the wool merchants and gentry of these parts. William Myddelton, brother of Thomas Myddelton, and a cousin once removed of the William Myddelton who was with Tomos Prys, lived in Flanders, and was married to a Flemish woman. His brothers and other members of his family used to visit him. Tomos Prys was there with the Earl of Leicester and the younger William Myddelton. Richard Myddelton, a close relative of William, was trading wool abroad, in the Netherlands, Portugal, Leghorn and the Canaries in the middle of the seventeenth century. As late as 1713 Roderick Lloyd gave some Flemish work to the church.

Lloyds lived and died in the Machno Valley throughout many centuries. The Evan Lloyde who diddled Ffoulke Vaughan is almost certainly the same Evan Lloyd who served with the Earl of Leicester in the Netherlands campaign in the 1500s and was knighted for his services. His eldest son, John, was also there and appears to have received his own separate recognition.

In later times the family had much bad luck. In 1727 Ellinor Lloyd died. and her son Lewis Lloyd followed in 1730,[76] there being a stone to her memory in the church. A year later, in 1731, her daughter Margaret died, followed by her husband the Rev. Evan Ffoulkes in 1736, and their daughter Elinor lived only until 1757. All of the last named lived at Hafod-dwyryd, which was built not later than 1678 and is still in occupation.

Fedw-deg (on Iwerddon) dates from the sixteenth century, but Gruffydd ap Dafydd Goch lived in a house on the same site. Still occupied and dating from the sixteenth century is Coed-y-ffynnon, while Benar, Dylasau-isaf, Pen-y-bryn, Tŷ-mawr, Blaen-y-glasgw and Dugoed all date from the 17th century, a former house on the site of Dylasau-isaf having had a pew reserved in St Tudclyd's Church.

But all these relate to times that are modern in relation to stones now stored in the church. One, about 2$\frac{1}{2}$ feet high, dates from the fifth or early sixth century. It bears the Chi-Rho sign of the early Christians, and is inscribed *Carausius hic jacet in hoc congeries lapidum* (Carausius lies here in this pile of stones). It was found in the churchyard.

It is sometimes stated that Carausius so remembered was the great commander of the Roman Navy in the waters between Britain and the Continent, who declared himself Augustus and Emperor of Britain and Northern Gaul — but that cannot be so if the stone is correctly dated at the fifth or sixth century, which there is no reason to doubt. That Carausius lived two centuries earlier, and was "Emperor" from A.D.287 until he was murdered in A.D.293. It could not, either, be the mysterious Carausius who appears on coins in Britain between A.D.354 and A.D.358 as Carausius II, but who is nowhere else recorded. It must, therefore, be a much less eminent Carausius, a local dignitary or man of wealth of a later century, as likely as not a "Welshman" of the post-Cunedda Wledig era, in the days of Cadwallon Lawhir.

There is also another pillar in the church, split longitudinally 3 ft 3 ins long inscribed *Fili Avitori* and *In tempore Iustini Consulis*, which tells us that another body was buried in the year of Justinius the Consul, which was the year 540, more than 150 years after Macsen Wledig had taken the last of the Roman legions over to Gaul, and 85 years after the Vandals had sacked Rome. England was already lost in the dark ages of the invasions by the barbarians from the continent. Hengist and Horsa had landed in the east 90 years earlier, and for forty-five years Cerdic and Cynric had been overrunning south-eastern Britain, and had taken over the Isle of

Tŷ Mawr

Wight. But this part of Wales was maintaining a Celtic-Roman civilization and administrative system, for another stone of the fifth or early sixth century, 2 ft 11 ins high is inscribed *Cantiorix hic jacet venedotis cives fuit consobrinos* and (on one side) *Magli Magistrat*. Two other stones have inscriptions which are less complete. All five date from the times of Cadwallon and Maelgwn — or of Rhun ap Maelgwn, Rhun Hir, Rhun the Tall, who had taken an army from Gwynedd as far as the Firth of Forth against the invading armies of the north, Clydno Eiddin and Rhydderch of Strathclyde, when Maelgwn was the Prince of Gwynedd and was rebuilding the castle of Deganwy.[77] Still in operation was the Roman system of magistrates, or what we should now call Justices of the Peace.

There are no main roads from Ysbyty Ifan to Penmachno and to Dolwyddelan now, although they were once important routes, linked with that which went via Nant Gwynant to Beddgelert. They formed from the days of Carausius and before the means of passage from Gwynedd-is-Conwy, the Cantrefs of Rhufoniog and Tegeingl to the Cwmwd of Eifionydd and the Llŷn Cantref, from the castles of Flint and Rhuddlan, Ruthin and Denbigh to those of Dolbenmaen and Cricieth and Cae Fadryn, and in between to Dolwyddelan and Dinas Emrys. Along these routes passed many a messenger with tidings good and bad, a friend to visit friend, a foe to harass foe, travelling preacher or bartered bride to leave behind her childhood home which she might never see again. Not for them was the comfort of a modern car on well made road — instead a progress of two miles or three in any hour, on foot or sweating horse, or bumping in springless long-wagon or cart, parched in the summer's heat, bemused uncertain of direction in mist or fog when every sound was of the *Tylwyth Teg*[78] or *Ysbrydion*[79] or in winter frozen near to death.

With the days of the Stuarts came the coaches: the first stage coach in Britain ran about 1640, and in 1664 springs began to be fixed to ease the ride. In 1663 the first Turnpike Act was passed for the proper provision and maintenance of roads. A coach came through Penmachno from Llanrwst to Ffestiniog. But for Penmachno those same years of progress brought change and loss of trade. The prime industries had always been the production of wool and its preparation. With that had grown up a thriving trade in knitted hose, the height of fashion in the Tudor times; but fashions changed, and by the early 1600s machines were knitting stockings. Hard times befell Penmachno until later came demand for slate, though the trade in fleece and yarn continued for two centuries or more, and some woollen cloth was made for export.

The slate trade grew with demand from the growing towns of England and abroad. The great slate quarries and mines are further up the valley,

Above: Penmachno Village
Below: Guidestone on the old way to Dolwyddelan from
Penmachno where it leaves the road to Tŷ Mawr

and a new community grew to house the workers, Cwm Penmachno, some $2^1/2$ miles to the south, off the old Ffestiniog road. Once a main route for wagons and for coaches, it is now not much more than a track which goes steeply up the hills for some three miles or more, to a height of 1,400 feet and on to 1,600 feet, higher than the Bwlch-y-ddeufaen or the Crimea Pass, to join the old road from Denbigh and Ysbyty Ifan to go to Ffestiniog and the south. Before the road was made through the Crimea Pass, this was still the coach road from Conwy and Llanrwst to Ffestiniog and Dolgellau, and where it joins the old Ysbyty Ifan road there is a building and a well. It has stood there for many a year, and bears an inscription which when translated means *Drink and be thankful.* Many a man and horse and even dog will have been thankful to obey.

That road to Ysbyty Ifan is to be visited at another time. For the present we shall return by way of Penmachno village to Penmachno Mill, near the crossroads and the chapel. This mill is a survivor of the valley's pandies, which had been brought into the present age by harnessing the power of the Afon Machno to drive turbines instead of water wheel, to generate electric current to power machines which stage by stage converted the fleece of sheep into cloth for gowns to bedeck the rich of the capital cities of the world, as the cloth of a score of centuries ago bedecked the rich of Athens and of Rome. But here also were made coats and sweaters, scarves, gloves and bed spreads.[80]

From the mill we could go to Ysbyty Ifan by the old road which we explored before. We will, however, go on to rejoin the Telford road, the present A5, and there turn right towards Pentrefoelas and the east. After three miles there is a turning on the right, the B4407 leading south-west to Ysbyty Ifan. By local standards this road is modern — it does not appear on maps of even a hundred years ago.

The village to which we come should by rights be called Dolgynwal, for that was the name of the place to which the knights of the Order of St John[81] of Jerusalem came towards the end of the twelfth century to set up a hospice[82] as a resting place for travellers. They came at almost the same time, if not exactly so, that the Cistercian monks came to the banks of the Conwy. The monks and the knights received grants of land, those of the knights becoming known as Tir Ifan. Their territories met somewhere along the line of the Telford road just here.

It is most often assumed and said that the travellers for whom the hospice was established would be mainly pilgrims going to Bardsey, of which a papal edict had raised the status, so that a pilgrimage made thrice equalled one to Rome or two to St David's. But in fact the foundation followed within a score of years of the conquest of Ireland by the Norman Barons based in Wales, within a decade of Henry II travelling to Ireland to receive the homage of the Irish kings and chiefs, so that great flows of people were going and coming by way of Holyhead and the northern ports of the Llyn, and the ships across the Irish Sea. Some of these people have their place in history, although none have direct connections with Gwynedd and the Conwy Valley.[83]

The first of these was Nest, a seductive lady of great beauty, of extraordinary fascination and character, whose amatory exploits changed the course of history. But the story itself starts before her time, when William the Conqueror made a sortie into South Wales, and a few years later the Normans built a castle at Pembroke. One of the great Welsh lords of that area was Rhys ap Tewdwr, who lost much territory, and of course set out to recover it. Rhys was directly descended from Rhodri Mawr and the earlier princes of Gwynedd through Hywel Dda. His wife was Gwladys, daughter of Rhiwallon and a great-grand-daughter of Maredudd ab Owain, King of Gwynedd. She was also descended from Rhodri Mawr. To them was born sometime in the 1080s, a daughter, Nest.

Rhys was killed in very suspicious circumstances in 1093, and his daughter, who was just growing up, and was already a presentable and desirable young lady, was immediately taken into the court as a ward of William II. Whether she had already been seduced by Prince Henry, the king's brother, although she was only eleven or twelve (which was marriageable age) or whether the seduction took place after her arrival at court, is not at all

Ysbyty Ifan bridge in 1987

clear, but she bore the prince a son, who later became known as Henry Filius Regis. He was killed at the battle of Tal Moelfre, Anglesey, in 1157 after his troops had rampaged through the Anglesey countryside and desecrated at least two churches, Llanbedr-goch and Llanfair Mathafarn Eithaf.

As soon as he came to the throne in 1100, the prince, now Henry I, rid himself of Nest by marrying her off to Gerald of Windsor, Castellan of Pembroke, a brash Norman who must have been many years older than she, a man much her social inferior, but obviously (judging from subsequent events) very kindhearted, and as captivated by her wiles and charms as Henry had been. By 1109 she had several children by him, but then there came to the castle Owain ap Cadwgan, a young, attractive Welshman, son of the ruler of Ceredigion and parts of Powys, and an impetuous scallywag. He likewise fell for her charms, and later came back with companions. In true romantic fashion they tunnelled under the castle gates, set fire to some of the buildings, and in the fracas that followed, ran off with Nest and two of her children, taking them to Elyseg (now World's End), near Wrexham.

Gerald of course retaliated. He attacked Powys, and Owain's father lost much of his territory. Owain had to flee to Ireland[84] and two years after the elopement Nest was accepted back into the arms of her forgiving husband at Pembroke, where she seems to have remained at least until Gerald died about 1137. By him she had six children or more, John, William who became Bishop of St David's, Maurice, David and Raymond FitzGerald. There was also a daughter, Angharad, who married the Lord of Manorbier, whose children included Giraldus Cambrensis, the controversial historian.

Quite incorrigible, she also had a number of children by other Norman lords, including a son Robert (Robert FitzStephen) by Stephen who was the later Constable of Cardigan Castle. Robert FitzStephen was to feature later in Henry II's onslaught on North Wales in 1157, being in charge of the navy, when he was fortunate to escape with his life. He was also to be one of the benefactors who gave lands for the establishment of Strata Florida, from which the monks were to come in 1189 to set up the Abbey at Aberconwy.

The war which started after Nest's elopement dragged on for years with changing alliances of Welsh and English and Normans. Owain returned from Ireland, went to France with Henry I, and was knighted in 1115. The following year he was campaigning again in Wales on the king's behalf, and was killed near Abergavenny — but the feuding did not end, instead it became conflict between the Welsh on one side and the Normans and English on the other.

Prys (Price) and Salesbury Family Trees

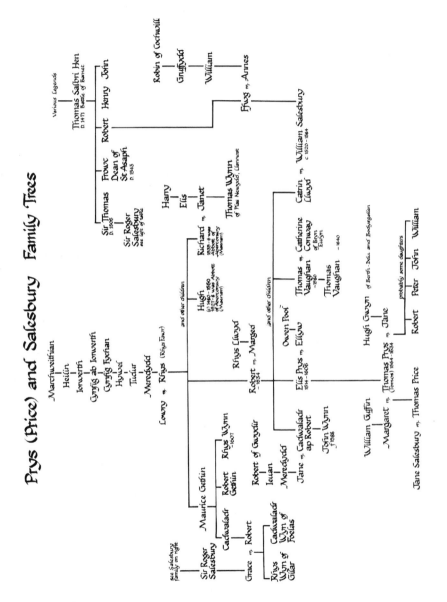

The next important man in the story was not even born until 1132, 23 years after the feuding began, but by 1165, famous then as the Lord Rhys, he had driven the Normans and English out of nearly the whole of south and middle Wales, as Owain Gwynedd had done in the north. Initially perhaps the Welsh were helped by the barional quarrels in England in the turbulent reign of Stephen, but the territorial gains continued in the reign of Henry II.

Lord Rhys was Rhys ap Gruffydd ap Rhys ap Tewdwr — in simpler language, he was a grandson of Rhys ap Tewdwr,[85] therefore a nephew of Nest, and cousin to her many children. Through Rhys ap Tewdwr he was descended, like Nest, from the princes of Gwynedd, and his mother, Gwenllian Nest,[85] was daughter of Gruffydd ap Cynan ab Iago, both Gruffydd and Iago being former kings of Gwynedd. Gruffydd's wife Angharad was daughter of Owain ab Edwin of the Perfeddwlad. Rhys married Gwenllian, daughter of Susanna who was a daughter of Owain Gwynedd. Not surprisingly with all those close connections with Gwynedd, the Lord Rhys' daughter Gwenllian married Ednyfed Fychan. So it was that the Tudurs and the future kings and queens of England and Wales were descended from the Lord Rhys. Rhys' mother, it may be noted, was a cousin of Llywelyn Fawr. But we have digressed.

In the wars between the Welsh and the Normans, Lord Rhys became leader in the south, while Owain Gwynedd was the leader in the north. The sons of Nest were on the Norman side — after all, their fathers were Norman — and in 1165 the Lord Rhys took at least three of them prisoner — Maurice and Raymond FitzGerald and Robert FitzStephen — not long after the latter had escaped capture by Owain Gwynedd.

In 1167 Rhys had sent Welsh and Flemish[86] troops to Ireland to help Diarmait Mac Murchadha, King of Leinster, to recover his kingdom from Ua Ruairc and the Connacht kings.[87] They were only partly successful, so in 1168 he released his cousin Robert FitzStephen, and sent him with further Welsh troops to assist Mac Murchadha — there can be no doubt that the blood relationship influenced him. These fared much better giving Murchadha control of the Danish cities of Waterford, Wexford and Dublin, as well as the whole of his own Kingdom of Leinster. The following year Lord Rhys released Maurice FitzGerald and Raymond de Gros to go with more Welsh troops, and they were followed in August by Richard de Clare, the subjugated Earl of Pembroke (Richard FitzGilbert, known as Strongbow) with another Welsh army. Uprisings in Waterford, Wexford and Dublin were put down and Dublin was burnt. FitzGilbert married Mac Murchadha's daughter, Aife, and became King of Leinster when Murchadha died in 1171. They had one daughter, Isabel.

The whole of Ireland then united against the Norman/Welsh invaders, but under the leadership of FitzGilbert and Nest's sons the forces of Leinster and Wales conquered most of the country. Henry II of England was faced with the prospect of virtually all Wales and Ireland developing into a power owing allegiance to Lord Rhys, which could be a threat to the very throne of England. Accordingly in 1172 he crossed to Ireland with some 400 ships and 5,000 men, and accepted the homage of the Norman/Welsh lords, their Welsh armies, and the Irish chiefs.

After all, even in Wales Rhys and Owain Gwynedd found it very convenient to feign acceptance of Henry's overall sovereignty. In return FitzGilbert was recognised as steward or seneschal, virtually viceroy, of all Ireland; Maurice FitzGerald was granted control of Kildare, where he and his family settled; Robert FitzStephen was given the kingdom of Cork, where he and his family settled. Raymond and other members of the family were rewarded and the sons of Nest became the leading families in Ireland, eventually almost more Irish than the Irish, and may be said to have done very well for themselves.

Ties between Wales and Ireland had already been close for many generations, and intermarriages were not uncommon (even Owain Gwynedd's grandmother Ragnhild was a daughter of Sistric of the Silken Beard, Lord of Dublin), but with the conquest the to-ing and fro-ing across the Irish Sea increased.

But in the south of Wales the Lord Rhys had died and the peace that he had established was being disturbed by his quarrelling sons. Passage that way to Ireland was not as safe as passage through the north, by way of the ports of Llŷn and Anglesey. So it came about that in the same year that Henry II died and that the monks of Strata Florida came to Conwy to set up Aberconwy Abbey, the Knights of St John of Jerusalem obtained lands at Dolgynwal and established the Hospice of St John, Ysbyty Ifan, for the benefit of travellers, some of whom would be those bound to and from Ireland, as well as Bardsey Island.

The right of immunity of the Knights of St John applied to the whole of Tir Ifan. No officer of the crown was permitted to go into those lands to arrest criminals or any others who might seek sanctuary there. The Hospice continued for $3^1/2$ centuries, until dissolved by Henry VIII.

The village lies on both sides of the Conwy, crossed by an early eighteenth century bridge of two spans. Until the 1974 changes in local government boundaries and organisation, the river was the boundary between Denbighshire and Caernarfonshire, so that there were two county, two district and two parish councils concerned with the administration of local affairs, sometimes with comic results. The parishes of Tir Ifan and Tre

Brys were in Denbigh County, Eidda was in Caernarfon. At one time, when water rights and land for a reservoir for the benefit of the area as a whole had been donated, the authorities fell out about implementation of a scheme, and in consequence one authority went ahead on its own. Half the area got its water supply, the other half did not. Now the whole area is in the County of Conwy, and Tir Ifan, once taken over by Elis Prys and his family, is owned by the National Trust. Much of Tir Ifan and Tir Eidda (probably more of Tir Eidda) was part of of the Penrhyn (Bangor) estate but in 1953 was given to the National Trust.

It is a very close-knit and active Welsh community, famous as the birthplace of several Welsh poets of renown before and since William Cynwal was buried here in 1587 or 1588. Small though it is, it still holds its annual eisteddfod. It was one of the first places, it seems, where the Women's Institute held all its proceedings in Welsh, despite the fact that the first W.I. was founded in the Principality, at Llanfairpwll on Anglesey, the world-famed place to which the Victorians attached the so-called longest name, Llanfairpwllgwyngyllgogerychwyrndrobwllllandysiliogogogoch.

Ysbyty Ifan seems to have been one of the first places in Wales to have its own electricity derived from local water power. The electricity was supplied by the local mill owner, Thomas John Roberts, who used a turbine for the purpose. It is recorded that the residents were charged so much a year for each lamp or power point in their houses, and could use as much current as they liked, and if the supply was poor when Mrs Jones was doing her ironing, she would dash out and shout to Mr Roberts, who would open up the sluice gates a little to speed up the generator.

What the population was in the distant past is unclear; in 1801 it was 645, which grew amazingly to 892 by 1851, when nearby Pentrefoelas had grown to 561. Four chapels were built in that same time.

There is no visible trace of the old hospice now, which stood north of the church, which was, no doubt, an integral part of the hospice precinct. It was in 1530 that the Order was suppressed by Henry VIII in England and Wales, and the next that is heard of it is that the lands of Dolgynwal were given to Robert ap Rhys, probably about 1540, and that Tir Ifan was granted to his son, the Red Doctor, Elis Prys, in 1560. Whether the legal immunity of the lands was claimed officially still to exist, or whether its continuation was just locally assumed, is not clear, but for a long time the old hospice buildings appear to have become a refuge for all kinds of scoundrels who terrorised the countryside. The farm house Hafod Ysbyty (or Hafod Ifan), half a mile south west of the village, just off the Ffestiniog road, is said to have been a meeting place for outlaws; part of the fifteenth-century building there still remains.

On the suppression of the Order of St John, the old church of the hospice became the parish Church, but the last remnant of the hospice was finally destroyed when the old church was demolished, and the present rather plain building was erected in 1860; however, the effigies of Rhys ap Meredydd and his wife Lowry, and of their son Robert were transferred to the new building.

Rhys ap Meredydd, who was known as Rhys Fawr (Rhys the Great), lived in the fifteenth century, and was a great supporter of the Tudurs, wealthy and a strong military man, who raised a force to assist Henry Tudur. According to Polydore Vergil, Official Historian to Henry VII, Rhys the Mighty (Rhys Fawr) came from Golgynwal (Dolgynwal) in the uplands of the Conwy Valley and joined Henry Tudur with a contingent of troops from the Perfeddwlad before he reached Shrewsbury. At Bosworth Field he stood near Henry, and when Richard III charged at Henry and in the process killed William Brandon, the official standard bearer, Rhys Fawr retrieved the standard and held it aloft. His home is thought to have been Hen Foelas, and he is said to have traced his family back to Marchweithian. It was because of his help at Bosworth that Henry gave him lands in the Tir Ifan area, so that he and his family became important and appear much in the history of the Valley for a long time.

His second son succeeded him at Tir Ifan, Sir Robert ap Rhys — the Sir only indicated that he had taken holy orders. He took great advantage of his father's favour with the king, and he became Chancellor of St Asaph, and then Vicar General in 1507. Before he died in 1534 he had become cross-bearer to Cardinal Wolsey. He persuaded Henry VIII to give him lands at Dolgynwal on the disbandment of Ysbyty Ifan, and parts of Penllyn. He married Marged, daughter of Rhys Llwyd of Gydros, Llanfor, Meirionnydd. He was an unpleasant character, who acquired the stipends of about 18 ecclesiastical livings, maintained what amounted to a private army, and threw anybody who displeased him into prison. It was he who built Plas Iolyn on the Tir Ifan lands, which is now but a ruin some 2 miles north east of Ysbyty Ifan, in what used to be Tre Brys.[88] He had a number of children, two of whom were of importance to the history of the Conwy Valley, but Cadwaladr,[89] the eldest, was of more importance in the Meirionnydd area.

Almost unknown was Hugh Prys, brother of Robert ap Rhys, though he was abbot of Aberconwy Abbey at Maenan — he died in 1528 and was buried at Saffron Walden. He had succeeded Sieffre Cyffin only a year earlier.

Better known was another of Robert's brothers, Richard Prys, who was the last abbot of Aberconwy, taking over in the year of dissolution to replace Abbot Sieffre Johns who had succeeded Hugh Prys in 1528: it is notable that he seems to have lent a willing hand to his nephew, Elis Prys, in closing the Abbey, arranging for its total demolition and destruction, one or both of them arranging that a large part of the estates passed into the hands of family and friends. As we heard before, Richard was given the living of Cerrigydrudion and a pension of £20 a year after the dissolution.

But it was the second son of Robert ap Rhys who became in the long term perhaps the most well known member of the family —Elis Prys, the Red Doctor. Educated at Cambridge, he gained an Ll.B. in 1533 when he was only 21, and a D.C.L. in the following year which entitled him to the red robe or cloak from which his nickname derived. We have already learnt something of the offices which he held, and of what he did. He was just as unpleasant as his father, and one complainant to Cromwell said *"he rides about openly with his concubine which he took from her mother"*. He was accused (probably justifiedly) of retaining for his own use items of value which he took from the monasteries which he closed down for the king and Cromwell. He was a party to robberies by Dudley, Earl of Leicester, Lord of Denbigh. Tomos Prys, the privateer was his son, and carried on, it appears, the family reputation.

One of Elis Prys' sisters was Catrin, known as Catrin Llwyd by reason of her mother's maiden name, and it was she who married William Salesbury of Llanrwst, translator of the New Testament, of whom we shall learn more.

From such a prolifery, it would be expected that there should be in the Ysbyty Ifan area some vestige of family still, but it seems that after the next generation none remained, and Plas Iolyn became an ordinary and undistinguished farmhouse, a ruin in the grounds of a more modern building by the time of investigation by the Royal Commission of Ancient Monuments in 1911.

Continuing along the road to Blaenau Ffestiniog from Ysbyty Ifan, the river is on the left; the valley and the road are attractive, but perhaps not outstanding. Five miles from the village the Pont-ar-Gonwy takes road over river, and here the Conwy rises a mile to the north, in the lee of Pen-y-bedw, as an outflow from Llyn Conwy. But to the south of the road is Migneint, the "Swampy Place", two thousand acres and more of upland marshes in the lea of Carnedd Iago and Arenig Fach from which flow the waters of the Afon Serw to join the Conwy. At the confluence of the two rivers is the cave to which the harpist was lured by the Tylwyth Teg and was never seen again. The music of his harp can be heard further down the Conwy Valley, to lure the unwary to a similar fate. It is descendants of those fairies, no doubt, who may be seen dancing across the rocks in the Fairy Glen.

If we continued along the Ffestiniog road, the old toll and coach road, we should come to Ffynnon Eidda, at the head of the road from Penmachno.

Returning by the road on which we came, to rejoin the Telford road, we will turn right to Pentrefoelas, for the Merddwr stream and its many tributaries feed the Conwy; but Llyn Alwen and that which is now Alwen Reservoir (into which a monster pulled the oxen when attempts were made to pull him out), flow to the east, to feed the River Dee.

A third of a mile along the Telford road, on its northern side is a field known as Beddau, not obvious to any passer by, of which the interest is that when the road was being built, the workmen found a stone inscribed

BROHAMAGLI
IAM IC IACET
ET UXOR EIUS CAVNE

In that form it reads "Of Brohamaglos here lies already and his wife Caune". But maybe Iam was Iatti as some suggest, for the inscription is far from clear, and "Brohamaglos son of Iattos lies here, and his wife Caune", sounds much more sensible. Brohamaglos died in A.D.662, and the Roman influence still remained.

It was here on the upland plains that Idwal ap Meurig, grandson of Idwal Foel, was defeated and driven into exile by the forces of Maredudd ab Owain in the year 986. In that battle some say Meurig himself was killed. Idwal was not destined to be king but his son Iago was to return 27 years later to rule over his father's kingdom. Ironically here also Llywelyn ap Seisyll, who seized the kingdom on the death of Maredudd ab Owain, having married Maredudd's daughter Angharad, was himself to be killed by the forces of another upstart, Rhydderch ab Iestyn in the year 1023. This Maredudd was the great-grandfather of Gwladys, wife of Rhys ap Tewdwr. It is to Llywelyn ap Seisyll that some attribute the upright inscribed stone found on Foelas Hill, at Pentrefoelas, but on the other hand the stone may commemorate Llywelyn Fawr or Llywelyn the Last.[90]

Hen Foelas, to the north of the village of Pentrefoelas, the traditional home of Rhys Fawr, is old, as are some of the other houses and buildings here, but the Pentrefoelas village which we see today really owes its existence to Robert Lawrence and his express coaches between London and Holyhead, and to the later road built by the Capel Curig Turnpike Trust, and then improved by Telford. To the west is the more modern mansion of Foelas, and the estate.

To the east of the village lies the old Tre Brys, through which flows the Afon Meddwr to join the Conwy near the new Ysbyty Ifan road. Tre Brys

The old road to Ffynnon Eidda from Cwm Penmachno

was on the borders of the lands of the Aberconwy Abbey and those of the Knights of St John. The road south from the Pentrefoelas crossroads leads to the old road from Ysbyty Ifan through Rhydlydan to Corwen and the east. A short distance along that road is a bridge across the Afon Meddwr, alongside which there was as recently as the end of last century the small Capel-y-fedog, erected, it is thought, at the time of the closing of the Hospice of St John.[91]

To the south, but approached by roads from Rhydlydan, are Plas Iolyn and Giler, farmhouses and accompanying parts of ruins of the homes of those names of the Prys and Price families of four centuries ago.

Returning to Pentrefoelas crossroads, our route lies north, across the sheeplands to Nebo, on the coach road of 1777, of the time of Lawrence, and we will follow it for the views it affords across the high Carneddau, taking the left fork half a mile beyond Nebo to bring us again to Llanrwst — but not to stay. By turning left as we come into the town, by the old toll house, we join the modern valley road to Betws-y-coed, the first short length of which was the road to Capel Garmon and Ysbyty Ifan, the old road to the south before the 1777 toll road was built or Betws-y-coed became the place where bridges crossed the Conwy.

---

71. *See pages 80 - 81.*
72. *Gallt Pandy — "Fulling Mill Hanger" — the wooded hillside of the fulling mill.*
73. *For a long time the area specialised in costly knitted stockings.*
74. *This John was a great grandson of Rhys Fawr, see page 118.*
75. *Pen Nant Machno — the headstream of the Machno, or the top of the Machno Stream.*
76. *See page 110.*
77 *See page 249.*
78. *Tylwyth Teg — the little people, the fairies good or bad.*
79. *Ysbrydion — ghosts.*
80. *The mill closed in the late 1990s and is currently vacant.*
81. *Latin Iohannes became both Ioan, John and Ifan, Evan.*
82. *Latin Hospitium became hospital in English, ysbyty in Welsh.*
83. *See Table page 250.*
84. *Sistric Lord of Dublin was grandfather of Gruffudd ap Cynan, Prince of Gwynedd.*
85. *See Table on page 250.*
86. *There were a great number of Flemish settlers in the Pembroke area.*
87. *That was immediately after Mac Murchadha had appealed to the Merchants of Bristol, but had turned down their terms.*

88. *Brys, mutation of Prys — the area was named after the Prys family.*
89. *See page 110.*
90. *See page 51 .*
91. *It was not included in the Religious Census of 1851, which would suggest that no regular services were held.*

Tŷ Mawr, near Penmachno, now in the hands of the National Trust

The road from Betws-y-coed towards Bangor is the Capel Curig Turnpike road, built in 1803 where none existed before other than a track for horses; improved by Thomas Telford, and widened in recent years, it is now the A5. At the end of the village, a mile from the Royal Oak, is Pentre-du, just past the school. Here the eastern Roman road came into the valley from Tomen-y-mur, and the west coast and the south, Moridvnvm (now Carmarthen) and Nidvm (Neath). It then turned up the Llugwy Valley to the north and west, some three miles to where the fort was built at Bryn Gefeiliau.[92] On the right of the main road here at Pentre-du is an unusual sloping footbridge over the Llugwy river, known as the Miners' Bridge. The present structure is modern, but there have been such bridges here through the ages, from Roman times if not before. When the fort Caer Llugwy stood at Bryn Gefeiliau, this bridge would have served as a way from the lead mines near Bryn Elin, a short cut to the Tomen road and the route to the south. No doubt it was also used by those who travelled in haste from Canovium to the south who had no need to stop at Caer Llugwy Fort while it stood, nor at the community which remained in the later times of the Roman occupation. Perhaps Elen's armies used it in their race from north to south, or south to north again, and gave her name to the hill where the lead mines had earlier been.

The bridge has been replaced and maintained for untold generations, as pack trail and way to work, for in later days, the second half of the nineteenth century and the first part of the last century, the miners of the lead mines lived in the valleys rather than in the remoteness of the hills, and some may have done so in earlier times.

Along the Telford Road we come next to the misnamed Swallow Falls, where the road has been widened and made more straight, and has provided parking for visitors' cars. The *Rhaeadr Ewynnol*, the foaming waterfall, is a name to understand, where the waters of the Llugwy cascade and boil their way through the rocks, but the Victorians, to whom any language but English was a joke, translated Rhaeadr y Wennol, and called the

Top inset: Family coach. Bottom inset: Buzzard

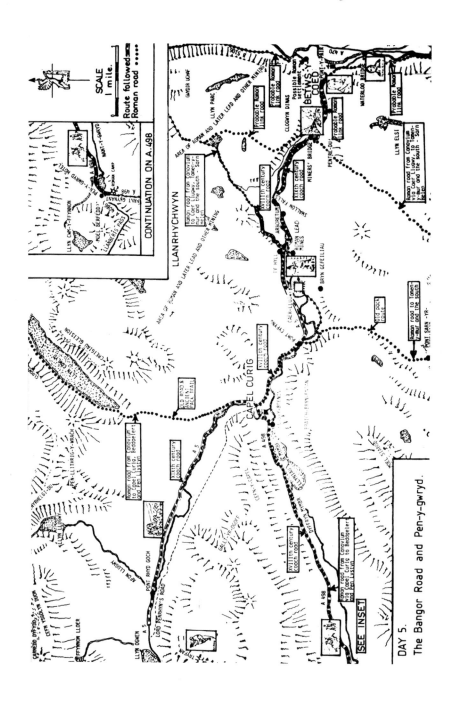

DAY 5.
The Bangor Road and Pen-y-gwryd.

foaming waters the Swallow Falls — a name which sticks today. They are more spectacular than the falls on the Conwy and the Machno, and it is worth stopping to see them, as no doubt travellers have done in every age before. It is here in the foaming and seething waters below the falls that the soul of Sir John Wynn is doomed to toss forever in expiation for the way he treated his tenants. There are now a little terraced path and steps which are safely fenced, and for a small charge one may follow them. The falls are owned by the Betws-y-coed Community Council, which inherited them from the enterprising Betws-y-coed Urban District Council, destroyed like many another in the local government upheavals of 1974. They were granted on very long lease to the council of the district by the local landowner, the Earl of Ancaster, in the year 1913, and the council developed them so successfully as an attraction for tourists from all over the world that the income received from the charges enabled them to abolish rates for their local needs.

From here it is a few hundred yards to a car park and picnic site on the left, provided by the Forestry Commission. There mounted on a large board is a map, which shows the walks to be taken through an adjoining arboretum. Even those whose interests may not be in trees, or the varieties of them, should follow some of those walks, for they show glimpses and views of the Gwydir Forest to the north, the fringes of the Carneddau and the Glyders which attracted the visitors of the century before last almost more than those of the twenty-first.

A short distance further on, the modern road, that built by Telford, crosses the river, where the earlier road built by the Capel Curig Turnpike Trust continued on the southern side for almost a mile on the line of the Roman road from Pentre-du to Bryn Gefeiliau and on beyond to Pont Cyfyng. Maybe there was a bridge to the northern side then, as there is now, for the Roman road from Bryn Gefeiliau to Canovium followed the northern bank, to climb out of the valley towards Llanrhychwyn, Gwydir and Llanrwst. A short distance along the road on the south of the river, on the left, are the remains of a Roman lead mine, but little trace is visible.

Across the bridge, beside the Llanrhychwyn road, is a most extraordinary building, the fourteenth-century Tŷ Hyll, the Ugly House, the Hideous House, some say the Spikey House from an old meaning of the word hyll, referring to the way the stones stick out all round the building. Why and how did those who built it use such massive stones, in the days of power of man and horse alone? Perhaps, of course, it would be less easy for marauding gangs to push down such a structure than one of normal build.

If we go up the road to the north, the Llanrhychwyn road, we are on the old road to Llanrwst — the road of the early days of coaches, of the times of the Tudurs and of the ten centuries of the princes of Wales, and of the age of the Romans and Celts. Of Llanrhychwyn not much can now be found, but in the past it was a substantial community exceeding in population all those around. It is a place we will visit another day — for now we will go only as far as a car park on the right, again provided by the Forestry Commission. Climbing this steep road, one has to sympathise with those who put shoulder to wheel of the wagons and coaches which came this way, or heaved and hauled to control the whole as it came down the slopes on the journey back. How easy is our lot, with our cars and our central heating, telephones and supermarkets, compared with that of those who lived before; and yet they could enjoy as much as we the beauty of all around, and maybe with more leisurely rate of travel, or need to rest on the mountain climbs, they saw and enjoyed much more than we. Looking out from the car park over the valleys of the Llugwy and the Conwy, and over the Denbigh Moors to the Cantref of Rhos, we can, perhaps, understand a little those who fought and retired, and came back to fight again, Celts and Romans, Welsh and Normans, to possess and keep such land as this.

Beyond us are the lead mines, but those we will visit another time, and for now will return to the main road, the A5, to continue our journey west; but we shall not go far before we shall stop again, for it is less than a mile to Bryn Gefeiliau.

Here it was that the armies of Agricola in the year A.D.78 set up a camp on the south side of the river, and fortified it with a timber wall. They were to stay, and build it again in stone, and to keep a garrison for a little over half a century, when it was reduced to strengthen those of the northern borders against the Picts of Scotland, and invaders from Europe. But Romans stayed at Bryn Gefeiliau for nearly three centuries, and they had, it seems, a large community here and nearby. By the river, adjacent to the fort, they had a big building with a hall some 60 feet by 20 feet, and an adjacent hall some $18^{1}/2$ feet square, with pillars of stone, suggesting a building of significance, such as only the house of a local governor, or a community of wealth and importance, would have in a land and age where timber was the material of building. The lead of the mountains, the beauty of the valley, and the confluence of roads were no doubt the factors which led to such development.

The existence of this fort seems to have been long forgotten, until the end of the eighteenth century. It was referred to in 1798 by Edward Lhwyd,[93] and by Richard Fenton who lived from 1747 to 1821, but whose works were largely unpublished until 1911; a Pembrokeshire man, he lived for a time at Machynlleth. Samuel Lysons who investigated the site between 1799 and 1801 reported that "Abundance of materials have been taken from these remains, for several years past". It was not until 1920, 1921 and 1922 that the site was again partly excavated and examined by J.P. Hull, W.J. Hemp and G.H. Higson, and their excavations were left open. Erosion has now exposed rather more than they did, but has also destroyed much of what they found.

Here was a camp of more or less the standard type, about 400 feet square as close in parts as 40 feet to the present course of the river. To the west, also close to the river, was another walled enclosure 400 feet by 300 feet, lightly defended only, within which was at least one building covering a site of 120 feet by 110 feet. A large hearth at one end has been said to indicate some industrial use, but other suggestions are that it was for the heating plant for a luxury building, or for baths. The site has been robbed a great deal at various times in history, so that much is lost, but on the other hand neither it nor the surrounding area has been systematically examined.

The location of the fort would have been very odd if, as many have assumed, the only Roman road here lay through Trefriw from Canovium to Tomen-y-mur and the south; its line from Canovium has been traced over the mountains at Llanrhychwyn to where Tŷ Hyll now stands, and again to Dolwyddelan from Pentre-du, two miles down the valley. If that was the only road, why should the Romans have come up here to build a fort? The answer must be that such road was not the first they used, but came at a later date when the wells at Trefriw and the mines at Llanrhychwyn were established, with, perhaps, a quay at Llanrwst. They must first have used the road to which our travels will later lead, that built by the Celts before them which climbed out of the Conwy Valley at Llanbedr-y-cennin near Canovium to skirt Llyn Cowlyd on its north-western side and continue to Capel Curig, going on from there through Nant-y-gwryd to Beddgelert and the coast. For 50 years at least they had a fort on the Llŷn near that coast at Pen Llystyn. From Capel Curig another road came down the Llugwy Valley to Bryn Gefeiliau probably crossing the Llugwy where Pont Cyfyng now is, on round the western slopes of Mynydd Cribau to the Lledr Valley and Dolwyddelan, and so to Tomen-y-mur. Along that route have been found the remains of roundhouses and of long-huts which survived the pillaging for the building of the miles of walls and the Afon Ystumiau is crossed by a bridge known as "The Roman Bridge".[94] That road appeared on the first of the Ordnance Survey maps of 1841, and was marked as a through coach or carriage route on maps of less than half a century earlier, John Evans' maps of the late 18th century. If, as seems likely, the Romans had a road from Viroconium by way of Ysbyty Ifan and the upper Conwy Valley to Betws-y-coed, that would have followed the line south of the Llugwy past the lead mines to Bryn Gefeiliau, passing Pentre-du, on the way to Segontium.

The road on the north of the river, from Llanrhychwyn past Tŷ Hyll would be part of a totally different route in Celtic times, for the stone-age men, the Iberians and the Celts had a complex system of routes of travel, just as we have in our time. One such route would be from the Great Orme via Llanrwst to Beddgelert.

Of course the people of those ages did not know such names as we have given in more modern times, but we do not know the names they used, so we must use our own.

At a later time came another road built by the Romans from Llanrhychwyn by way of the Miners' Bridge and Pentre-du to Dolwyddelan to provide a shortened route to the south for armies, for carriers of ores, and ordinary travellers.[95]

From Segontium (Caernarfon) to Tomen-y-mur they had a road which passed through what is now Beddgelert, and there was a link road from Bryn Gefeiliau by way of Pen-y-gwryd (which we shall later visit) to Beddgelert which evidently went on to Pen Llystyn, and to Porthmadog and Cricieth, where they had holiday villas overlooking the sea, and more than one community of size. While they had a road from their great City of Deva (Chester) by way of Bala and Tomen-y-mur to those seaside resorts, the route by way of Varis (St Asaph) and Canovium, Bryn Gefeiliau and Pen-y-gwryd would have provided an attractive alternative.

Maybe the fort was set up on the site of an earlier one, defence by the Celts against incursors from foreign lands, who came over the mountains from the coasts of the Irish Sea. That would fit in with W.S. Hanson's conclusions in his book *Agricola*. The Romans may even have chosen the site for the sheer delight of its setting. There is no doubt they had here industry, the smelting of ores, the founding of iron, and legend is that they had a fair amount of luxury, as would be expected for those in charge of an important centre of mineral workings, slate and other quarrying, and timber trading.

One of the reasons why the relationship between the Romans and the Celts was good was that unlike the Goidels of France and the Goths and Vandals of middle Europe, the Brythonic Celts had much in common with the legionaries Agricola had sent. While prepared to fight when need arose, or sometimes for the sheer joy of it, they were also kind and hospitable. The Romans of the first century A.D. were not just those who lived at Rome, but were in fact made up of a multitude of races. The forces which

Agricola sent, from the Legio XX Valeria Victrix, were probably recruited largely from the Celtic west of Gaul [96] and from the Iberian Peninsula. They would regard as almost kith and kin, those whom they found living here. They would find much similarity in language, as there is today. They fraternised and intermarried. Though prior to the time of the Emperor Septimius Severus (A.D. 193-211) legionaries were not officially allowed to marry, many did in fact take wives from local population in areas where they were stationed. After that time marriage was officially sanctioned. When they retired, the legionaries became entitled to call themselves Roman citizens, and the entitlement, with all its attendant rights extended to their families. Their sons were therefore able to join the Roman regular army, and rise in rank, and it would be they who formed the Legio Segontientes. Many on retirement stayed, or having been posted elsewhere, returned to live in the lands of their wives, and a resident "Citizen" population became established.

All these, and the bureaucrats and scribes, provisioners and traders, with all their families, mingled with the free Celts, even with the serfs and slaves and the Iberians, to form the people that became the Welsh, and in so doing built up in an area such as this a sizeable community. As relics found suggest, it probably spread to the Betws-y-coed of today, to Llanrhychwyn and to Capel Garmon.

The Telford road leads on through Capel Curig, a scattered village, once a haven for artists. For these the old coach houses were extended and rebuilt, which had formerly provided for those on passage locally and for the quarrymen of the area, and of more recent times for Lawrence's express coaches, and the Irish Mail which came five years later. After Telford's road on the coast, and later the railways, reduced the Holyhead traffic, it was the tourists, the artists and the climbers who kept them going, as it is today, though the artists now do more with cameras from Japan than with brushes and canvas.

Those who wrote of the times before 1790 tell us that there was no road for vehicles before then through the upper valley of the Llugwy, or through Nant Ffrancon. Although a road is shown on John Evans' maps of about that time, along the north and east side of the Llugwy and the Ogwen, by way of Llanllechid, it was, as it had always been, only fit for travel on foot or on horseback. But in 1791/2 Lord Penrhyn built a toll road from Bethesda on the other side of the two rivers, the western and the southern side, which was extended as far as Capel Curig by 1800, to join there the Beddgelert to Llanrwst road. It linked Capel Curig and Bangor with a road on which vehicles could pass. It made a great improvement in communications, and enabled coaches and wagons to go that way from

Shrewsbury to Bangor on the Holyhead route, but in part its gradient through Nant Ffrancon was 1 in 6, which meant hard hauling for the horses, and pushing for second class passengers on the south-eastward run. This was the road to which Robert Lawrence's coaches were diverted when the Capel Curig Turnpike Trust linked it with the Shrewsbury to Pentrefoelas road in 1803, with the Beaver Bridge over the Conwy at Betws-y-coed. He then reduced the time of travel from London to Holyhead to 38 hours. That road can still be walked, but only disconnected lengths are fit for any kind of vehicles.

Plas-y-brenin at Capel Curig, which is now an Outdoor Pursuits Centre and National Mountaineering Centre, was built at that time by Lord Penrhyn as a sixty-roomed hotel for those who travelled on his road, and no doubt for those on the Beddgelert road as well. It was then The Royal Hotel. It is now a place for instruction in climbing and canoeing, in sailing and ski-ing, and in an increasing range of outdoor sports and skills.

Within thirty years of Lord Penrhyn's road came that of Telford, who chose to follow the opposite side of the two rivers, where the Llanllechid horse-track had been to Llyn Ogwen, but beyond that on a totally new route cut in the mountain-side to Bethesda, by-passing Llanllechid. His road was a godsend to all, for the horses could maintain a steady trot with a fully-laden chaise. That is the road which carries all the modern traffic.

From Capel Curig this road climbs steadily between the Carneddau on the right, and the Glyderau and Gallt yr Ogof on the left. At Rhyd Goch, the Red Ford (for that is what the name means) which served the ancient horse trail, was replaced by Telford with a bridge, the Pont Rhyd Goch, and here in the middle of nowhere is a chapel. Out on the high cynefin, we are at the limit of the watershed of the Llugwy and the Conwy's tributaries; a mile and a half to the north is Ffynnon Llugwy, from which the waters flow, fed from the slopes of Carnedd Llywelyn and Pen-yr-helgi-du.

If we walked back, or rode a horse, we might feel something of the awe with which the travellers of old came through this land, except that in those days there was no constant stream of traffic. In a whole day which it would take a man to walk from Llanllechid through to Betws, except in Capel Curig he might meet but one, or maybe two such travellers as him-self, the occasional shepherd, one or two on horseback, but not a wheeled vehicle. Here it was once wooded, but overstocking sheep ate all regenera-tion, so that by the days of the coaches it was, as now, bleak, forbidding on a stormy night or in winter snow, and when the passage of the Irish Packet had been rough and hazardous, and the drive across Anglesey had been raw and cold, the coachmen and the passengers, or those who rode in private carriages or on horseback, must have been truly thankful to see the lights of

Capel Curig, of Lord Penrhyn's Hotel and the older, lesser hostelries.

Those who on such trips from cold or sheer exhaustion went to sleep, if they were those who rode outside the coach, were apt to fall off and suffer injury or death — they were the ones who "dropped off" and gave origin to that expression. Even the guard and coachman were not immune, and there are recorded cases of coaches arriving safety at their destinations with the coachman or his guard frozen stiff and dead, or even missing.

But arrival at a village or a hostelry on a mail coach or express did not for passengers or crew mean much respite, unless it be at meal time, for the halt would be only enough to change the horses, and good ostlers could change a team in less than a minute, the recorded fastest being 45 seconds.

From Capel Curig there is a road to the west, through Nant-y-gwryd, on the line of the old Roman road to Beddgelert and the seaside villas of Tisobis Flumen and beyond. The Roman villas on the coastal lands to the east of Cricieth, and along Traeth Bach, and the port where Porthmadog is now, all were associated, no doubt, with the great training camp they had at Tomen-y-mur, as well as local industries. This was the road in later times which led from the castles of the Princes of Gwynedd at Deganwy

Moel Siabod from Caer Llugwy

and from Trefriw to Dolbenmaen and Eifionydd in the southern Llŷn, the road also in later times from Llanrwst and Gwydir to the shire town, Caernarfon. This is the true Eryri, the land of the eagles, Snowdonia; but no eagles now will fly overhead as we pass between the Glyderau and Moel Siabod, though there may be buzzards, or even a far-roaming kite. But mostly there will be sheep, the ubiquitous Welsh sheep, which turned the lush forests and glades of all but the highest land into bleak and desolate moors, though they brought wealth to the hearths of the people of Penmachno, Ysbyty Ifan and Llanrwst. Through the appetites of the sheep, the warmth of the past has gone, and even where, in other parts, trees have been planted, they have not been the native oak and ash, or elm and sycamore, but the hardier conifers which in an age where all is haste yield faster crops and profit, but poison soil and streams alike. But this valley has none of this, and is a land of heath and heather all the way to the Pen-y-gwryd Hotel.

For how long has there been a hostelry here? This was the meeting point of main routes from the Conwy Valley to the western coast and Llŷn, with routes from the south to the Menai Strait and the crossing to Anglesey from the earliest times, through those of the Celts and the Romans and right up to the nineteenth century. The Roman forces of Agricola stopped here and built a camp a few yards from where the hotel is now. But those who passed along these roads in later Roman times would not all be soldiers. There would be those who carried messages, civilian as well as military; the agents of the army provisioners; men of professions and of trade, with scribes and stewards and their servants; magistrates and civilian administrators; and families with their retinues of slaves and staff going on before, to visit friends, enjoy a holiday, or take up residence on long or short term basis. For them would be the carriers who took the household baggage, the pottery and the silver, pewter and lead, the furniture and linen and the women's gowns, for when they moved house they had just as much to move as we today, but no pantechnicons with rubber tyres and smelly engines, just men and horses and sheer muscle which when they came to here would welcome ale and bread and cheese and food and water for the animals. So maybe there was an inn here in those early days, at which no doubt the soldiers of the camp, perhaps in winter wishing themselves back in warmer climes, would seek conviviality.

To the right is the road to Llanberis, through Nant Peris, the Llanberis Pass at the foot of Snowdon, but that lies outside the catchment area of the Conwy and its tributaries. The Gwryd stream flows from Llyn Cwm-y-ffynnon, at the foot of Moel Berfedd, north-west of the Pen-y-gwryd hotel.

Betws-y-coed has been of small account in history, but every road which leads from it goes into lands steeped in the history of the Medieval Welsh and their Norman and English foes, of the later Wales of Tudor expansionism, of the days of coaches and industrial prosperity; but also the history of the Romans and the Celts before them, and the Iberians, of whom the Brythonic Celts survived, absorbing by marriage the strangers who, having come in war or trade, settled to rule or mingle. From the earliest times their culture, their cloths and jewellery, their pottery and works of art, were most sought in Europe; they ensnared and beguiled, and their hospitality has been renowned. Of their early homes they left little more than the bases of their great round-houses and they kept their records by word of mouth, and not by writing.[97] Masters in the arts of war, equipped far better than their Roman[98] or Danish foes, or than the Normans who followed, when they succumbed, it was to guile and deception, rather than skill, to their own good nature and rules of conflict to which the ruthless empires of the Mediterranean had not subscribed, nor the Normans in the next millennium. To the Danes and the Angles and Saxons they did not succumb.

Though they built in wood, and the circle was their plan rather than the square or rectangle, the houses of their princes and their nobles have, through all the generations from Macsen Wledig and before, been referred to as mansions of some magnificence. We know not if they were of single storey, or of more. But before those days, before even the Romans came, the legends of their wealth were rife in Rome.

But so were legends of the Druids, the spiritual and cultural leaders of the people; they were given a reputation for human sacrifice, for which no evidence exists but the literary exaggerations of some historians of quite recent times. What Tacitus had to say we consider elsewhere. It is notable that in the Brythonic Celtic areas the Romans did not establish arenas for their gladiatorial and other murderous and bloody entertainments, as they did in Italy, in almost every other area which they overcame and occupied, even in some parts of Britain. It is most unlikely that the Celts would have agreed, let alone turned up to watch. There was an amphitheatre at Tomen-y-mur, but it has been shown that it was used only for training troops, and not for public "games" of such a type.

92.   *See footnote 95 below also. The name was spelt "Bryn Gefailio" in 1801, which was then translated as the "Hill of the Smithy". "Gefailio" was a Latinised-Welsh invention, and "Gefeiliau", plural of Gefail came into use, although originally only one smithy was involved.*

93.   *Edward Lhwyd (or Lhuyd) 1660-1709. Botanist, geologist, antiquary, philologist. Second keeper of the Ashmolean Museum, Author inter alia Archaeologia Britannica 1707.*

94.   *See page 88, footnote 58.*

95.   *W.J. Hemp, F.S.A., who assisted early this century in the excavation of the Roman Fort in the Lluguy Valley, named Caer Lluguy in the absence of knowledge of the Roman name, reached the conclusion that there were many roads in the area. He found there to have been four between Dolwyddelan and Trefriw, which he described —*

a)   *The direct route through the fort and Llanrhychwyn,*

b)   *Through the fort and Betws-y-coed,*

c)   *A possible direct road which may have been used by "through traffic" which had no need to visit the fort, and also after the fort had been abandoned, and*

d)   *The direct route through Pont-y-pant and Betws-y-coed.*

He also expressed the view that the road to Caerhun may have crossed the Conwy by a ford at Trefriw, and continued down the east side of the river to the Caerhun ford.

His conclusions did not include the road now known to have existed between Caerhun and Caer Lluguy by way of Llyn Cowlyd, and his map excluded a road which verbally appears to have been included, that between Pentre-du and Llanrhychwyn via the Miners' Bridge.

Archdeacon Evans suggested a Roman route between Pentrefoelas and Llanrwst, and tradition attributes two bridges on the road south of the Conwy between Pentrefoelas and Betws-y-coed to the Romans.

There was, of course, a road between Caer Lluguy and Pen-y-gwryd, and on to Beddgelert.

Caer Lluguy, like Caerhun, was therefore evidently quite a centre for travel, and with the presence of lead mines both north and south of the Lluguy, the iron-foundry nearby, the evidence is increasing that the whole area from the Lluguy Valley, through the Conwy Valley and on its western slopes at least, probably as far as the Creuddyn, was a populous and busy area in Roman times, with mining extending throughout, and very considerable agriculture, and probably trading in timber, slate and perhaps fruit.

Was this part of the lost Genouni area of Roman Britain?

96.   *Agricola's mother Procilla came from those parts.*

97.   *They were fluent writers in Greek, but still did not keep many written records, unless Edward I destroyed a lot.*

98.   *See Caesar, de Bello Gallico, the Invasion of Britain.*

Saying farewell to Betws-y-coed, we go over the Pont-y-pair and down Mill Street, onto the medieval pack trail along the west side of the Conwy River. On the right are the broad fields of the fertile valley, with a few ancient farms dotted here and there. This was the old free township of Bettus and Comlannerch mentioned in the fourteenth-century Record of Caernarfon, but the title of Cwmlannerch Farm goes back to Wyrion Eden and the days of Iorwerth, the grandfather of Ednyfed Fychan in the twelfth century, before even the days of that other Iorwerth known as Drwyndwn, the father of Llywelyn Fawr. On the left are the wooded slopes of Gwydir Forest, where in part the rotation of forestry cropping and some too-easily started forest fires have left the hillside bare until new crops can cover them. But the bareness of these slopes belies the forest's size, its interest and its history.

We shall come in time to the Forestry Commission's Information Centre, where may be bought a booklet by Donald Shaw; his father before him and he in later times, have played a most important role in the establishment of this forest. Mr Ian Niall has written a most fascinating book about the father, Mr J.L. Shaw, which is called *The Forester.*

Mr Niall starts his book with Shaw's early days in forestry far away from here, and with his appointment as Head Forester. He gives a vivid description of the family's journey in the hey-days of the railways, and its arrival one dark evening at Llanrwst railway station. He proceeds through the hard days of the development of the forest, the life of the family through all, the set-backs, great fires, restarts, and changes in methods and equipment. He takes the reader through from the days of manpower and horse-power to the times of mechanisation, which has, of course, advanced even more since the days of which he wrote.

The names Shaw and Gwydir in these times must surely be synonymous, as in the past were those of the Wynns and the Watkin Owens with that of Gwydir Castle.

Further along the road, past many a recess in the forest wall for timber loading, we shall come to a raised semi-circular stone platform or terrace. Its history and its purpose are best described by an extract from Thomas

Top inset: Gwydir Castle

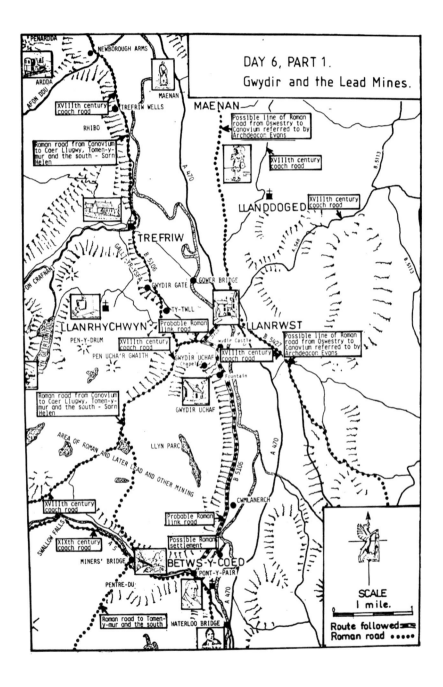

DAY 6, PART 1.

Gwydir and the Lead Mines.

Roscoe's *Wandering in Wales"* —

At a bowshot from Gwydyr Castle stands the fountain of St Albright. The stream which at this place offers its cooling waters to the lips of the traveller, as it issues through the stone conduit, is supplied by a large cistern constructed for that purpose at a considerable distance up the mountain. An open elevated court, of semi-circular form, stands close to the roadside, backed by a stone wall of corresponding figure, surmounted in the centre by pedimented blocks; a narrow channel perforated in the blocks opens a passage for the pure element, through which it issues all day long in one unceasing stream. The opening of the fountain to the public was celebrated by Lord Willoughby in a grand invitation to all the poor old men and women of the neighbourhood, who were plentifully regaled with tea and cakes, and flowing flagons of good ale, and sent merrily home at night with a small portion of money in their pockets.

That was written in 1836, eighty years before the Forestry Commission acquired Gwydir in 1920. The Wynns and their successors, the Willoughbys had owned it since Maredudd ab Ieuan bought it from Dafydd ap Hywel Coetmor about 1500. It was Hywel's father, Gruffydd, whose effigy and tomb we saw in St Michael's Church at Betws-y-coed, and Hywel's own coffin lies alongside the empty stone coffin of Llywelyn Fawr in the Chapel at St Grwst's Church, Llanrwst.

Sir John Wynn

A short way beyond the fountain, on the left a steep track leads up the hillside to Gwydir Uchaf, which is now the Information Centre for the Forestry Commission, and its local office. The original house on this site was built in 1604 by Sir John Wynn, but in 1804 that was described as derelict, and the present building is a much less magnificent restoration.

The Wynns by that time lived in Gwydir Castle, which John Wynn ap Maredudd had started to rebuild half a century before, in 1555 in the reign of Queen Mary. Much of the timber came from Maenan Abbey, dissolved 19 years earlier, as it was hastily and completely demolished. John ap Maredudd died in 1559, and the building was finished by his son, Maurice Wynn. It was this John and Maurice whom we found were buried at Dolwyddelan.

Maurice Wynn was Member of Parliament for Caernarfonshire in 1553, 1554, 1559, and 1563-67, and High Sheriff of the County in 1555, 1570 and 1578. In that he followed in his father's footsteps, for John ap Maredudd had been Member of Parliament for the County from 1551 to

1553, and High Sheriff in 1544-45, 1553-54 and 1556-57.

On August 18th, 1580, Maurice Wynn died, and the estates passed to his son John, who became Sir John. He and his son, Richard, are of the most interest in the history of this part of the valley. John was born in 1553, went to Oxford and was at Furnival's Inn in 1572 and the Inner Temple in 1576, staying in London until his father's death, when he returned to establish himself in the County. He carried on some of the family traditions, becoming Member of Parliament for Caernarfonshire in 1586-87, and Sheriff in 1587-88 and again in 1603. However, his loyalties were not as much with the County as those of his family before him, and he became Sheriff of Meirionnydd in 1588-89 and 1600-01, and of Denbighshire in 1606. In 1608 he became a Member of the Council for the Marches. For his general services, and perhaps for some of his son's work also, he was made a Baronet in 1611.

He tried, usually unsuccessfully, to advance the commercial interests of the Valley and of the County as a whole, no doubt still with an eye to his status with the people and to possible financial gain. Among other schemes he tried to get Hugh Myddelton,[94] who had considerable experience in land drainage in England but who had lost a lot of money on a similar scheme on the Isle of Wight, interested in a scheme to reclaim Traeth Mawr, off Cardigan Bay, and in mining various ores in the Llanrhychwyn area behind Gwydir. He made a more laudable effort to set up the manufacture of Welsh friezes in the valley. Changing fashions had hit the area. Long woollen stockings had gone out of fashion for men with the passing of the Elizabethan era, and also in 1589 William Lee of Woodborough had invented the knitting machine which was rapidly adapted to make the hose that were still wanted, far more quickly and cheaply than they could be knitted by hand. But to add to the problem, the men and women of the court had taken to wearing silken hose, even though they cost £1.5s a pair.

There was at the time great demand for friezes, rough woollen cloths made in southern Wales and the Cotswolds, for export from both Bristol and the growing port of Liverpool.

Sir John could not afford to finance such schemes, for his interests in Parys Mountain, before the great bonanza, had lost him money — in fact, he seems to have had a great aptitude for losing money, while living quite extravagantly. He was frequently in debt to John Williams, Thomas Myddelton and others (see later). He was, in fact, not a pleasant man, as may be gathered from the legend of his soul being condemned to the pool below the Swallow Falls at Betws-y-coed. Some further idea of the man can be obtained from papers which he left, such as one giving instructions to his chaplain, John Price, on his appointment, which included —

> After dinner, if I be busy, you may go to bowles, shuffel bord or any other honest decent recreation, until I go abroad. If you see me void of business, and go to abroad, you shall command a gelding to be made ready by the grooms of the stable, and to go with me... Avoyd the alehouse, to sytt and keepe drunkards company there, being the greatest discredit your function can have...

Sir John had eleven sons and two daughters, so that it is no wonder that his family became connected with many of the great families of Wales, and yet the male line and the title were to die out within three generations, on the death of the son of Sir John Wynn of Plas-y-llan, Eglwys-bach. Sir John of Gwydir was succeeded in 1627 by his second son, Richard, his eldest son, John, having died in 1614.

In order to take advantage of the accession of Henry Tudur to the English throne in 1485, and the removal by him of Edward I's prohibition against Welshmen holding any office under the crown, many Welshmen of standing became at pains to establish their credentials in the succeeding centuries. Of the Wynns, Richard, who was not even born until 1588, a century after Bosworth Field, both before and after the death of his father, was particularly desirous of doing that, for his aspirations were to national office, where his father's had been to local office.

Richard, therefore, sought to get the best of both worlds, and what he traced, and later set out for all to read on the walls of Gwydir Chapel at Llanrwst stated —

> Sir John (his father)... was son and heir to Maurice Wynn, son and heir to John Wynn, son and heir to Meredith, which three lyeth buried in the church at Dolwyddelan, with tombs over them.

That established the immediate local connections. The next point was to establish the fact that the family had its roots deep in Wales, while at the same time maintaining connections with the Royalty. He went on, therefore, to trace the family back ten generations to Owen Gwyneth (Owain Gwynedd), Prince of Wales, and younger brother (as he said) to David Prince of Wales, who married E'me Plantagenet,[95] sister to King Henry III. Owain Gwynedd, from whom he traced direct descent, was father of Iorwerth Drwyndwn, who built Dolwyddelan Castle. But Richard was not content to let the matter rest there. He proceeded —

There succeeded this David three princes, his nephew Leolenus Magnus who married the daughter of King John, David his son, nephew to King Henry III, and Leolyn — the last Prince of Wales of that line — who lived in Edward I's time.

Really the whole recital did not show that he had any Tudur blood, but only that at two stages in the past, relatives of his family line had married relatives of the Norman kings.

The Anglicised, or Norman French spelling of some of the names is amusing, and cannot have helped his relationship with the local Welsh. Also amusing is the anxiety to show the (very tenuous) association with King John and King Henry III, no doubt because King James was also connected with the house of Tudur, for both his father and his grandmother were grandchildren of King Henry VIII, son of Henry Tudur — who had himself female descent from Norman and Welsh kings and princes.[96]

His efforts had success, but showed that his loyalties were more to himself than to the Conwy Valley. He was educated in London, at Lincoln's Inn, and in 1608 he entered the service of the Lord Chamberlain. He became Member of Parliament for Caernarfonshire in 1614, the year of his elder brother's death, which must have taken him away again to London. From 1617 to 1625 he was Groom to the Bedchamber of Charles, Prince of Wales, and travelled around with him, including going to Spain. In 1620 the County rejected him as Member of Parliament, no doubt because they never saw him, so in 1621 he stood for, and was elected for, Ilchester. In 1625 he became Treasurer to Queen Henrietta Maria on the accession of Charles to the throne, and to her at that, or a later, time he gave the largest pearl ever recorded as found in the River Conwy. In 1629 he became Groom to the Bedchamber of the King and Queen. He became Member of Parliament for Andover in 1640, and for Liverpool from 1640 to 1649, in which year he died. The Conwy Valley saw little of him, and in spite of the benefits he had obtained from Charles, both as Prince of Wales and as King, he seems not to have supported him in the Civil War, but instead supported the Parliamentarians.

While we have digressed we have arrived at Gwydir Uchaf. It is doubtful if it was finished in the same year as its erection was started, for a lot of work was put into it. When completed it was said to be the finest house in Gwynedd. Very likely it was not erected for the Wynns to live in — it seems to have been built rather to glorify the Wynns in the eyes of the crown and the powers that be in London. In

Henry Tudor (Henry VII)

145

those days one route to Ireland would be by Denbigh to Llanrwst, and thence to Caernarfon, Newborough and Holyhead, and it would fall to the Wynns to provide good accommodation for Lords Deputy, Royalty and others of high station when they passed through. It may be that the family did not particularly like having all those people arriving often unannounced at Gwydir Castle, lording over all the children and the servants, sometimes, perhaps, when Sir John or his wife were away. The house would be ideal for their accommodation, and it could not be said that they were being pushed into an inferior annexe. In 1690 the Duke of Beaufort was housed here when he was making a tour of North Wales. In due course the house seems to have become more popular with the Wynn family than the castle.

It was presumably in connection with the responsibilities of the family to look after the interests of the crown and its agents when in the area, that Sir Richard was involved in the reconstruction of Pont Fawr in the 1630's.

Sir Richard had no children, and the estate and title passed to his brother Owen in 1649, and it was he who in 1653, as Sheriff of Caernarfonshire, proclaimed Cromwell as Protector. Three years later he was Sheriff of Denbighshire. He died in 1660 and was succeeded by his son, Richard — the second Sir Richard Wynn. He had been involved with his cousin Sir Hugh Myddelton[97] in Royalist plots in support of Charles II in the days of Cromwell in 1652 and again in 1659, and was imprisoned — his political views must therefore have been the opposite of his father's. In 1673 Richard started building Gwydir Uchaf Chapel here (not to be confused with Gwydir Chapel at St Grwst Church, Llanrwst). The design of this, like that of some other buildings in the area, and like Pont Fawr, is often ascribed to Inigo Jones, but he died in 1652. However, the first Sir Richard would have known him well when he was serving with King Charles, and it may be that the design was prepared in those days. It has a rather plain exterior, but the inside, especially the ceiling, is well worth seeing, which requires arrangements at the Forestry Commission Offices. Originally for use by the family and guests, there is no record of it ever being consecrated. Nevertheless until 1920 there were regular services, recorded in 1851 as "open to those who may chance to attend".

Owen married Sarah, the daughter of Sir Thomas Myddelton, grandson of the Sir Thomas Myddelton who financed Sir John Wynn, but died in 1674 with no male heirs, and the estate passed to his 13-year-old daughter, Mary. It was at this time that Watkin Owen was appointed as agent for the estate. When she was 17, in 1678, Mary married Robert Bertie, Baron Willoughby de Eresby, who later became Duke of Ancaster (how the title became Earl of Ancaster at a later date is another story). Mary only lived until 1689, eleven years after her marriage, but the estate remained in the hands of the Dukes and Earls of Ancaster until 1895. As we have already learnt at Eglwys-bach, the title passed, on Richard's death, to John Wynn of Plas-y-llan, and died out with the next generation.

The castle of today is not that built by John Wynn in 1588 and the years that followed. In 1816 part was pulled down and new work was erected, and in 1922, two years after the Forestry Commission acquired the estate it was severely damaged by fire, and part lay derelict for twenty years or so. In 1943 it was purchased by Mr Arthur Clegg, who spent the rest of his life carefully restoring and furnishing it. He was followed by his son, Richard, who owned it until 1982, after which there was a somewhat chequered history until the present owners took over, and re-opened it to the public. The gardens are noted for their peacocks, of which some are often to be found on the road — a hazard to themselves and to motorists.

Just beyond the castle the road joins the B5106, the toll road built in 1777 from Llanrwst to Conwy — though its line has changed since then. Most curiously the road from Betws-y-coed to Gwydir bears also the number B5106. To the left is another road, leading steeply up the hillside to Llanrhychwyn, which earlier was the road to Trefriw, the Roman road to Canovium, and for thirteen hundred years the only road through the Conwy Valley on either side of the tidal river. Another branch from the same road, three hundred yards or so up the hill, was the Roman road to Bryn Gefeiliau, Caer Llugwy, and for untold years the only route for vehicles from Trefriw and Llanrwst to Beddgelert and Caernarfon. This was part of the famed Sarn Helen, along which the armies of Macsen Wledig[98] marched against the raiding Scots and Danes, before crossing into Gaul and on to Rome. Here also marched the troops of Elen, of later Cunedda Wledig, and those of many a later generation. But before that, many a party of Romans and Celts, in chariots and on horseback, with servants on foot, must have passed on their way to enjoy a holiday on the shores of the Celtic Sea, at Cardigan Bay.

The river valley was liable to flooding, as it is to this day, but the present main road down which we came from Betws-y-coed to Gwydir is above such level. Why then did the Romans not follow that far easier line? But maybe they did. Maybe with the importance of the mining they had several routes. W.J. Hemp, who we heard before assisted in the excavations at Bryn Gefeiliau, was of the opinion that they did have such a road along the valley floor on the west of the Conwy River as well as the roads to the Miners' Bridge and to Tŷ Hyll. If they had a camp or a settlement at Betws-y-coed where the Llugwy joins the Conwy as well as the fort at Bryn Gefeiliau, such a road, along the riverside would, by any standards, be a real necessity, to get from that settlement to Caerhun, or to their friends at Trefriw or in Canovium, to bring supplies in from the fields at Farchwel and at Ardda, and from the quays at Caerhun, Trefriw, perhaps Llanrwst. These places will all be visited in the coming days. A road in the valley would, of course, avoid the snows of winter to a great degree.

There is a maze of lanes between Gwydir and Llanrhychwyn and Tŷ Hyll, on the hillsides above the Conwy and the Llugwy, the relics of mining through two thousand years and more. Many we know date but from the last two centuries, but lead was mined before the Romans came, a fact supported by two sources of good evidence. The first is information given by writers who lived before the days when the Gwydir Estate allowed almost uncontrolled prospecting under a "take note" system, and extensive stratching around and working for lead, zinc, sulphur and silver destroyed evidence previously there to see. They tell us of age old workings and other relics which then still existed. One such writer was John Williams of Pentre Felin, who wrote *Faunula Grustensis*.

The second is that despite the spate of speculative working, some quite significant remains have come to light. It is from those that we know that the Romans had a road in the vicinity of the Miners' Bridge on a line between Llanrhychwyn and Pentre-du, as well as their main road to Bryn Gefeiliau. From those also we know that they mined near Coedmawr, just off that road as well as by the Llugwy near Tŷ Hyll. But other indications have been found, and much may yet remain to be discovered beneath the lead waste heaps, maybe just in the thickets which abound between them. They mined further afield, at Trefriw and at Henryd, for sulphur and for lead, and, of course, for copper on the Orme.

But back here at Gwydir they would certainly prefer to move the heavy ores by water instead of on their wagons. Though they had learnt from the Celts to harness teams of horses to wagons whose front wheels could swivel for bends, they still used in the early years of occupation their two-wheeled carts, or ungainly steerless wagons.[99] They had their main harbour on the river at Caerhun, and it is evident that they also had a quay at Trefriw, but there is reason to believe that they also had some form of harbour at Llanrwst, to which in those days the tide still came. For that they would have a road to the mines, and the road from Gwydir could be the line. The continuation of the same road across the hill to Caer Llugwy with its bridge or ford, defensive camp and fort, on a line which served for so many a century, would have been Roman engineering logic.[100]

The mining activities from here to Henryd in the later middle ages, and on into the nineteenth century and the first half of the twentieth-century, were very extensive, and great numbers of people worked in the industries.

Not only, therefore, were there communities of the Celts and the Romans which have disappeared under the rubble and scrub, but even villages of the past which some alive can still remember. This area, which now looks so sleepy — a land of conifers and sheep and old waste heaps — has in the past been an area of great activity in mining, in forest products in the days when hardwoods covered the hills, in sheep and wool, and the by-products and service requirements of all. No wonder Llanrhychwyn, which tomorrow we may have difficulty in finding, had in the year 1801, 87 houses, and a population of 376, when many a town of today had less. In those days, whole families of a dozen or a score would live in just one house, and in the larger ones there would be servants also.

We can wander the lanes, and enjoy the views — the small ones across the little pools, the greater ones across the Conwy Valley— and we could stay all day enjoying beauty, but we must in time go on our way, return again by Gwydir to Llanrwst, and we will come to Llyn Geirionydd another time.D

94. *Hugh Myddelton was son of Richard Myddelton of Denbigh, and brother of Thomas Myddelton.*

95. *Emma was in fact an illegitimate daughter of Geoffrey of Anjou, and therefore only half sister of Henry III.*

96. *See page 251.*

97. *This was grandson of the Hugh Myddelton referred to on page 143.*

98. *Maximus Magnus.*

99. *They were levered with poles to change direction.*

100. *Reference has been made to W.J. Hemp's investigations and views about valley roads from Canovium (Caerhun) to the Lluguy Valley. In the Conwy Valley there was at least one road between Canovium and Bryn Gefeiliau and another branch which led to the Miners' Bridge, Archaeologia Cambrensis III, Vol XI, page 215 in 1864 described the former as follows — "at the foot of the cliffs on the west side of the Vale of Llanrwst as far as Trefriw, then over the moor behind Gwydir". W. Bezant Lowe, in "The Heart of Northern Wales", 1912, page 126, says a later conjecture, however, is that the road kept some little way up the western hillsides, fringing the valley, passing over the Ardda uplands, thence to the upper extremity of what is now Trefriw village, thence ascending to Llanrhychwyn, and thence past the sites of the old quarries in a southerly direction over the moor, past Bryn-y-Fawnog to a point east of Ty'n-y-Mynydd and then along the existing road in the direction of Ty Hyll". Archdeacon Evans in his History of Pentrefoelas recorded that "the line of road from Oswestry to Corwen, Cerrig-y-Drudion, Pentrefoelas, Llanrwst, and from Caerhun by Bwlch-y-Ddeufaen to Aber, frequently formed the line of march of troops, whether for invasion or defence". That suggests a link between Llanrwst (then perhaps Grwgystu) and Sarn Helen more or less on the line of the road up the hill, and favours a line for Sarn Helen near to that suggested in Archaeologia Cambrensis, rather than one further up the hill. However, the area seems to have been well populated, with industries, spa and agriculture, timber and mining, and it may be that there was a complex system of roads criss-crossing the area, and that all those propositions are valid.*

In the seventeenth and eighteenth centuries in particular, Llanrwst was a busy town. In 1698, when the population of the whole of Britain was only six million, it had 60 houses and 300 inhabitants. From then on it grew rapidly so that 90 years later it was approaching 2,000, since when it has grown at more or less the same rate as Wales as a whole, but less than most urban areas. By the last decade of the eighteenth century, when coaches had for over a hundred years replaced the old covered wagons, and when the new toll road of 1777 was bringing coaches from London on the way to Holyhead,[101] as well as the previously established coaches from Denbigh, Beddgelert and Caernarfon, it was not only prosperous and comparatively large, but was also fashionable. It had not less than ten alehouses, of which three, perhaps more, were recognised coaching and posting houses. As we learnt on our earlier visit, in those days it had many shops and industries. There were cabinet makers and jewellers, saddlers, hatters, shoemakers, glovers, tailors and dressmakers, cornmerchants and oilmerchants (the equivalent of the modern ironmongers), butchers and bakers, as well as the other usual small trades of a town. There were ten qualified doctors and lawyers, and there were banks, schools and a number of other establishments, including a hospital. Its annual wool fair was an event of great importance to which came merchants from far and wide, including some from over the seas, and it fixed the price of wool throughout the land.

Its manufacturing and primary industries included tanning, brewing, dyeing, harpmaking and the usual service industries associated with farming, such as wheelwrights and cartmakers, farriers and smiths, sawyers, and other small industries, soapmaking, caskmaking and the like.

In the Square the old Town Hall has gone, part of Denbigh Street and all of Plough Street and Scotland Street have been demolished, and other

detrimental things have happened, but there is still enough left of the town of those days, of over two centuries ago, to imagine the times of the dawn of Llanrwst's greatest prosperity, at the height of Georgian elegance, the summer

Top inset: Tŷ-hwnt-i'r-bont, Llanrwst. Bottom inset: Pont Fawr

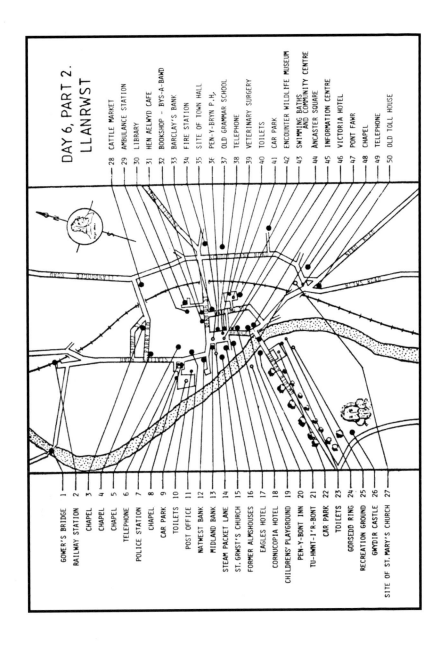

**DAY 6, PART 2.
LLANRWST**

1 GOWER'S BRIDGE
2 RAILWAY STATION
3 CHAPEL
4 CHAPEL
5 CHAPEL
6 TELEPHONE
7 POLICE STATION
8 CHAPEL
9 CAR PARK
10 TOILETS
11 POST OFFICE
12 NATWEST BANK
13 MIDLAND BANK
14 STEAM PACKET LANE
15 ST. GRWST'S CHURCH
16 FORMER ALMSHOUSES
17 EAGLES HOTEL
18 CORNUCOPIA HOTEL
19 CHILDRENS' PLAYGROUND
20 PEN-Y-BONT INN
21 TU-HWNT-I'R-BONT
22 CAR PARK
23 TOILETS
24 GORSEDD RING
25 RECREATION GROUND
26 GWYDIR CASTLE
27 SITE OF ST. MARY'S CHURCH

28 CATTLE MARKET
29 AMBULANCE STATION
30 LIBRARY
31 HEN AELWYD CAFE
32 BOOKSHOP - BYS-A-BAWD
33 BARCLAY'S BANK
34 FIRE STATION
35 SITE OF TOWN HALL
36 PEN-Y-BRYN P.H.
37 OLD GRAMMAR SCHOOL
38 TELEPHONE
39 VETERINARY SURGERY
40 TOILETS
41 CAR PARK
42 ENCOUNTER WILDLIFE MUSEUM
43 SWIMMING BATHS AND COMMUNITY CENTRE
44 ANCASTER SQUARE
45 INFORMATION CENTRE
46 VICTORIA HOTEL
47 PONT FAWR
48 CHAPEL
49 TELEPHONE
50 OLD TOLL HOUSE

of the year 1780. The town had recovered from the depression of the previous century following the collapse of the stocking industry. The new turnpike road from Shrewsbury through to Conwy had been in use for just three years, and was starting to really benefit the inns and the warehouses, and through them the shops and every other trade.

The Grand Alliance of France and Spain and Holland in support of the rebellious colonists in far-away America was not of great concern in this comfortable corner of the Principality, which had seen many great events of history come and go. What was there to worry over? Admiral Rodney had shown the Spaniards at St Vincent who really ruled the seas: Gibraltar had been relieved, and he was on his way to teach the French a lesson. The success of General Washington against the King's armies on the American mainland would be short-lived.

It was just ten years since Daines Barrington, the Circuit Judge for Meirionnydd, Caernarfonshire and Anglesey from 1757 to 1777, had edited and published Sir John Wynn's history of the Gwydir family, and had revived old legends, memories and controversies. Those who favoured the memory of the Wynns were still complaining of the closing off of Gwydir Chapel from the Church by panelling over the doorway. The harpist Thomas Parry had become the leading town musician since the death the year before of David Roberts.

These were things that mattered on a sunny market day which had attracted the local gentry and their wives from as far as Ysbyty Ifan, Penmachno and Pentrefoelas, from Trefriw, Eglwys-bach and Llangernyw. They had come in four-in-hand or family coach, with flunky and footman and coachman. With them had come their stylish sons and animated young ladies sporting parasols, riding in modern gig in front where the girls were under watchful parents' gaze. Here on the streets they mingled with the farmers in sturdy homespun and their wives and daughters bedecked with bonnets and bows — with miners from Betws-y-coed and Llanrhychwyn and the Ardda uplands, and with professional people in their business best. In the coffee rooms of the local hostelries the prospect for the season's wool was the common subject of conversation among the men. The women talked of fashions new from London, of garden parties past and yet to come, of matches and engagements and of who might be invited to a local wedding. Among them all, in the streets and in the hostelries, dashing hither and thither, delivery boys and apprentices, all rubbing shoulders with shepherds from the hills, shop assistants, market-stall holders, and now and then outside a herd of cattle or flock of sheep or even goats or geese on their way to or from the auctioneers' pens.

On the market stalls was the food of the smaller farmers and the artisans — milk, coarse bread, goats' meat, fresh-water fish, potatoes — butter for the better off at six pence a pound, the cost of a good dinner in a country inn when a labourer's wage was a shilling a day, but a room in a coaching-house with food and heat was half a guinea a day.

Of a sudden, across the valley came the echoing sound of horns, as Lawrence's coach from London came rushing down the new toll road from Nebo, while that from Bangor dead on time came through the valley by way of Trefriw. There was hustle and bustle to clear the way, to have all ready at the coaching houses in Bridge Street, to get the change of horses harnessed and finally watered. From nowhere impish urchins appeared, ready to hold or carry a bag for a farthing, or just hope for a morsel to eat. With the coach there might come gentlemen, or even more venturesome ladies, on horseback, perhaps in a gig or a chaise, preferring to travel in company with the coach than venture alone where there might be highwaymen or thieves. A coach from the east or west from Denbigh or Beddgelert might come as well, to meet up with the London coach or that for the Irish passage.

With the coaches came the news. From London it told of disturbances, of a mob led by Lord George Gordon the Protestant fanatic, of the anti-Catholic riots and the firing of the Newgate prison and rumours that 300 had been killed. The conversation was of the turning of the tide against Lord North and the Tory government. Word of all this passed quickly round from mouth to mouth throughout the town — but London was in England, far away, and what mattered there was not of import in this market town, so the talk returned again to rearing sheep, to the latest fashions in the milliners' and the gown-shops, and the watches in the Owens' shop, their new idea said to be unique of having a dial above the face of longcase clocks to tell the phases of the moon, even the date. Protestant or Catholic, in Wales it mattered not, for both were united in abomination of the system that appointed English bishops and clergy to the wealthy livings of the Principality, and gave only poorest livings to the Welsh: the great days of the chapel building had not quite arrived. Likewise whig or tory, rich or poor, had no significance, for local interests affected all, the national did not.

The air was full of the smells of the tannery and the soap works, the brewery and the wool dyeing, of horses and of sheep, of meat stalls and fish shops, pie houses and mussel booths. The middle-aged could recall when the Vestry had occasion to notify the tanners that their skins must not be hung in public places, from the trees, or in the churchyard.

To some the Square was still Bryn-y-boten (Pudding Hill), as it had always been before the days of the Ancasters. The clock in the Town Hall was still a novelty, and the building itself The New Town Hall. The business premises in the Square, in Bridge Street and in Denbigh Street, had their signs, the cut-out bottle for the apothecrary who served as dentist, striped pole for the barber who was also surgeon, sheep and ox for the butcher, the man in frock coat for the tailor, and those of all the other trades, the cow, the plough (Siop-y-plow moved from Plough Street to Denbigh Street and to where it is now in Station Road not long ago, but no longer sells the wares of old). There were Father Time with his scythe, the Harp, the leathern saddle and the signs of the hostelries, the eagle and the hand.

The modern shops, in London fashion, now had big windows, with squares of glass behind which their wares could clearly be seen (how very good it is to see the style returning). The talk was of a new road to be made from town to Tal-y-cafn on this eastern side of the Conwy River, and even of a proper road from Gwydir to Pont-y-pair.

In the shops, even on a board outside the town hall, were notices produced by the new printing works of Dafydd Jones at Trefriw, and the copies of his books could now be bought — *Y Ddadl rhwng Pob America a'r Llywodraeth - pris 2 geiniog* (The debate between the people of America and the Government, price 2 pence), and *Histori yr Iesu Sanctaidd - pris swllt* (a shilling), and others. In Denbigh Street the shop of John and Watkin Owen was displaying for sale lantern and longcase clocks, and watches. Elsewhere were gloves in local leather, both fashionable and utilitarian, the crafts of local goldsmiths and silversmiths, the finest wine cupboards and dressers, chairs and tables, made by the local craftsmen of Gwydir oak or imported mahogany. All the signs of wealth were to be seen — or could be found by those who knew, smuggled brandy, tea, tobacco, brought in by John McCullough or Randle Podmore from Roscoff [102] under the noses of Collectors' men, carried by night on backs of horses from the smugglers' landings on the Orme, or among the marshes Rhuddlan way: the wealth of the woollen merchants, the landed gentry, the general traders and the farmers ensured demand to meet supply, and the smugglers were more liked by poor and rich than were the King's Collectors' men.

This was the Llanrwst of the 1780s, eighth largest town in Wales with nearly 2,000 population, a town of then unusual learning and of culture as well as wealth. Its respected grammar school would soon celebrate its 175th anniversary, for it was founded in 1608, together with the almshouses, with money provided by John Williams, son of William Coetmor of Dolwyddelan, styled in 1623 as "late His Majesty's Goldsmith". The supervision of the work was entrusted to his son, John Williams, and

Sir John Wynn. John Williams the younger was also a Member of the Goldsmith's Company in London, presumably with a business in Llanrwst, since he could spend a considerable amount of time here. Sir John Wynn was in the habit of borrowing heavily from the elder John Williams, who was a very wealthy man.

The Wynns set out in later years to show that they had provided the money for the charities — they were always out to gain any credit or glory there was to be had — but in 1678 the Crown determined that it had been John Williams who had provided it, and who had promoted the scheme. Many a long proceeding before commissioners was to follow, but the matter was never resolved in any way different from the Crown's decision. At this time, a century later, official circles therefore credited John Williams, while the local people were conditioned to most of the Wynn family's ability to credit Sir John, the argument all stirred up by Daines Barrington's book. The general state of Sir John's finances (he was for ever borrowing, as we have already heard) definitely suggests John Williams to be rightful claimant.

The culture was long established — it was two hundred years since the days of the Morgans and the Salesburys and the Pryses of whom we learnt before. Of those, the Salesburys had lived in Llanrwst, at Plas Isa, having moved there from Llansannan.

The family of Salusbury was established in the Vale of Clwyd by the mid-fourteenth century — the spelling of the name varied from time to time. One Thomas Salusbury, or Salbri, of Lleweni, a man of great estates, was a Lancastrian supporter who was killed at the Battle of Barnet in 1471. He had five sons of whom Robert ap Salbri settled at Plas Isa, Llanrwst, and acquired extensive estates. On his death his son Ffwg, already married to Annes ferch William ap Gruffydd ap Robin of Cochwillan, moved from his home at Llansannan to Plas Isa. William was the second son of the marriage, and he was born at Plas Isa about 1520. He may have started his education under monks at Maenan Abbey, and have gone on to Gwydir school after the abbey was dissolved. He then went to Oxford. As we learnt, he married Catrin Llwyd, daughter of Robert ap Rhys ap Meredudd of Hiraethlyn, and a sister of Elis Prys, the Red Doctor — she was therefore a niece of two of the last three abbots of Maenan.

Catholicism returned with Queen Mary from 1553 to 1558, but when Elizabeth came to the throne William was invited to assist the Bishop of St David's, Richard Davies, in the translation of the whole of the New Testament into Welsh, and, it seems, the prayer book. No doubt this largely came about because of family connections, for Bishop Davies was the son of Dafydd ap Gronw, Curate of Gyffin [103] (Conwy) and his wife, Jonet, both of whom belonged to families of the gentry of the Conwy Valley area: also, William's second cousin once removed, Sir John Salusbury, had been a friend of King Henry VIII, and was his agent in Denbighshire. Nevertheless William had the necessary qualifications, for he was undoubtedly one of the foremost scholars of his age.

He was personally responsible for most of the translation, although some of the minor books were translated for him by others. The Prayer Book and the New Testament were both published on 7th October, 1567. Willam had even organised the actual printing and publishing, although the licence for *Y Testament Newydd* was issued in the name of Humphrey Toy, who financed the publication. The ork of printing was done by Henry Denham, who had his business "at the Sign of the Helmet" in St Paul's Churchyard, London.

It is generally assumed that the Humphrey Toy was the man of that name of "St Paule's Churchyarde" in London, who was a bookseller and publisher, because William stayed at his house in 1567 while publication arrangements were in hand. It is, however, much more likely that it was that man's father, Humphrey Toy of Carmarthen, a man of considerable wealth who had been a friend of Bishop Davies when he lived at the Bishop's palace at Abergwili, 1 1/2 miles from Carmarthen. He would have met William there, and it would have been quite natural for Toy to have arranged for him to stay with his son in London, and no doubt to get his

An old market day in Llanrwst

son to give William some assistance. The friendship led to the son publishing other books for William in that and later years. The father's interest in Welsh church matters, his great wealth, his friendship with Davies,
all favour him as being the financial backer and licensee.

London printers were used for this work, and for the Bibles of 1588 and
1620, because until 1698 all printers had to be licensed, and licences were
only issued to people in London and the major English cities, none at all
in Wales.

Another matter which would no doubt have influenced Bishop Davies
in his choice of William Salesbury was that he had already written and
published books, starting with *A Dictionary of Englyshe and Welshe in*
1547, *Oll Synnwyr pen Kymbero Ygyd*, also in 1547, followed by at least
five others. The first-named was a collection of Welsh proverbs, and it
was printed by Nicholas Hyll of London on a paper suitable for writing in
pen, so that readers could add notes for themselves. His *A Playne and
Familiar Introduction, teaching how to pronounce the Letters in the
Brytishe Tongue, now commonly called Welsh* proved so popular that it
ran to a second edition. It was published first in the same year as his New
Testament, which may have influenced its popularity, for there is no doubt
that the Testament (and the Welsh Bibles of 1588 and 1620) did much to
save the Welsh language from the oblivion into which officialdom was
trying to drive it. In 1551 William published a translation into Welsh of
the Lessons used in the Communion Service, under the title *Kynniver
Llith a Bann*, which was printed by Robert Crowley in London.

The connection between William Salesbury and William Morgan, which
led to the use by the latter of Salesbury's New Testament in his Bible may
have arisen from the fact that his father-in-law in 1540 acquired from the
Crown the estate of Dolgynwal, and in 1560 his brother-in-law acquired
Tir Ifan, which included lands at Penmachno, where Morgan lived.

The exact date of William Salesbury's death is not known, but it is believed to have been about 1584.

The roar of a graceless juggernaut brings us back from the past to today, belching forth its stinking fumes of diesel fuel, shaking the old buildings to their foundations. We will escape by going down Tan-yr-Eglwys,
beside the Eagles Hotel. On the right are the almshouses, now a museum.
These are the ones that were built, as we have heard, in 1610 at the ex-
pense of John Williams; apparently he intended first to establish the charity at Dolwyddelan, his father's home, where maybe he himself was born;
for some reason that proved too expensive, and he changed to Llanrwst.
The almshouses, which became known as The Bowles, were *"with twelve
rooms for eleven men and one old woman for their bedmaker, and £5 a*

year for each of them." The adjacent school, long demolished, was associated with the almshouses to the extent that the master was to give certain religious instruction to the inmates, while the usher of the school was to read prayers daily for the inmates and the scholars together.

Each almshouse occupant had a room 12 feet square, and although old, they must have needed to be agile, for nearly every room was approached by a little flight of steps, and the only washing and toilet facilities were on the other side of the back yard. They were, however, much better off than they would have been at the local workhouse, and they must have had considerable freedom; for example, Rowland Griffith, last of the Llanrwst harpmakers, lived here in the late 18th or early 19th century, and was able to make harps on the premises. It seems that he would never finish a harp here, for he said that the ceaseless chatter of the women around would get into the soul of the harp, and ruin its tone! One may wonder who the women were — were they inmates, where the charity provided for men? Were they friends of the bedmaker, or perhaps of the other inmates? Were they patients in the hospital? Or were they the women in Ancaster Square?

Through the churchyard gates, Gwydir Chapel is on the right; but to the left is the river, beyond a small part of the ancient churchyard. Looking across that way, or at another time looking to the church from the other side of the river, it is difficult to imagine a more beautiful setting for a church, or any other building. Even today, so near in footsteps to the trafficked A470, it is a haven of quietude, as it was in the past (except, perhaps when the tanners were hanging their skins on the churchyard trees!). This chapel, the Gwydir Chapel, is another building ascribed to Inigo Jones. The church itself having been built in 1470 and ensuing years, following destruction of its predecessor by marauding Yorkist troops, the chapel was added by the first Sir Richard Wynn in 1633, by which time he was Groom to the Bedchamber of King Charles I and Queen Henrietta Maria, no doubt in frequent contact with Inigo Jones on the King's behalf. If, as seems likely, Inigo was born in this area, he would no doubt have been delighted to help with this work, with Pont Fawr and the later Chapel at Gwydir.

The tower and the north aisle of the church were added in the nineteenth century. The interior we will examine later.

Many of the Wynns of Gwydir are buried in the chapel, but ironically Sir Richard, who built it and set such store by it, is buried at Wimbledon. There are within brass engravings of many members of the family, which were once bedded in the floor, but are now better preserved. Here is the monument to the Wynn family bearing the family tree prepared by Sir

Richard, which we heard of before. The tomb of Sir John was brought from London by his own anticipatory arrangement in the *Hopewell*, many years before he died! Beside the coffin of Llywelyn Fawr is the effigy of Hywel Coetmor, a captain of a hundred troops at the field of Poitiers, who owned Gwydir before the Wynns, and probably built an earlier castle.

The chapel is kept locked now, but may be seen on request. Here in this chapel hang the spurs of Dafydd ap Siencyn (in modern times, he would be David Jenkin), who was descended on his father's side from Marchudd,[104] and on his mother's side from Llywelyn Fawr. He was a Lancastrian supporter who kept the Yorkists out of Nant Conwy until 1468, when the Earl of Pembroke's forces made a successful foray and did so much damage. He was variously described as "a Captain in the Lancastrian Forces", and "an Outlaw", the difference depending on whether you were a supporter of the House of Lancaster, or that of York. He was a poet as well as a warrior, eight "englynion" being attributed to him. He is said to have lived on Carreg-y-gwalch, the hill to the south of Gwydir Uchaf.

There are as many legends about him as there are in England about Robin Hood, and many may be read in Welsh in little books which can be bought at Bys a Bawd in Denbigh Street. If they were translated, we should no doubt soon have a Holywood Dafydd on our television screens. As with such characters in the countries of Europe, he was reputed to be such an excellent shot with a bow and arrow that (in his case) he could shoot the quill pen out of the hands of a man about to sign a document of which he did not approve; and like his peers elsewhere, he is reputed to have taken from the rich to give to the poor.

Taking us further back into history, here is the effigy of one Goch, who owned Gwydir estate before even Hywel Coetmor, and was renowned for his prowess with a battle axe. He was killed in Flanders in 1388.

While the chapel may contain the history of the top families of the area, the church itself has the beauty. The tracery of the east window, the old stone font, some of the panelling, the reading desk and the reproduction fresco on one wall, must not be missed, nor, of course, the carved rood screen which came from Maenan Abbey. In the churchyard was buried on January 10th, 1663, John Salusbury at the age of 113.

If we go now across the Square and up Denbigh Street, on the right are premises where the Owens had their first clockmakers' shop. Beyond, by C.L. Jones' shop of today, John Jones set up his printing works in 1836, having come first to No. 29 Little Bridge Street (now Station Road) from Trefriw in 1825 — the business had outgrown those premises. Of his earlier days, and of his father and grandfather we shall learn when we visit Trefriw.

Here, in Denbigh Street, Jones operated under the name of the Venedocian Press,[105] not only designing and casting his own type to supplement that which he bought, but also inventing and building machines for the printing trade. At one stage he printed ultra-miniature hymn books for children, which were presented as prizes to new pupils at Sunday School. From at least 1830 he was including art plates in his books. He died in 1865, the business then passing to his son, Owen Evan Jones, who already had his own printing business in Porthmadog, and therefore left his brother John Evan Jones to manage the Venedocian Press, as he had been doing in the father's later years. Steam power was introduced, and the name was changed to O. Evan Jones and Co., The Venedocian Steam Printing Works.

John was good at the work, but he died in 1887, the management then being taken over by John Lloyd, nephew of Owen Evan Jones, a well trained printer, but no good at business management. Owen therefore returned to his home town in 1894, and took charge of the works until his death in 1918. John Lloyd died in 1935 and the business came to an end.

It was just around the corner, at No. 2 Watling Street, then later at Cowlyd House, No. 12 Watling Street, that William J. Roberts had another printing works from 1862 to 1897. Better known as Gwilym Cowlyd (his Bardic name), we shall learn more of him at Trefriw. In the annals of printers Roberts was important only for employing in 1878 a twenty-two year old assistant by the name of John Lloyd Roberts from Bangor, who later married his niece, causing a family rift. John Lloyd consequently left W.J. Roberts after the wedding, and set up his own business in the Market Hall, taking business from his former employer as well as from other printers in the town. He later added insult to injury by buying cheaply all his former employer's equipment at the bankruptcy sale of 1897. Later, after J. Lloyd Robert's death in 1936 the business was bought by his apprentice, Ted Jennings, who moved the business to Willow Street and, in fact continued printing until his retirement in 1984, having started working for J. Lloyd Roberts as an apprentice in 1922.

There were other printers in the town, including Evan Pugh and R.J. Jones in Denbigh Street, but none with the inventive genius of Dafydd Jones and his successors, and none with the business acumen for their businesses to survive into the present age like that of John Lloyd Roberts and Ted Jennings. Evan Pugh did have the distinction of having a linotype machine.

Continuing on our way up Denbigh Street we come to School Bank Road. Along here, on the left, is the school, where stands today the building of the Grammar School, founded in 1608, where generations of the Valley children have attended, and still do. We come next to the Wildlife Museum, and beyond that the old Free School. On the opposite side of the road is the churchyard of St Mary's, where the church is now demolished. Built in 1841 and 1842 on land given by Lord Willoughby de Eresby as a Chapel of Ease to provide for more services for English visitors than could be fitted in at St Grwst's, its popularity diminished in recent years. Falling attendances, cost of maintenance, and other factors, caused the Parochial Church Council to abandon services, and later to commence demolition — a process completed in 1984. Some few years before that, Aberconwy Council took over the responsibility for the building, and there was talk of preserving the ruin as it then stood, but that came to nought.

Within the ruins there was a plaque inscribed *Sacred to the Memory of Admiral John Wyatt Watling, of Fron Ganol. Born April 9th, 1787, died November 28th, 1867.* He came from Leominster, and he served with Nelson, almost certainly being with him at Trafalgar. After his first wife died he came on a visit to Llanrwst and he met a local woman whom he married. He later settled in the town, and made such a significant impression that it was after him that Watling Street here was named, when it was extended with buildings a hundred years or more ago. The name has nothing to do with the Romans! The plaque is now at the Wildlife Museum.

The Gwyneddigion Society established eisteddfod traditions in the town about 1791, when the first National Eisteddfod was held here, yet a further indication of the culture of the eighteenth century. The next National Eisteddfod here was in 1951, and the Eisteddfod Dyffryn Conwy dates from 1924. The National Eisteddfod came again in 1989.

The prosperity of the town in the eighteenth and nineteenth centuries is further shown by the chapels. There are three in Station Road alone, of which two are massive, imposing buildings, set to rival St Grwst's Church. The largest, Capel Seion, had seats for 965 and standing room for 300 more. Others are in Scotland Street and Parry Road.

With the fall of evening we can look inside some of the ancient hostelries, of which perhaps the Pen-y-bont is the least changed from the days when it was a coaching inn. The Eagles shows the contrast of the prosperity of the end of the Georgian era, when it was extended and "modernised". The Victoria (demolished mid 1990s) showed the optimism of the Victorian days, built for the coming of the railway, with the expectation that the station would be where the Central Garage now stands. The Cornucopia, another of the sixteenth century or earlier posting houses, retains much of its original character. Other hostelries of the past, such as the Pen-y-bryn while still as old, have changed in character, but the delightful little restaurant Hen Aelwyd[106] is much as it must have been four centuries ago.

For those who wish to shop, there is not much that cannot be purchased in the town, as those who seek and enquire will find. For a Rolls Royce or a mink coat, you might have to wait, but in time it would arrive. If we explored all that is here, it would take us many a day, but our schedule takes us on our way tomorrow.

101. *To avoid conflict with London coaching houses, passengers had to change coaches at Shrewsbury.*
102. *Roscoff in Brittany — the age-old link between the Celtic nations again revealed.*
103. *Gyffin was a perpetual curacy.*
104. *Marchudd was a forebear eight generations removed of Ednyfed Fychan, Seneschal of Gwynedd.*
105. *Venedocian derived of course from the tribal name Venedotes.*
106. *Hen Aelwyd. One of the few places where coffee and cream really still is coffee and cream.*

Day 7, Part 1 - Trefriw

From Llanrwst we continue our journey by crossing again Pont Fawr, to travel down the western side of the river on the Llanrwst to Conwy toll road of 1777. There have been a few changes — at Gwydir in particular — but generally this road must be now much the same as it was then, though at that time the surface was waterbound, and not firmly bound with tar as now. Those who travelled in coaches, on horseback, on foot or in any other way in the eighteenth century must have been able to enjoy the same views of the hillsides, the tender greens of the springtime, or the wonderful reds and golds and yellows, browns and blues of autumn heralding the onfall of winter. Some of the oak trees which now stand in the lowland pastures may even have been there then, perhaps young saplings nurtured in the hedges by caring hands of farmer's labourer, long before the days of the ruthless cut of the modern hedging machines, back in the times when hedges were layered with the utmost skill by craftsmen, and post and wire were quite unknown.

The toll house is still there, Gwydir Gate, two-thirds of a mile from the Gwydir junction; but no longer is there a gate, and no old crone now comes for fee to use the road. Tŷ'n Twll stands back from the road before Gwydir Gate, as did Hen Dyrpeg now gone, for they served the road as it used to be when the route from Tŷ Hyll to Llanrwst met the roads from Trefriw and from Llanrhychwyn part way up the hillside behind Gwydir, the Trefriw and Llanrhychwyn roads parting company south-west of the house now called Whitebarn. Gwydir Gate became the toll house when the present length of road from Gwydir towards Trefriw was built across the marsh.

The farms are there, but some are now just houses, the land run by another farm or syndicate. The stone walls beside the road were then quite beautious, proud evidence of the skill of mason and of waller, and so maintained with loving care by many a generation of highway lengthsman. Now they are gracelessly neglected in a wasteful and untidy age, disclaimed, unwept perhaps, by the successors to the highway trust, but their destruction hastened by the pounding of a myriad cars and lorries, coaches and tractors which now pay tax instead of toll. The tax no

Top inset: St Mary's Church, Trefriw

longer pays for walls, and men who would take the pride are unemployed, so soon they will be no more, supplanted by unromantic post and wire, and no-one seems to care.

Trefriw to which we come is a straggling, strange and mixed community, now with the appearance of an overgrown village. It was once a market town, not much less in population than nearby Llanrwst. It was the administrative centre of the Cantref of Arllechwedd, which comprised the Commotes of Arllechwedd Uchaf, Arlechwedd Isaf and Nant Conwy, stretching from Llanfairfechan to the River Conwy, and from Tir Ifan to the Orme. It had a court and it had a palace. Through the ages it has been a centre of lead and silver mining, and of sulphur and perhaps of tin. It was here that for many years Llywelyn Fawr had his home, a palace for his royal wife. It has been a port for ships that plied the seas, a spa, and just a home for people.

The changes have come and gone, some to return again in a later age, to overlap and intermingle, so that at no time could it be said that Trefriw was this, or that, or famed for such a man or thing, and yet until quite recent times it has been for 2,000 years or so a most important place.

The Romans were here, and they were probably not the first to come and settle. One of their roads from Canovium to Caer Llugwy and the south passed through, and the road to the seaside villas and the ports of Cardigan Bay passed near. They found the orange-tinted waters from the springs on the slopes of Clogwyn Mawr, and appreciated the medicinal values, which they exploited. Before even the Roman troops were withdrawn from the forts in A.D. 140 or thereabouts, they tunnelled into Allt Goch, and constructed pools to gather them, perhaps even to bathe, and those may still be seen.

In the river they cultivated pearls, which the Celts had done before, and it has even been said that Caerhun was first constructed to guard the pearl beds. Like the Celts and earlier Iberians, they farmed the lands in this part of the valley, and on the uplands to the north and west, and traces of their fields can still be found. Some of their houses were no doubt of great magnificence, built with the help of Celtic craftsmen from the oak which covered the hills from the valley floor to 1,200 feet or more, with slate for roof and maybe for floors cut from the quarries in the nearby hills; most likely in the Roman tradition, their gardens were tended with loving care.

There would be, for sure, legionaries and officers who, paid on their discharge, built lesser homes and stayed with Celtic or Iberian wives like those in the Betws-y-coed surrounds. They would ply the trades and industries which such a place required, and their descendants would rank

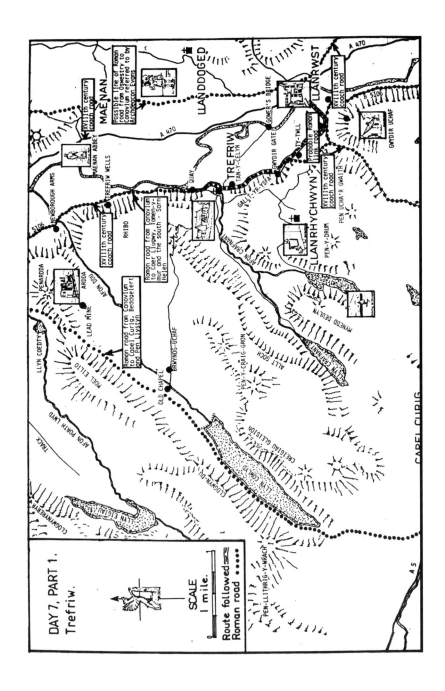

as Roman citizens, and would form the Segontian Legion which went with Macsen Wledig to the gates of Rome, and the armies which destroyed the invading Saxon hordes. Here we know in later times were Celts of high degree and station, whose homes though based on the round, not the square, may well have vied with those of the Romans in their magnificence. Maybe the Mabinogion did not exaggerate, of that same Macsen Wledig —

> And he came straight into the castle and into the hall, and there he saw Cynan son of Eudaf and Gadeon son of Eudaf playing at gwyddbwyll,[107] and he saw Eudaf son of Caradawg sitting in a chair of ivory, carving pieces for the gwyddbwyll. The maiden he had seen in his sleep he saw sitting in a chair of red gold. (Translation by Gwyn Jones and Thomas Jones — see bibliography).

Their round rooms opened one out of another in some cases, as much as forty feet across with lesser size for the retiring rooms. Of their height we know nothing — some may have been of more storeys than one. Separate groups of buildings served as kitchens[108] and servant's quarters, but all would be within one walled enclosure. Their furnishings have been

"Gwydir Gate" — an old toll house

described as including cushions of brocaded silk, the women's gowns of similar material. Gold clasps for the women's necks, and for the men's plaids, have been discovered, and their pottery and jewellery was not inferior to that of the high-rank Romans. Examples have been found within short distances of here.

The Romans developed the mines, for sulphur as well as lead and zinc, silver and maybe tin, and great galleys came with wares, and to take away the ores, the wool and cloths, maybe timber also, perhaps even slates, and tied up at the quay below the hill. No doubt on a summer evening the Roman and the Celtic ladies would be escorted along the river banks to enjoy the views, the wildflowers and the birds, or up the hillside tracks, and the lesser folk would watch, children would play under parental or nanny's eyes, for social life went on, as well as commerce and trade, in those past days, and families were families with children, with love of nature and with lives to live just as families of today.[109]

These are the lands of Nefydd Hardd, legendary founder of one of the fifteen tribes of Gwynedd, of Taliesin, and no doubt of some of those of whom the Mabinogion relates. For many a year Llywelyn Fawr lived here in the palace which he built. He brought his wife, the Princess Joan, daughter of John the King of England, and for love of her, and respect for John, it is unlikely that he chose a place of little culture, lacking in population or communications. We may therefore assume that in medieval times there was still, or perhaps again, a community of substance and society which Joan could enjoy. In those days Trefriw was the centre of the Cantref.

Of Joan we have not enquired before. The date of her birth is not determined, but she was a natural daughter of King John. According to the Annals of Tewkesbury her mother was Clementia, one of the Court staff. Of all his legitimate and illegitimate children, Joan seems to have been John's favourite throughout his life.

The turn of the eleventh and twelfth centuries was a time when allies of one year were the enemies of the next. It followed shortly after the conquest of Ireland by the sons of Nest, a time of mixed marriages of convenience between Welsh and Normans and English, and of consequential divided allegiances. All the combinations of alliance had come about between the King, the Marcher Lords, Gwenwynwyn Lord of Powys, and Llywelyn, in which Llywelyn had come off best. King John sent the Archbishop of Canterbury and the Chief Justice to Chester in 1201 to discuss terms of peace with Llywelyn, following the latter's support of Gwenwynwyn against aggressive and oppressive

King John

Marcher Lords.

It seems likely that the arrangements for the marriage were made then. Whether Llywelyn had met Joan at that time we can only surmise. The final betrothal took place in 1204, which suggests that Joan may have been very young. In 1201 John himself was only 34, and Joan was almost certainly born after John's first marriage, which took place in 1189. Joan may therefore have been ten years old or less in 1201, and only about thirteen when the marriage took place late in 1204 or in 1205. The marriage seems to have been very successful. She was certainly very clever as a diplomat, and in Llywelyn's later struggles with the King, when first one was in the ascendancy and then the other, between 1211 and 1232, she seems to have been an intermediary of tremendous skill. The fact that both John and Llywelyn loved her so deeply no doubt aided her greatly.

That love saved her when in 1229 and 1230 she lapsed from grace with a liaison with one of the Marcher Lords, William de Braose. For that she went to prison for a short while, but was soon reinstated to favour; William was less fortunate, for he was hanged on Llywelyn's instructions on 3rd May, 1230. But so strange were the times to our eyes that a marriage which was arranged between Isabell, one of William's daughters, and Dafydd, son of Llywelyn and Joan, before William was hanged still went ahead within less than a year.

Joan also seems to have had a great deal of influence with others than the King and her husband, for in 1229 she persuaded Henry III (her much younger half-brother) to agree that when Llywelyn died his younger son, her son Dafydd, should assume the overlordship of the whole of Wales, to the exclusion of his older half-brother, Gruffydd, who was an illegitimate son of Llywelyn by Tangwystl, daughter of Llywarch Goch. Under Welsh law, Gruffydd had a right to succeed. It was probably she, rather than Llywelyn, who arranged the marriages of their daughter, Gwladus Ddu, to Reginald de Braose, and Margaret to John de Braose, Lord of Gower and Bramber, who succeeded to the titles of William on his execution — he had no sons of his own. When Reginald de Braose died, Joan arranged for Gwladus Ddu to marry Ralph Mortimer.

Their son Roger was later to come into dispute with his cousin Llywelyn ap Gruffydd (Llywelyn the Last) about lands in Brecon, Radnor and Pembrokeshire. He was heavily defeated in battle by Llywelyn in 1266, and by the Treaty of Montgomery he had to surrender a great part of his territory. It is generally believed that it was the son of Roger, Edmund Mortimer, who murdered his father's cousin, Llywelyn the Last, at Builth in 1282.

Joan also arranged the marriage of their daughter Gwenllian to William de Lacy, and Helen to John, son of Ranulph, Earl of Chester. Margaret married Walter Clifford on the death of John de Braose.

These alliances with the greatest of the Norman families, those of the most powerful and wealthy Marcher Lords, illustrate that the Welsh of those times were not wild and woolly savages opposing cultured and superior Normans, as an English history book would make believe. They were better educated and more genteel than the warlike Normans, who clearly considered it an honour to marry into their families. Llywelyn was called in as one of the signatories of Magna Carta. His court was one of poetry and music, learning and culture when at Trefriw as well as elsewhere, and Trefriw must have benefitted then and for generations after, perhaps helped by the exclusion of Welsh people from Conwy by Edward I and his successors, despite the vandalistic destruction which that conqueror wreaked. That destruction was no doubt responsible for the disappearance of Llywelyn's palace and, no doubt, the houses of others, and buildings of earlier times, like the courts of the Cantref.

Llywelyn and Joan used to walk to church up the steep path, possibly even then a road as it had been in Roman times and is now, to Llanrhychwyn. By the time she was in or near her forties she found it hard going, and Llywelyn therefore built and endowed a church at Trefriw. That was about the year 1230.

Joan died, comparatively young, in 1237, at Llywelyn's palace at Aber (Abergwyngregyn), and she was buried at Llanfaes on Anglesey, where Llywelyn founded a Franciscan Friary in her memory. It is believed that on the dissolution of the Friary in 1536/7 the remains were transferred to St Mary's Church at Beaumaris; a stone coffin there is said to contain them.

No part of the original church remains at Trefriw, unless it be some parts of the walls; it was rebuilt in the fifteenth and sixteenth centuries, and again last century. Here in the churchyard lies buried Ieuan Glan Geirionydd, who was born at Tan-y-celyn on the main Gwydir road out of the village. We shall learn more of him at a later time.

In the village also lived the remarkable Thomas Wiliems, physician, student of Brazenose College, Oxford, author and lexicographer. He claimed to have been born at Ardda'r Myneich, near Trefriw in 1545. He was the son of Wiliem ap Thomas ap Gronwy and his wife Catrin, who was an illegitimate daughter of Maredudd ap Ieuan. He was therefore a nephew of Sir John Wynn of Gwydir.

At Oxford he probably obtained a degree of MA in 1573, in which year he became Curate of Trefriw. He is reputed to have been a papist, and was charged on that score at Bangor in 1607. As such he is believed to have known of the plot to blow up Parliament and to have persuaded Sir

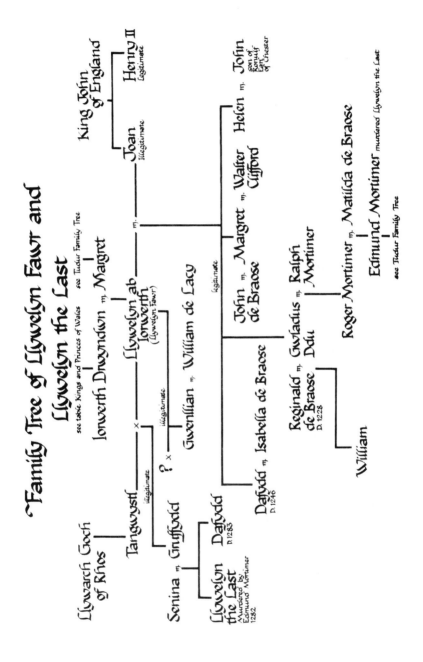

Family Tree of Llywelyn Fawr and Llywelyn the Last

see table Kings and Princes of Wales   see Tudor Family Tree

Llywarch Goch of Rhos

Iorwerth Drwyndon m. Margret

King John of England

Tanguystl
illegitimate

Llywelyn ab Iorwerth
(Llywelyn Fawr)

Joan
Illegitimate

Henry II
Legitimate

× — *illegitimate*

Senina m. Gruffudd

? ×

Gwenllian m. William de Lacy

m. — *legitimate*

Helen m. John
son of Ranulf Earl of Chester

Dafydd
D.1283

Dafydd m. Isabella de Braose
D.1246

John m. Margret m. Walter de Braose   Clifford

Llywelyn the Last
Murdered by Edmund Mortimer 1282

Reginald m. Gwladus m. Ralph de Braose   Ddu   Mortimer
D.1228

Roger Mortimer m. Matilda de Braose

William

Edmund Mortimer *murdered Llywelyn the Last*
see Tudor Family Tree

John Wynn not to attend.

He set up in Trefriw as a physician, but whether he was in any way qualified is sometimes said to be open to doubt, although Sir John Wynn accepted him as such. The originator of that doubt was Sir Roger Mostyn, who resented Thomas' friendship with Sir John. There was strong antipathy between the two because Sir Roger was married to Mary, the eldest daughter of Sir John, a great grand-daughter of Maredudd ab Ieuan on the legitimate side, while Thomas was a grandson of Maredudd, but on the illegitimate side.

Much could be written about Thomas and his collection of manuscripts, his writings and other matters, but his main interest is that he prepared a voluminous and extraordinary Latin-Welsh dictionary. He died, however, in 1622, leaving the manuscript on which he had worked for fifty years to his cousin, Sir John Wynn, who promised to get it published. As in many other things, Sir John broke his word, and gave the manuscript to John Davies, Rector of Mallwyd who, instead of publishing it, used it as the basis for a Latin-Welsh/Welsh-Latin dictionary which he published as his own work.

Although Sir John had been dead for three years before the work was published, he must have known what was going on before he died.

That John Davies had other connections with the people of the Conwy Valley, for in 1621 he published a grammar, *Antiquae Linguae Britannicae — Rudimenta,* in the preface to which he claimed to have assisted William Morgan in the translation of the Bible into Welsh. He was about 20 when the work was published in 1588 and admits to a minor role, describing himself as an 'unworthy assistant'. However, he lived at one time near Llandaf, possibly when William Morgan was Bishop there between 1595 and 1601, and assisted him in carrying out revisions of the original publication. The work continued after Morgan's death in 1604 and John Davies helped his brother-in-law, Richard Parry, Bishop of St Asaph, prepare the Bible published in 1621, generally known as Richard Parry's Bible. Experts are of the opinion that John Davies contributed a great deal towards the grammatical correctness of this translation.

Bishop Wm Morgan

Richard Parry himself had connections with the Valley. While he was Bishop of St Asaph he not only retained two of his former parish livings, but also acquired three others of which Llanrwst was one — he held it from 1616 until he died in 1623. He was also involved in trying to settle a dispute between Sir John Wynn and his tenants at Dolwyddelan, which seems to have had the effect of exacerbating the matter.

At Trefriw on the 23rd of February, 1831, was born James Hughes, son of Robert and Ann Hughes of Ysgubor-gerrig, who played the harp, the violin and the flute; he built his own harps. He lived part of his life at Llanrwst, but died in Manchester in 1878, his body being brought for burial in Trefriw churchyard.

While there had been a quay at Trefriw for untold numbers of years, and large Roman ships came here, followed, it seems, by medieval and other traders up to the seventeenth century and later, there came a time when slow silting of the river made it impossible for larger boats to get past the rocks, "Yr Arw", at Tal-y-cafn except at favourable states of tide. Nevertheless the *"Topographical Dictionary of the Dominion of Wales"*, published in 1811, says of Trefriw that...... "It is a settlement upon the River Conwy, and here numbers of small Vessels are built and sent down the river at the spring tides". That same publication gives the 1801 population as 301. Before the rocks were blasted seagoing ships, trading with Chester and Liverpool, came when tides allowed. Afterwards ships of up to "80 tons burthen" are recorded, quite a sizeable ship by the standards of the times. At one time one merchant here was shipping 42 tons of Dolwyddelan slates regularly to New Orleans. Other outgoing cargoes included grains, wool and hides, and oak from Gwydir. The ships brought in various cargoes, including wines and coal. By 1851 the population had grown to 428.

But long before that Thomas Pennant reported the existence of boatbuilding in the second part of the eighteenth century, and said that boats were engaged in transporting lead and calamine from Ffloyd's Mines above Gwydir Uchaf round the coast to Bristol. Records at the Port of Bristol [110] for that same period show that many of the small North Wales coasters brought consignments of wines on their return journeys on specific orders for the landed gentry of this area and Anglesey, naming the consignees. Coal supplies and fertilisers for Llanrwst and Trefriw seem to have been included in those return cargoes, as well as in cargoes from Chester and Liverpool — sometimes, it appears, in the same boats as the groceries!

Copies still exist of plans prepared in 1908 for the construction of a railway from Conwy up the western side of the river, by way of Ro-wen and Tal-y-bont to Trefriw. That was at the time of the construction of the Dolgarrog works, which no doubt was a factor being considered. The last ships to ply the river were the paddle steamers from Conwy and Llandudno, which stopped in 1939.

In 1833 the old Roman mineral water caves were excavated, and efforts were made to attract people to Trefriw as a Spa, but it was not until 1863 that Lord Willoughby de Eresby built a small bath house. That was replaced in 1873 by the present Tudor style building on the Dolgarrog Road. The medicinal powers of the waters were advertised widely, all over the country, and a great effort was made to establish Trefriw in opposition to Bath and Baden-Baden. A fashionable Liverpool medical specialist, Dr Hayward, described it as "probably the best spa in the United Kingdom". The original Gower's Bridge was built to link the spa with the railway station at Llanrwst; it was a timber-trestle bridge which horse-drawn carriages could use.

Trefriw prospered, and hotels were developed. People came in large numbers, and many houses were built, in the process of which perhaps some of the old historical remains were destroyed. There were a number of shops, two village halls, two chapels and other facilities. There was a fair held on the 12th of May, 3rd of September and 7th of November.

The Edwardians flocked to Trefriw, and by 1910 it was a leading social centre in summer, with facilities and functions provided by the Trefriw Improvement Company. There was a band playing regularly on the riverside lawns, and parading of chaperoned young ladies before the fashionable young men, and the middle-aged and elderly looked on and walked the lanes and streets. There used to be a proper path alongside the Crafnant River, and it was a favourite route to take to the Conwy's banks, or through the then well-known Fairy Glen and the Crafnant Valley to the lake of that same name, where there was, as there is now, a place to get afternoon tea — in those days splits and lots of cream and jam, with cakes to follow. Were the summers longer and hotter, and did the sun shine more in those Edwardian days, or is it all nostalgic dream?

But the spa boom died with the First World War, and Trefriw reverted to being a place for homes, a place for residence and retirement, for professional people from Llanrwst, Conwy and Dolgarrog, with a declining tourist trade, which now shows signs of some revival.

A printing works was set up here in 1775 by Dafydd Jones, of whose descendants we learnt at Llanrwst who ran the Venedocian Press. He was born about 1703, but first appeared in Trefriw in the 1730s, marrying Gwen ferch Richard ap Rhys in Trefriw Church on the 27th of January, 1735. For most of his life he was a poet who published books by himself and by others, initially through Sion Rhydderch's Press at Shrewsbury. Sion Rhydderch (John Roderick) was a Welshman from Cemaes in Montgomeryshire who had been in the printing business from about 1701, and died in 1735.

It was not until he was in his seventies in 1775 that Dafydd Jones acquired a small hand printing-press and set up as a printer on his account at Tan-yr-yw, opposite Trefriw Church — a tablet in the wall there commemorates him. Some authorities say it was the first printing press in

North Wales. He had been some 55 years old when his son Ishmael was born, his wife then being in her late thirties, so Ishmael was about 18 when Dafydd started his printing business — it may well be that it was for the son that he did so. By 1782 Ishmael had adopted the name of Ishmael Davies, and he became a partner in the business, probably both at the same time as he married. The press was then moved to Bryn Pyll Isaf, Ishmael succeeding to sole ownership when his father died in 1785. In 1817 the business passed to Ishmael's son John, who had always used his grandfather's name of Jones — he came to be known as John Jones Pyll. He was trained in the background crafts of printing — smithing, foundry work, etc. — after which he went on to learn the printing trade itself in Liverpool. When he came back to Trefriw he constructed an iron-framed press with a firm, flat slate bed. The basic design may have been by Alexander Ruthven, but the realisation and construction were entirely John's work. The press and some of his other equipment, including patices and matrices for his type, are on exhibition at the National Science Museum, South Kensington. Another of his presses, in pieces, is at St Fagan's. We learnt of his later history, and of that of the succeeding generations of the family, at Llanrwst.

Trefriw now has its famous Welsh Woollen Mills. In past ages wool was spun and woven in people's houses, and then taken to a fulling mill to be washed and finished. In Welsh a fulling mill is a pandy. Quite early in the

Three steamers and launch at Trefriw

nineteenth-century a water-driven pandy was established here, and in 1859 Thomas Williams bought it. Cloth from the hand looms was here washed, finished and dried, the last process being carried out by stretching the cloth on tenters in a field, as until not so many years ago was done on such a big scale at Witney. From that to the present mills has been a steady process of development well described in a small booklet which can be obtained at the Mill. There is a large shop, which none should miss, selling cloth and finished clothes, bedspreads, rugs, table mats, purses and many other colourful items, and there is a very considerable export business to all parts of the world. The whole of the works may be inspected, and all the processes watched.

If we have wandered the lanes and streets of the village, inspected spa, church and woollen mill, and stopped to admire the wonderful views in all parts of the place, it will be time for a belated lunch.

107. *A game which seems to have had some similarity to Halma.*

108. *This was a common practice even in the castles and houses as late as the Tudor era, to reduce the risk of fire.*

109. *Letters handwritten in ink on paper-thin sheets of wood found close to the fort at Vindolanda on Hadrian's Wall include correspondence and invitations to a birthday party, etc., exchanged between the wives of commanding officers, proving that Roman ladies accompanied their husbands on tours of duty . Peter Salway comments on page 512 of "Roman Britain" — see Bibliography.*

110. *Referred to before on pages 59 - 60.*

Day 7, Part 2 - Llanrhychwyn, The Lead Mines & Geirionydd

This part of our tour is into the lands of Taliesin, and of the eisteddfodau of Gwilym Cowlyd. We will start by going up the narrow route which all must have used for the past two thousand years, the hill which leads south now past the Roman Catholic Church from the Prince's Arms Hotel — opposite where the quay has been for untold years — the quay which was probably built first by the Romans, used through the middle ages, and extended at the time when Yr Arw was blasted out at the beginning of the last century. After the last of the trading ships came, the quay was used by the paddle steamers which came from Conwy and Llandudno, and a building there was used as a Spa Treatment Room; there were lawns which were open for the public to use, and part of the area was a cricket ground. The fashion parades of the past, the leisurely cricket, the jolly bustle of the steamer passengers, have gone these many years, and are not likely to return in this age of haste. The last of the paddle steamers came in 1939, and all that remains now as a reminder of the romantic past is a pair of fine brick gate pillars, and gates that might again be brought to their former glory.

This was the road which Llywelyn and the Princess Joan used to walk to Llanrhychwyn church, climbing up the slopes of Gallt-yr-Ysfa for a mile to the crossroads by the house Tai Isa. The road straight on now ends as a cul-de-sac for any vehicles at Tan-yr-Eglwys farm, but a footpath still exists along the valley of a stream, through the old Llanrhychwyn slate quarry, on past old lead mines to Tŷ Hyll. To the left is the road to the valley floor, perhaps the old Roman road by which they took their ores to the boats on the river at Llanrwst, of which a part — not quite a mile —was also the road from Canovium to Bryn Gefeiliau. This road by Tai Isa at Llanrhychwyn was the only road for passage from Trefriw to Gwydir and Llanrwst before the construction of the turnpike road in 1777.

The road to the right at the crossroads — the road signposted to Llyn Geirionydd — leads to the church. We go in by the lychgate, built in the comparatively recent times of 1762. To enter the church we go round to its south side. The building has two aisles, that on the south being the older, probably built in

Top inset: Church of St Rhychwyn, Llanrhychwyn. Bottom inset: Heron

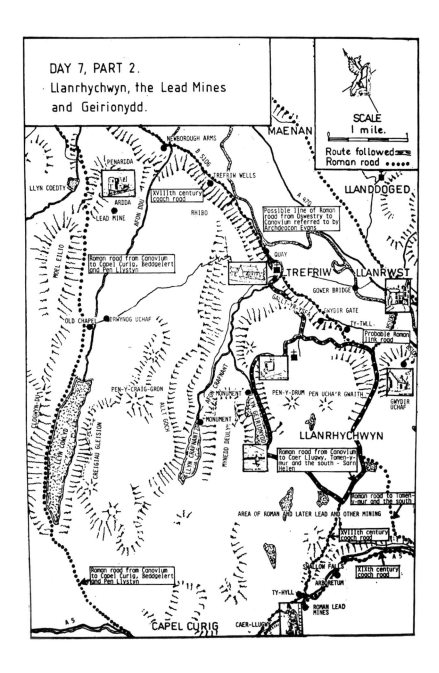

the late eleventh century; it stands on the site of a church of very much earlier date, possibly as early as the sixth century, for it vies with Llangelynnin in the age of its establishment. The chancel was probably added in the thirteenth century, when the building was re-roofed. It is thought that the north aisle was added in the fifteenth century, or early sixteenth, by Maredudd ab Ieuan, not long after he bought Dolwyddelan Castle, built Penamnen and Dolwyddelan Church — it is most likely that he did so after he bought Gwydir from Hywel Coetmor in 1500.

The font should be examined; it is believed to be the oldest in the country, dating from the eleventh or early twelfth centuries, before which baptisms were carried out by total immersion in rivers — not, perhaps, a pleasant experience in a Welsh mountain stream on a cold day!

The one-piece pulpit and reading desk are dated 1691, and from their date and form one wonders if the parson of the day had it constructed so that he could adopt the London fashion, and prop himself up most prominently in an apparently standing position in the pulpit, while his clerk, more lowly seated so that he could just peer over the reading desk, would read the sermon — perhaps an hour or two, or even more. Samuel Pepys records that in those days it was not unknown for a morning sermon to be adjourned part way for all to go for lunch, to continue for another hour later. More than one parson in that way is said to have dozed loudly off in the middle of his own sermon, written by another and read in this manner by his clerk, so that he heard not a single word of the rest of it, nor ever knew its content.

The bell is inscribed with a fleur-de-lys, and a crowned capital bell; it is of the fourteenth century, and it may have come here from Maenan Abbey.

It is fourteen centuries and more since Rhychwyn set up his enclosure, and there is an atmosphere of sanctity in the old church which has to be sensed to be understood, but services are now held monthly in the summer only.

From here we can wander round many lanes and tracks and footpaths, map and compass in hand or we may get lost. This is now a land of conifer forests, where in the past were oaks and other hardwoods. In those forests would have been clearings or glades, in which would be the homes of the workers in the mines, with their cattle and sheep and goats around. The mines were small and many, and the lanes and tracks criss-crossed from home to work, from mine to road, from mine to mine, and from homestead to homestead. Some, even parts of the Roman system, where the roads were no doubt paved, have disappeared altogether, but who knows what may turn up as thicket and mound are cleared in years to come, as in past years, some not so far back, have bits of paved roads and other kinds of works.

About A.D. 370 the Romans went, but they left many of their kind settled in the local community. Many others, no doubt, going in the Segontian Legion with Macsen Wledig, told their wives they would soon return, but perished in the Balkans, or before the walls of Rome, or stayed with Cynan with the Celts in Britanny.

The story of Macsen Wledig — Magnus Clemens Maximus —and his march from Wales to become Emperor of the Western Roman Empire, and eventually reach Rome, is one for a book on its own, and is only briefly dealt with in the final chapter of this. It was at Siscia on the Saone and at Poetovia on the Danube that he was finally defeated, being captured and executed by his enemies at Aquileia in 388. It was his Welsh wife, Elen, who returned with part of his armies to North Wales, with her son Cystennin. Her brother Cynan stayed with the Brythonic Celts in Brittany, and was largely responsible for the development of the intensely independent character of Brittany, and its lasting affinity with Wales which was to lead to refuge there for Henry Tudur for fourteen years before he returned to claim the English throne.

Elen's other brother, Gideon, returned with her to North Wales, but Macsen's other son (by an earlier wife) was killed with him at Aquileia.

The Celts by that time had long ago given up the nomadic way of life, and lived in settlements, but the nomadic way in part returned in later centuries with a more intensive farming system of hafod and hendre. There were still Iberians, intermarried with the Iberians who had come with the armies of Agricola, but all the races had welded by the times of Elen to form the people we now call Welsh. The obsession of the Romans for orderliness, for recording all in writing, had mingled with the Celtic art and culture, and had been influenced by those of other lands, the homelands of the legionaries. Christianity had come in the third century, but was much extended by Elen and Cystennin after their return from Tours and Nantes, where they had been so influenced by their friend Bishop Martin. In Wales it never suffered setback as it did in England.

That such is so would be evident if alone, as many say, such men as Taliesin came from hereabouts. But who was Taliesin? Was he one man, or were there more by similar name? Taliesin was in Powys, and he was at Strathclyde; he was at Deganwy. He was in the fifth century, but he was in the sixth. Reputedly like Moses he was found in a basket among rushes — in this case by Elffin ap Gwyddno in the reclaimed marshes between Llys Euryn and the sea. All we really know is that there is preserved a manuscript of 1275, Llyfr Taliesin, and of that we do not know if it may have been a copy of earlier works, or was compiled from legends passed down by word of mouth. But there seems complete justification that a bard of that name, and of some fame in his time, lived hereabouts, most likely on the banks of Llyn Geirionydd, which was not then poisoned with lead. Nearly two centuries ago, the *Topographical Dictionary of the Dominion of Wales* reported "Near a small Pool in this Parish, called Llyn Geirionydd lived the celebrated Bard Taliesien".

Here also is the reputed home of Nefydd Hardd, founder of one of the legendary fifteen tribes of Gwynedd from whom so many claimed their lineage.

Taliesin was a bard; Nefydd Hardd was a warrior. Neither would be found in an area that was not civilised and populous. The bards like to sing and recite their poems of the history of the past to great groups of people in the houses of the gentry and the princes, but they would only stay where they thought their music and songs, poems and legends, were understood and appreciated. A warrior needed his armies and his courtiers, and all that followed on.

In later times, at the beginning of the 19th century, this community had as we learnt before, 87 recorded houses, and a population of 376, when more famous Trefriw had much less. In 1851 it was 586, for the lead mines flourished as they had never done before, unless it was back in Roman times. Silver, zinc, sulphur, all were found and mined, and all required labour, and labour needed homes, so the number of houses grew. All demanded transport, services and shops. Why did all these depend on Llanrwst, on Trefriw, and on Betws-y-coed, when they had not so done in earlier times? Perhaps we may never discover the answer — or perhaps it lies simply in the Willoughby and Ancaster ownership of lands.

In our wanderings we shall come to Llyn Geirionydd, and alongside it a fallen monument, re-erected in 1995. Baddeley and Ward's *North Wales, Vol. 1*, says of this —

> "an upright slate slab, surmounted by a cross and supported by steps — the whole about 25 feet high.[111] The monument to the 6th cent. poet was erected by the late Lady Willoughby D'Eresby. The earliest record of Taliesin is like that of Moses, if we substitute the mud of the Dyfi estuary for the bulrushes of the Nile, a coracle for a cradle, and Elphin, son of Gwyddno, for Pharaoh's daughter; the latest record, owing to a mistaken idea respecting this memorial, reminds us of Macbeth, for like that monarch he is made by some to have been buried in two different places, 40 miles apart — by the shores of Llyn Geirionydd, and among the hills between Aberystwyth and Machynlleth."

Those words were first written in the very early days of the railways, although repeated in later publications of the guide. It seems, therefore, that those who ascribe the date of the monument to 1830 may well be right. But the original purpose of the monument, and the man whom it was intended to recall, are less important locally than events which followed.

In 1828 there was born in Ardda, a community which has long disappeared, at a house called Tyddyn Wilym, one William John Roberts. He became highly respected under his bardic name of Gwilym Cowlyd. He enjoyed high regard as an adjudicator and historian, and he won the Chair at the National Eisteddfod at Conwy in 1861. Later he came to disagree with the rules of the Gorsedd of the National Eisteddfod of Wales, and he associated with one Robert Williams; together they organised a rival eisteddfod in 1863, held round this Taliesin monument; it continued annually with great success under the name of Arwest Glan Geirionydd, attracting entries from all over Wales and from afar.

Gwilym Cowlyd required very high standards before honouring competitors with bardic names, and the monument, as the centre of the Eisteddfod, came to be regarded as a symbol of the cultural history of Wales. It was one of the great attractions in the hey-days of the Trefriw Spa. He lived until the 5th of December, 1904. With his passing went all the drive behind the eisteddfodau, and the last was held in 1912.

As William J. Roberts, Gwilym Cowlyd was a poet, a printer and a bookseller, and he published the works of Owen Gethin Jones of Penmachno,[112] and of his own uncle, Evan Evans. If he had paid as much attention to the running of his printing works at Cowlyd House in Llanrwst as he did to the Eisteddfod, perhaps he would not have found himself sitting bankrupt in the road one day in July, 1897, ejected from his home and his business on a warrant of the local Magistrates' Court.[113] After that he lived in Scotland Street in that town until he died at the age of 76. He was buried in the churchyard of St Mary's at Llanrwst.

Three years after the founding of the Llyn Geirionydd eisteddfod, the "Arwest Farddonol", the *Illustrated London News* found it to be of sufficient interest that it published a picture of the event on 26th August, 1865 (see page 183) drawn by Mr George Hayes of Glyn Afon, Trefriw, together with a short report.

Among those reported as being present was Clwydfardd, David Griffith, a clock and watch-maker from Denbigh, son of Richard Griffith of the same trade in that town. David was also a Wesleyan lay-preacher who had been appointed as an Arch-druid in 1860, but was not licensed to be an Arch-druid of the Gorsedd until 1876. Another who was there was Gwalchmai, Richard Parry, a wealthy Calvanistic Methodist who had earlier been Minister at Henryd and Conwy, and later founded the Calvanistic Methodist church in Llandudno — curiously he was buried in Llanrhos churchyard when he died in 1897.

Yet another was Owen Gethin Jones, the master-mason who built Betws-y-coed railway station and Gethin's Bridge in the Lledr Valley. He was well known as an historian and a poet. Also there was the Robert Williams, "Trebor Mai" (I am Robert in reverse), who was born at Ty'n-yr-ardd near Llanrhychwyn, the son of a tailor who later moved to Llanrwst, where Robert worked with him in his shop and continued in business until he died in 1877. He was well known as a writer of Englynion and was William J. Roberts' main collaborator in the founding of this eisteddfod.

The article confirms that the Taliesin monument was erected by the de Eresby's, but attributes it to Lord Willoughby de Eresby, not to his wife.

Evan Evans was more known under his bardic name of Ieuan Glan Geirionydd. He was born on the 20th of April, 1795, at Tan-y-celyn on the main road at Trefriw. He went to the church school in the village, and from there to Llanrwst Grammar School, where he learnt music. After the failure of his father's farm due to huge rent rises by the Gwydir Estate, he became a schoolmaster at the nearby Tal-y-bont village school in 1816. He moved to Chester to become a Church of England priest in 1826 and did not return to Trefriw until 1852. He compiled a number of books on church matters, and was the translator of others. He died on the 21st of January, 1855, and was buried in Trefriw churchyard, and therefore did not live to see the eisteddfodau inaugurated by his nephew.

The meeting of the bards at Llyn Geirionydd

For a number of years Llyn Geirionydd has echoed to sounds other than bardic poetry and music, for the lake is used for water skiing, as well as quieter sailing and canoeing. The waters are sterile, poisoned by lead seeping from the heaps of mining waste which here abound. In one part only, where the lake is fed by a small stream, do a few hardy trout and plants exist — such is the price of the demands of civilisation as the centuries roll on.

Among the mines we shall suddenly come to an old slate quarry, or one for stone, for the area has been plundered by countless generations over many thousands of years for its wealth of rocks and ores. But those ores can now be got in far away places at much less effort, and cheap concrete tiles are favoured more than lasting slates, while concrete blocks have superseded stone.

Long before the Celts there were people living in the uplands between Llyn Geirionydd and Llyn Cowlyd, for many cairns and roundhouses and longhuts have been traced, of which a few that remained in 1956 were recorded by the Royal Commission on Ancient and Historical Monuments in Wales. Roads which existed and are shown on maps of the 19th century leading to farms and cottages no longer used maybe followed tracks which the people of those times first used. In places parts remain of walls which divided their fields, but they, like the huts and cairns, were plundered in medieval and earlier times for walls and buildings, and again in the eighteenth and nineteenth centuries for the Enclosure walls.

But time has passed with unexpected haste while we have wandered and pondered, and it is time to return to Trefriw for the night.

111. See plate on page 183. 112. See page 84. 113. See page 161.

The Village, Trefriw

Old Trefriw

Day 8, Part 1 - The Lands Of Lakes & Sheep

The Carneddau — the cairns, the heaps, the mounds, the tumuli — we can take our pick, for all describe the lands into which we go. They cover near 100 square miles, with now no real road, although they abound with roads and tracks of the past. A hundred square miles of heaps and mounds, with vales and valleys in between, with placid lakes and foaming streams — heaps and mounds that reach for the sky, to 3,000 feet and more. Lands of sparse, rough grazing, settlements abandoned 40 and 4,000 years ago, of cairns and tumuli, burial places of the stone age, the bronze age, and of the iron age, and of long abandoned quarries; lands which tempt with golden sunlight on a glowing summer eve, but lie buried under an all-concealing blanket at times of winter snow.

This is an area of great beauty, or one of great terror, according to when and how it is seen, not one to enter into ill prepared, in fog or blinding rain, whether it be to explore the high rhosydd[114] and the snow-capped crags and peaks, or to wend one's way into the deep valleys in between.

We will go up to the rhosydd first, starting from Trefriw on the road to Llyn Crafnant, but at once turning right up the steep hill past the cemetery. On and up, and up and on we go, to 1,000 feet, 1,200 feet, 1,300 feet, 1,400 feet, then gently down to the broad, shallow valley of the Afon Ddu, the dark river, the black river. The track gets rougher, but is still sound, and with care we may go to Garreg Wen, just before Llyn Cowlyd, to which we may walk; as we do so, we shall be on the line of the Roman road from Canovium, which they built up through Llanbedr-y-cennin, between Penardda and Moel Eilio, to cling precariously to the slopes of Clogwyn Du along the banks of Llyn Cowlyd, and from there over the top to fall to Capel Curig, to Caer Llugwy and the road to Tomen-y-mur and the south. This, maybe, was the first great road they used from Caerhun, after the road from Deva (Chester) to Segontium (Caernarfon) — it was probably already an ancient pack route or Celtic road which the Romans used as a route to Pen Llystyn.

No doubt the importance of this route did

Top inset: The Lands of Sheep. Bottom inset: Curlew.

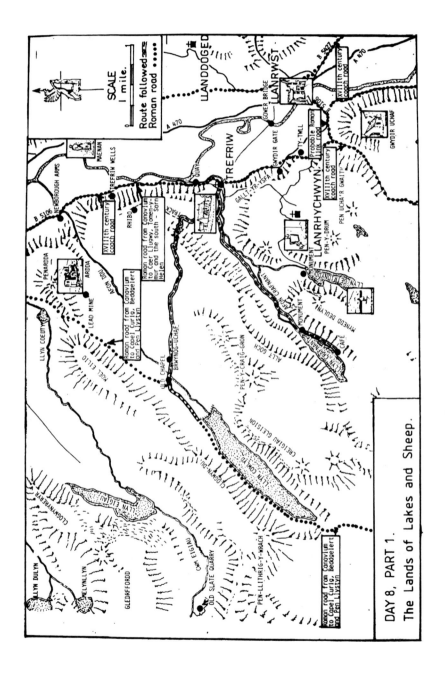

DAY 8, PART 1.

The Lands of Lakes and Sheep.

not lie solely in long range communications. The stone age and the bronze age men lived here, and many centuries of men since they. The Celts who were here when the Romans came grazed their cattle and their sheep, and tilled the land, above the belts of forests of the steep hillsides and the marshes of the valley floor. Here and throughout the whole Carneddau region they built their great enclosures, and within them their roundhouses of stone — unlike the earlier men, who had used earth piled up between rough stone faces, or just plain earth.[115] In the times of the Romans the garrisons of the Roman forts and camps at Caer Llugwy, Caerhun and Penmaenmawr, and of the Celtic fort of Braich-y-ddinas, and of all the lesser forts and camps, the miners of Llanrhychwyn and Henryd, the residents of Canovium and Trefriw, Dwygyfylchi and Aber, would all need to be fed, as would their wives and families, their followers and slaves, administrators and scribes, those who kept the baths and ran the sulphur springs, and all who provided the services, the shops, the entertainments. Of those who came from Rome or other parts of the Roman Empire, as soldiers or civilians, there would be, as happened everywhere, many who in retirement stayed as Roman Citizens to farm or trade, or just to live a life of leisure, gold and silversmiths, craftsmen in stone and timber, farmers and many more. There were very many mouths to feed in this then populous area — for such it was by the standards of those far off times— maybe more populous than it is today. This upland area, still of high production just a few generations ago, indeed within the memory of many still alive, could well have been the larder, the farm, the source of wool, and the roads the means of getting all to market. The basic needs of life, of commerce, have been the same in every age.

As we came we saw the remains, the ruins, of great farms and little holdings — such names as we shall find on the maps —Siglen, Brwynog-uchaf, Garreg Wen itself, and further away, Pen-bryn-brwynog and others we saw not, for they lay behind hills and humps. Many were in use within living memory, some even since the Second War. Within this area were complete hamlets, Rhibo and the larger Ardda, which prospered a hundred years ago and less, of which no more now remains than rubble walls.

At Pont Brwynog where the track goes over the Afon Ddu there was not long ago, a Calvinistic Methodist Chapel, built in 1836 to seat more than a hundred people. Nearby, adjacent to the Roman road, there was in the early part of this century still a lead mine, where maybe the Romans mined before.

Be that as it may, the Roman road was here, and it remained in use throughout history as a pack trail between Tal-y-bont, which we shall see, near Llanbedr-y-cennin, and Capel Curig, and the roads to Beddgelert and

Llanllechid, the west coast and the north, to Caernarfon and to Bangor, town and friary. It was still in use a hundred years ago.

Llyn Cowlyd has now been dammed at its northern end, and its waters with those of the ill-fated Eigiau, which we have yet to visit, supply coastal towns and local villages, and drive the turbines of Dolgarrog hydro-electric station, and power the Aluminium Works.

For years there were across these uplands plains light railways which served first the Eigiau Dam, and then Llyn Cowlyd. The line started by the Dolgarrog Aluminium Works, passing under the present road through a tunnel which can still be seen, then it climbed 800 feet or so at an average gradient of 1 in 2 up which locomotives and wagons were hauled by ropes. Originally in 1908 it went from there to the dam at Llyn Eigiau through the valley of the Afon Porth-lwyd, past the ill-fated Llyn Coedty, all of which we shall later visit. The Llyn Eigiau dam impounded then the waters for the Dolgarrog Hydro-Electric Station and the Aluminium Works.

Llyn Cowlyd, it may be recalled, had been used to supply Colwyn Bay and Conwy with water since the 1890s, its level being raised by the construction of a dam in the early 1900s. In 1916 a contract was let to increase its capacity very greatly by building a new dam, and raising the water level by some 30 feet, to supply extra water for the Power Station as well as for Colwyn Bay and Conwy. In connection with this work the railway was extended from Llyn Coedty some 4 miles round the foot of Pen Ardda into the valley of the Afon Ddu to Llyn Cowlyd.

The railway continued in operation until 1968 in connection with general maintenance of the Llyn Cowlyd dam and the great 4 feet diameter pipes from there across the uplands. It also served the contractors who constructed between 1917 and 1924 the mile-long tunnel which carries the waters of Llyn Eigiau to join the Llyn Cowlyd pipeline. There were a number of locomotives, some steam and one diesel operating on the uplands plains. The first was a 0-4-0 Bagnall Saddle Tank steam engine. The second was a German Orenstein and Koppel 0-4-0 Well Tank engine named *Eigiau*, which is now in Mr Alan Bloom's railway museum at the famous Bressingham Gardens nurseries near Diss in Norfolk. Photographs exist of a 0-6-0 saddle-tank and a 0-6-0 side tank of which the whereabouts have not been traced. The much more modern Simplex diesel locomotive which dates only from 1962 is now named *Deganwy* and hauls trains on the Llanberis Lake Railway. The track was finally

Top inset: 'Puffing proudly down the track'. Bottom inset: Eigiau

removed in 1984, men and materials now being taken up by lorry via the two roads from Trefriw and Tal-y-bont, each with in part nearly 1 in 3 gradient. The first we came up today, the second we shall visit tomorrow.

With our car, we can only return the way we came, and as we go we may wonder at the toughness of the children, the grandparents and earlier generations of those of today, who trudged this way to school, and back in time for tea. We may think of the ponies which held trap against the steepness of the hills, and ganged draught-horses pulling wains on the upward way.

Just below the hairpin bends, on the left is a track which leads north along the contours above Cae Coch to an old community, Rhibo, of which but one house, itself named Rhibo, now remains in occupation. On the steep slopes just below, approachable also from Cae Coch by Trefriw Spa, is an old sulphur mine, long disused. There is now no way through to further north, but some believe there was a road in Roman times which went by here across the Afon Ddu to Ardda and Pen-y-gaer, places to which we have yet to come.

At the bottom of the hill, beyond the cemetery, we will turn right along the road to Llyn Crafnant; here we are in quite a different scene, first among houses of the prosperous days of Trefriw Spa and the mining eras, interspersed with some of earlier time and some of the modern age. From hilltop and hillside we have come into the deep-set wooded valley of the Crafnant River, with lush meadows in the valley floor. The river, on its way from Llyn Crafnant joined by a tributary from Llyn Geirionydd, drives the turbines that power the Trefriw Mills.

Through this valley, at first on the other side of the river, was the favourite walk of the Victorian and Edwardian visitors, to which we referred before, and it may well have been a favourite in the times of Llywelyn and those of the Romans of long ago, for they will have enjoyed the pleasures of views, just the same as we do.

Before we reach the lake we come to a car park provided again by the Forestry Commission, where we must leave our car, to walk on proper road for a mile and a half, then, if we wish, on track and path far into the hills. But by the lake we are in the place where legend says that Nefydd Hardd had his house or palace. If he did live here, he chose very well, for this sheltered valley is one of beauty, and must surely have been so then.

The hills beside the lake rise up 600 feet, more soft than those at Cowlyd. Beside the water is the café of which we spoke before, and it may be open for coffee or afternoon tea. Before that we may see a column, which has upon it a plaque to record that the lake was granted to the Llanrwst

Parish Council on December 27th, 1895, for a term of 999 years at a nominal rent. The lease established a charitable trust for the benefit of the inhabitants of that part of the Parish of Llanrwst within the Special Drainage District called Tredre, as a supply of water for all. The grantor was one Richard James of Dyffryn Aur. The water rights passed to the Welsh Water Authority in 1974, but the lake itself and the lands which surround it are still owned for the residue of the 999 years by a charity administered by Llanrwst, now a town Council.

As we go beyond the lake, on the way to Blaen-y-nant where the metalled road ends, we may see yet another of the slate quarries of the past, and up the hills relics of search for lead and tin, perhaps for gold. We may not bring our car this far, although the road may tempt; not long ago it was sensibly concluded that if cars still came beyond where is now the car park, they would soon destroy that which the occupants wished to see.

Seeing Crafnant, the slopes of Gallt yr Ysfa on the way to Llanrhychwyn, the views of the Conwy Valley from all of Trefriw, the lands of the lakes and sheep which were then fertile farms, it is easy to see why Llywelyn Fawr, with all of Gwynedd at his command, chose here to bring his wife, to build a palace, to make a home, and why before him came Nefydd Hardd and Taliesin and those out-posted from Rome in the Empire days.

Our wanderings have taken us well into the afternoon, and we will find tea before setting out on a shorter trip today.

---

114. *Rhos, plural rhosydd — moor or heath; plain.*
115. *See also page 184. A very great number of the roundhouses of various ages have been found and examined in the Carneddau area, from which it is evident that during the Celtic and Roman times there was a well organised system of building, and of community living. Separate huts within an enclosure were used for spinning and weaving, meat preparation, cooking, smithing, living, sleeping, the chief's palace hall, and so on. At some stages the roofs may have been formed by lapping the stones inwards to form a dome, subsequently covered with earth, but at others there were great timber roofs, which, contrary to established ideas, were probably quite ornate in the main rooms. Some may have been, like the houses Caesar found, of two storeys and more in height. Unfortunately there has been much vandalising of these remains in the past to build enclosure walls, sheep pounds, and farms and farm buildings. Some have even been swept away in quarrying since they were first recorded and examined 200 years ago.*

North along the toll road, the B5106, these two places have little in common, but are linked by one feature, Llyn Eigiau. They are both, of course, astride the same main road, and many who live in Tal-y-bont work at Dolgarrog, share its British Legion Club, but it is Llyn Eigiau which matters.

That lake lies up in the lands of lakes and sheep into which we went this morning, to the north of Moel Eilio, but the only road for vehicles leads up from Tal-y-bont, which we will later follow.

Trefriw township is half a mile behind us when we come to the buildings at the Trefriw Wells. Another half a mile and we come to Dolgarrog, the old Dolgarrog. Beyond a little causeway tight between stone walls we find the Newborough Arms, an ancient inn of coaching days when here was a little village with houses, cottages and farms, and once, not much over a century ago, there was still a fulling mill, a pandy as it is in Wales. But they have all gone now, perhaps many of them sacrificed to make way for the railway which came to here, to meet with a tram track from the quarry up the mountain side, or perhaps they lost supply of water when the catchment of the Afon Ddu was crossed with gathering canals. That Dolgarrog is no more.

We come to the modern Dolgarrog along the road, of concrete houses strangely planned in two terraces on the contours of the hillside. It is older than at first appears, nearly all built quite early in the 20th century for the workers for the Aluminium Works and the Hydro-Electric Power Plant, which now dominate the Valley in these parts.

Just past where now is the village hall, and opposite the British Legion, is a little sheltered cwm in the hillside, where once was a charming village, Porth-lwyd.[116] Tracks came down from the mountains, from Rhibo and Ardda and the top-most Roman road, and here in the valley bottom was the lower Roman road. Across the Conwy was the Roman road by Llyn Syberi, which led to Llangernyw and the east.

The village had a church and a paper mill, and the Rhaeadr Mawr (Great waterfall) which people came from miles to see. It had been a place of habitation from early times, and there was a cromlech.

192

Bottom inset: Dipper

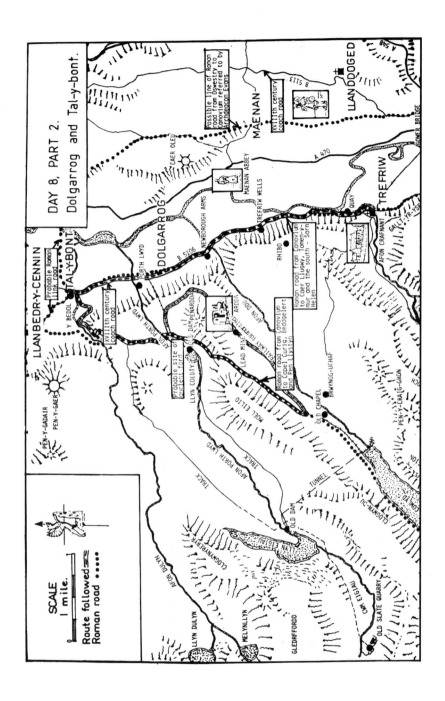

In 1908 came the Works, and the Hydro-Electric Power Plant for which were impounded the waters of the river, the Afon Porth-lwyd, and of the lake which fed it, Llyn Eigiau, far away up in the mountains. The dam was constructed in the way quite customary in those days, quite successful where it had been used. Mass concrete foundations were laid at some considerable depth, and a concrete and stone wall was built upon them, but they did not go down to bedrock base. The waters were let from there by controlled flow to Llyn Coedty, which was dammed in 1922 so as to form a reservoir not far from the old abandoned village of Ardda, nine hundred feet above Porth-lwyd. All went well for many years, though some people were beginning to question the wisdom of such construction except for very small impounding dams.

On Monday, November 2nd, 1925, disaster struck. Rain had fallen heavily and the lakes were full, the rivers flowing deep and wide, and still it rained. The evening was dark and forbidding, the moon mostly hidden by clouds, only shafts of light through infrequent breaks. About half past seven, no one knows exactly, the waters of the swollen Eigiau did what some engineers had feared and forecast — they filtered through the soft subsoil beneath the dam's foundations. Unable to go over the dam, not relieved by opened sluices, they filtered under, and as they filtered they took with them peat and soil to form an ever widening tunnel below the concrete, through which the water flowed at fast increasing speed. The rapid flow soon filled Llyn Coedty, and pressed against the dam above the village, and then that dam collapsed before the unaccustomed pressure. The waters came in a mighty torrent through the cwm, unheralded on the way to the Conwy river. They took all before them —boulders of terrifying size were tossed like pebbles, crushing whatever lay in their path. All came roaring on with mud and trees and debris of every kind, to sweep down upon the tiny village in the dark, and Porth-lwyd was wiped completely off the map, totally, entirely gone, with hardly a house left standing, and the bridge across the river was washed away as were church and school. Those that escaped were above the valley, and what was left can be seen today, the boulders and the stones from the buildings, all preserved among the birch trees just beyond the village hall, beyond the British Legion Club.

Incredibly, not more than sixteen people were killed, for it so happened that a travelling cinema had come to the village hall, just outside the fated area, and nearly all the population of Porth-lwyd was there.

That awful night is still remembered, not only hereabouts by families and friends, but in far away places, for the Dolgarrog disaster, as it became known, led to a change in British law about the design and inspection of dams, and reappraisal of recognised systems of construction around the world.

New houses were built for the people displaced, but in the new Dolgarrog, not in Porth-lwyd. A new bridge was built west of the old one, and the road was re-aligned — the old can still be seen for nearly a mile from Mac's Garage to the school, remaining, like the great boulders in the river valley, as a memorial to those who died.

From here we will go on to Tal-y-bont, to go up to inspect the reservoir, perhaps, if energetic, to walk to see Llyn Eigiau itself. We go up the lane before the school, continuing with a left turn each time the real road divides, a mile and a half to Bontnewydd, where proper road comes to a gated end. Here are two tracks, that to the right being the line of the Roman road, which later we shall follow; but first we will take that which leads to the left, which will bring us in two hundred yards or so to the head of the old Llyn Cowlyd railway. The metalled track has gone, but we can walk along its bed around Penardda's northern slopes, onto its south-western side. Two and a half miles along the track we come to what remains of the old medieval village, fields and dwellings of Ardda, between the leet and the Afon Ddu. All that now is clearly visible is one ruin of a farm, but in this settlement as recently as 1828 was born William Roberts — Gwilym Cowlyd, of whom we heard at Trefriw.

In much earlier times the settlement thrived, and it is mentioned in mid-fifteenth century Bangor Priory Records. A close examination still reveals remains of dwellings and of buildings associated with the field system of those times, field enclosure walls, and some more massive parts of wall which thirty years ago still stood eight feet in height in parts, no doubt remains of larger houses of an unknown era. The area covered by these remains is large, some 1,200 yards long and half as wide. The fields were evidently terraced, maybe by generations long before the medieval age, perhaps in Roman times, or perhaps before.

The origin of the name itself is of some interest. The Welsh word "ardd" is a mutation of "gardd", a garden, and since the lands were cultivated lands, that might appear at once to be the answer. But primitive ploughs that were used in Neolithic times and up to the times of the Celts were "ards". But then again in Roman times "ardua" were high up places, which no doubt was the origin of the "high" Welsh *ardd,* a hill or high place. And so one takes one's choice. However, expert opinion states that Ardda is derived from "arddu" - to plough - rather than garrd.

It is possible to walk along the track as far as Llyn Cowlyd, past the lead mines and Pont Brwynog, but we will leave it just more than a mile from the lead mines, near the ruins of Pen-bryn-brwynog, where another track leads east along the south-east side of Moel Eilio. This was the Roman road between Beddgelert and Canovium by way of what we know now as

Capel Curig and as we walk we may imagine the scene as it would have been — men with ploughs tilling the fields, singing to themselves, or shouting to cajole the oxen to greater effort, to keep in line, or to turn about at headlands. In another place a ploughman sitting down to eat some food, to take a drink, to rest the beasts, calls across to another still finishing a line, perhaps to taunt him that his furrows are not straight. Along the road towards Canovium a trio of carts also drawn by oxen is taking vegetables to the fort and to the market of the town. Towards the south goes a family bound for a posting or a belated holiday on the western

Trefriw Wells, pumproom and baths

coast, chariots and litters for the ladies and the children and horses for the men and for the guards who ride before and again behind, the servants and slaves on foot or in open carts or wagons, and last except the guards come the wagons with the baggage and the food for all. The other way comes a Celtic Lord in lighter, faster Celtic chariot on business bound, and elsewhere on foot a small line of soldiers is moving camp, or just out being trained. Above, blue skies, but over Penllithrig-y-wrach a threatening cloud foretells rain to come, and warns that winter is not far away. A wagon load of earthen pots all packed in straw in wicker carriers lumbers past, bound also for the markets of the town with two women and their children laden with handmade cloth to sell, or change for household wares or maybe a brooch or ornament for hair. All would look so different from a road today, and yet in purpose it would be the same, and all around the hills would look as now, the birds above would sing the songs they sing to us. Maybe there would be deer then, which long before our time died out, deprived of cover and of food by sheep.

So much would be as now, despite quite obvious differences, and so it would have been in much earlier Celtic times, in the later days of the earlier Princes of Gwynedd and in Llywelyn's time and after that, even as late as the times of the Georgian coaches — the maps of Victorian days marked this as a road to use.

But nowadays even the rough uneven track runs out to be a mere path to walk on foot, which after half a mile joins another track on which a vehicle may pass with care. A short distance on this joins another track for vehicles from north-east towards south-west, on the far side of which is Llyn Coedty, and along the track past that some two miles or slightly more is Llyn Eigiau, where the dam remains as it was that night of such disaster, except that more has washed away since then.

The Eigiau waters are now carried by tunnel to Llyn Cowlyd, and those of the nearby Afon Dulyn are carried by canals round to the reservoir. Those for the power station flow in pipes which come down the hillside above the Conwy Valley, and we saw them from the other side, looking for all the world like a cliffside railway. Rhaeadr Mawr is now a mere trickle.

On the return way to the valley, half a mile beyond Bontnewydd a track leads to the west, almost to Llyn Eigiau again, but through the valley of the Afon Dulyn, productive area of the past with now the ruins of farms, and sheep where cattle grazed and fields of corn were grown. A hundred years ago the track led past the Llyn three miles or more to a remote slate quarry in Cwm Eigiau, the Secret Valley of the Carneddau beneath the frowning cliffs of Pen-yr-helgi-du, and one must wonder at the men who trudged that far to work each day, and back at night, and carted slates from there to the boats at Trefriw when there were no such things as cars and tractors. But how old is the quarry? Did it perhaps provide the floors and roofs for the Celtic settlements of which there were so many in these upland territories through which the Romans used the road?

Continuing on the downward way from Bontnewydd to the valley we find Caer-llin Ford, where many say the Roman road crossed the Dulyn river — but others say that way was but an offshoot, a short cut, the main way going on as we shall do to Tal-y-bont. Probably both are right.

This little village has no claim to fame. It lies at the junction of two roads where an inn, Y *Bedol* (The Horseshoe) stands. The present inn dates from about 1650, when the first of coaches as we know them took the place of the long wagons of earlier times — but there may have been inns there long before, through many centuries of history, perhaps even when the Roman road came here from Trefriw on the shortest route to the fort and to Canovium town, and another road from the east led west to join the road from Tal-y-cafn through the Bwlch-y-ddeufaen. Maybe also, as suggested just above, the road by Llyn Cowlyd came down to here — there were, we know, a minor maze of roads, as befitted the approaches to an important fort and town, which will be discussed in the following chapters.

Some of the houses here are very old, Garth Maelog and Tyddyn and others, and a hundred years ago it had a school to which Tim Evans went. The mill behind the school, Gwern-y-felin, suggests that the place had some importance at an earlier time, no doubt to grind to flour the corn from the upland fields. Garth Maelog was named about 1600 as the home of a poet, William Burckenshaw, of whom William Myddelton wrote —

> while he is capable of writing a good cywydd,[117] he will never learn one good habit... Both of them, it seems, prefer making love to the fair sex, and tippling, and to procure gold, they live as wandering minstrels.

That was William Myddelton who was friend of Tomos Prys, the Privateer of whom we learnt at Ysbyty Ifan.

The Burckenshaw family must have had some standing for William Myddelton to have been writing of them — but William Burckenshaw whose habits were thus criticised went on to train for the church, and to make a name for himself as a poet some of whose works are preserved at the National Library of Wales. He only matters really because he composed a poem of interest to horologists, for it records a very early clock which John Trefor had at Trefalun in Denbighshire. Trefor had fought in the French wars of Henry VIII, and built Trefalun in 1576. He died in 1589, so the clock predated the introduction of birdcage or lantern clocks by a quarter of a century, and was three-quarters of a century before the introduction of the pendulum, and long before the days of the longcase (grandfather) clock.

The clock was also recorded by William Llŷn, Rhys and Morus Kyffin, so its existence is well authenticated. It was built of iron and steel, and it had a dial, and below that a wooden case. It was driven by weights and cords and had a striking mechanism.

Y Bedol, (The Horseshoe) Tal-y-bont

116. *'Porth' means 'opening' or 'doorway' (and also 'ferry') and Porth-lwyd is also the name of the stream, so it is almost certain that 'Porth' in this case does not mean 'ferry'.*
117. *Cywydd – a form of alliterative Welsh Poem.*

Day 9, Part 1 - Llanbedr-y-cennin, The Bwlch-y-ddeufaen & Ro-wen

The road to Llanbedr-y-cennin leads west alongside Y Bedol, to the church of St Peter among the leeks. Some would say it is among the daffodils. Huddled around the church is a village of great antiquity.

On the way, a hundred yards or so up the lane on the left is a tiny cottage, itself very old indeed, Ffynnon Bedr — Peter's Well[118] — set back beyond a small stream among trees. Here for many years came Angela Brazil, writer in the earlier part of the 20th century of books for schoolgirls. Her parents bought the cottage in 1883 as a holiday retreat. It was here in 1904 that she began to write seriously, her first book being *"A Terrible Tomboy"*. For a time she lived here, but later went to live at Coventry with her brother Walter and her sister Amy. She wrote her last book, virtually an autobiography, in 1940, and died in 1947, owning the cottage and visiting it almost up to the time of her death.

Through Llanbedr-y-cennin passed the Roman road which we found by Llyn Cowlyd and near Ardda, leading from Canovium to Bryn Gefeiliau. From the gates of the fort at Caerhun it came to Farchwel, where today is one of the oldest farms in these parts. In the 20th century the track existed as a usable road, but for many a year now it has been only a footpath. From Llanbedr it went virtually due south to the ford at Caer-llin, which we saw yesterday. But from Llanbedr also another road went west, up to the Bwlch-y-ddeufaen to join the main Canovium to Segontium road near Tan-y-braich — a ruin which is marked on the Ordnance Survey maps. The line of this road from Tal-y-bont is in direct continuation of the Roman road from Llangernyw and Llansannan traced in 1911 by members of the Nant Conwy Antiquarian Society.[119] It is therefore a reasonable assumption that there was a ford across the Conwy at the point which they indicated, but most likely it was not for the sole purpose of linking the Llangernyw road with Canovium, but also served to join up with this road to Tal-y-bont and Llanbedr-y-cennin.

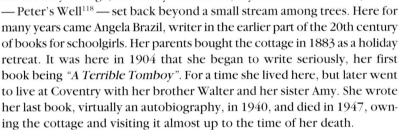

Evidently Llanbedr was important in those days, and earlier. On nearby Pen-y-gaer there was a Celtic fort, most unusually and strongly defended by an extensive and elaborate cheval-de-frise. At a height of 1,250 feet, surrounded by steep and sometimes precipitous slopes on all sides, it must have been both a look-out place,

200

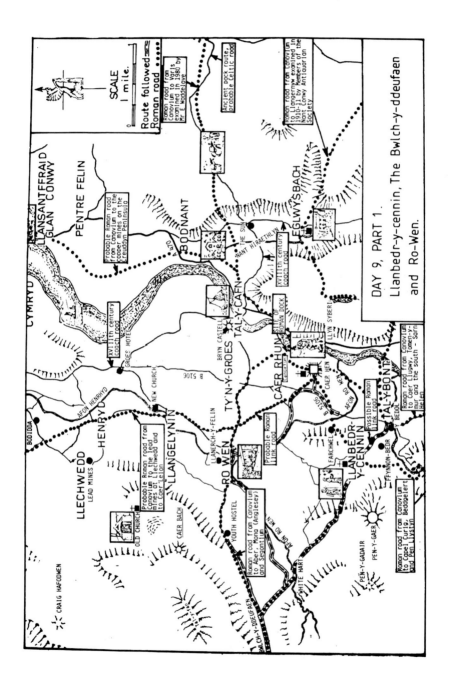

and one almost totally defensible, virtually impregnable.[120] Maybe the Iberians used it before the Celts, and certainly the Romans used it,[121] not to ensure that Celts or Iberians did not go back — more likely to keep watch on the Bwlch and the Conwy Valley.

The road to the Bwlch past Pen-y-gaer was perhaps an ancient track of some importance for long before the Romans came, as was that at the foot of its eastern slopes, which led to Caer-llin and the Afon Ddu, and over the mountains past Llyn Cowlyd. Both roads led to the uplands, and for that reason have remained of great importance until quite recent times. They could still be used by carriages and coaches in the latter part of 19th century.

The uplands supported sheep and cattle in summer, and produced crops in great abundance, but even in the days before sheep destroyed all vestige of trees in the higher parts they were bleak and inhospitable in winter. The lands between Llanbedr and Caerhun, and all those which lay near the Roman town, were soft and fertile and sheltered, and where forest was cleared, provided land for cultivation. They would grow the less hardy vegetables needed for the great population of this area, perhaps even of a much wider domain.

On the slopes of Pen-y-gaer, at heights from 600 feet to 1,150 feet, have been traced an ancient field system, the prehistoric largely destroyed by the medieval, so that the precise form of any age is lost, but here are relics of Celtic and earlier roundhouses and of medieval longhouses, of terraces, and of forms of cultivation through many a century still visible over an area of some 220 acres. But apart from that, there are relics of cairns and roundhouses, long-huts and longhouses in the valley of the Afon Dulyn and on the slopes of the Bwlch-y-ddeufaen, a community for which Llanbedr was for perhaps two thousand years the centre.

Leeks were vegetables of which the Romans were extremely fond — it was they who introduced them to these islands. These lands grow leeks very well, and maybe the farms at Farchwel and around, or the field systems of Pen-y-gaer, were established by the wealthy Romans and Celts to produce that crop in particular, so that when the Christian missionary or wandering monk came here to set up his Llan, enclosure or chapel, it was logical to call it the Llan or Church of Peter among the Leeks. The Peter may not have been St Peter the Apostle, but a wandering monk who had been called Peter from birth, or by adoption.

The present church is not the original on the site, but dates from only the 13th or 14th century, having been modified from time to time. There was a church before. The Bull Inn has its roots as far back, and parts of the building may be even older, as may the cottage opposite, Tan-y-fynwent, from which it is said that an underground passage leads to Ffynnon Bedr. What may be part of that passage was found in 1984 in the process of building alteration works.[122]

From days as early as can be traced by records or repute, there was a fair each year here in the autumn, in September or[123] October, the "Ffair Llanbedr". This had its origin and its popularity in the movements of the farmers, the stockmen, the shepherds, their families, and the cattle, the sheep, and in earlier times the crops of grain, down from the high ground, from the summer farms, the "hafodydd", to the warmth and safety of the winter quarters, the "hendrefydd" and the smaller "tyddynnod", and from the summer huts, the "cytiau" to the cottage homes, the "bythynnod". It was a time of great re-union and celebration, and of rejoicing and drinking. All turned up from far and wide, and while when it started it was autumn, when it finished all knew it was winter. There was much good fellowship, but also many an old score was paid off in drunken fights.

But Llanbedr has grown smaller — in 1801 its population was 420, by 1851 it was 327, and now without Tal-y-bont it is less. So "Ffair Llanbedr", like many a colourful tradition, has gone within the last half century — the last was held in the 1930s. The car and the tractor have made it possible to live all the year round in the valleys, and in the summer to travel daily to the sheep up in the mountains. Modern farming keeps cattle in near intensive conditions in the lower lands, and the rock-strewn, boggy uplands no longer suit modern cultivation and harvesting methods. Since the 1930s nearly all the hafodydd have been deserted, a few taken over in the 1940s or 1950s for holiday homes, and a few less taken over as retirement homes. Now when all have cars, and many would choose to live in those beautiful, if rugged, areas, planning administration, backed by unfortunate legislation, makes hard their use again for housing, and they stand so often as the ruins which we saw in the lands of lakes and sheep. There is now no great return to the homes of winter, no gathering in of stock to celebrate. "Ffair Llanbedr" is no more.

On the 9th of October, 1826, John Williams was buried in the churchyard, aged 66. He was a son of John Williams who was Agent to the Gwydir Estate, and he was educated at Jesus College, Oxford. In 1784 he was ordained and became curate at Betws-y-coed and master at the Free School, Llanrwst. He was appointed as Rector of Llanbedr-y-cennin in 1802, and served there until he died. He was responsible for the collection and preservation of large parts of the records of the Wynns of Gwydir, to which he had access through his father.

In 1868 William Owen Jones was born here, but his family moved to Blaenau Ffestiniog, and he is mainly associated with that town. He was destined to become choir-master of the great Soar Chapel in Merthyr Tudful, but returned to Blaenau Ffestiniog, where he died in 1928. Here also in 1877 was born Tim Evans, who was educated first at Tal-y-bont elementary school, going on to Liverpool Technical College, then to von Herkomer's school of art. He died in London on November 18th, 1939. He was a painter in watercolours, largely landscapes of Welsh scenery, but he also painted portraits.

Up the hill, on the way to the Bwlch-y-ddeufaen, is Ffynnon Gwrach, the witch's well, which nobody goes past in fog or the blackness of night, and beyond that is Tyddyn Robin, where a little maze of ancient lanes denotes a community of ages past, and maps of last century show many a house and building at the foot of Pen-y-gaer, the hill of the fort. Beyond the former village is a track to the south, up into the Bwlch-y-gaer, the pass of the fort, no doubt the road of approach up which on many an occasion the inhabitants in haste retreated to the heights when Celt, or Roman, or Dane, was sighted on the way. The cattle and the hens would go up as well, but the sheep would be driven into the open lands where, without dogs trained to the area, few would catch more than a straggling ewe. The danger past, the enemy gone, down all would come, to weep over homes destroyed, byres and fodder plundered and burnt, and to set to and rebuild, roundhouse where round-hut had stood, and in turn long-hut and longhouse on the foundations of what was there before. All would settle until, perhaps many years ahead, another foe would come. The tree-clad slopes of today, Ochr Gaer, were the security of the past.

The hill to the Bwlch gets steeper. What effort it must have been for man, and more for pack-horse, and yet more again for sweating team with heavily laden coach, or pair with small farm wagon; how endless it must have seemed for beasts with little understanding of the purpose of it all. We pass the White Hart Inn, where no longer can refreshing glass be filled, but must have been a place of rest and respite for many a traveller, man and beast. Where did it get its name? Was it from the deer which roamed to graze, as we have heard, in Llanrwst churchyard? Was it corrupted by Anglicisation from the old "high" Welsh *ardd*, a hill or high place,[124] or was it a place of cultivation. But then again, the white hart was born as a supporter to the arms of Madog ab Iarddur of Penrhyn, to whom maybe these lands belonged. Perhaps also like many a building hereabouts it was painted white. But colour may not have had anything to do with it, for while gwyn is white, gwyn is also holy, and wyn is gwyn, and hereabouts are many names with Wyn or Gwyn, or Wen. The little stream across which the road here passes is the Afon Ro, but also the Afon Ro-wyn, or now the Afon Ro-wen. The farm nearby was Hafodty Gwyn, now Hafoty-gwyn, and the bridge nearby was

Pont Hafodty Gwyn. Was this a holy place? Was this a holy river? Certainly the travelling monks and holy men came by this way in early Christian times, in the fourth and fifth centuries and those that followed. Did they use the stream to baptise converts?

We are here 900 feet above the level of the fords at Canovium. Half a mile on, and 300 feet higher, we join the main road of the Romans from Deva (Chester) to Segontium (Caernarfon) and to Anglesey, which crossed the river near Tal-y-cafn, and that we will follow, though before long we must leave our car, proceed on foot. We are here in the Bwlch-y-ddeufaen, where the road of old, now a track, climbs to 1,400 feet, before it drops again to Aber on the northern coast. For the Romans Aber meant the road to Segontium, the modern Caernarfon, as we just said, or it meant the alternative of the most hazardous crossing of the Lafan Sands [125] to Mona (Anglesey) and the copper mines, or Caergybi (Holyhead) and the Roman fleet. In medieval times and until Telford built his Menai Bridge in the nineteenth-century, it meant the same.

On a stormy night, the crossing of this pass must have called for very brave hearts, all knowing that ahead lay the hazards of those sands and the Beaumaris Ferry.

But long before that, this was a road of stone-age man, passing near the axe factories, the homes, and all that pertained to life of those people who left the cairns and the burial mounds of which there are so many still; they are there in their hundreds from where we stand to the site of Graig-lwyd, now blasted away by quarry working overlooking Penmaenmawr, and the other way extending to the topmost peaks of Carnedd Dafydd and Carnedd Llywelyn at 3,484 feet above sea level, and to many a lesser peak, Foel Grach and Drosgl and others. That these people were here for many a century is clear from the vast numbers of the cairns and mounds, and the variations of kinds and types. Of their houses, the types are as varied, from those which were evidently small mud-surrounded mounds to the other extreme of the complex roundhouses described before.

In spite of all that has been found, we know less of their houses, their communities, than we do of their graves. From time to time some further trace appears, of rings of huts, of place of fires, but most has gone, for timber rots, and stones about were handy for the houses of later genera-tions, for the walls of the ffridd, of the high cynefin, perhaps for the roads of the Romans, or those for the coaches of the Georgian era. But the men of some age when the quarries of Graig were worked marked a track to Dinas, to Graig, and between the two, and the line of the pass through the Bwlch, with standing stones and tumps, and piles of stones, rocks and mounds, and most significant of all, what we believe to be mourning stones. But the relics up here are not all of stone-age man, or those of the times of bronze, nor even just of Celts, for Roman remains, including swords, have been found in the highest places, on Carnedd Llywelyn and Carnedd Dafydd; they did not just march along the roads they built, but walked and climbed, perhaps for pleasure, as every generation has done before and since.

What was the purpose of the stones and cairns? Some, no doubt, were burial places; but why, in that event, were they built in such inaccessible spots? The lines of stones suggest that the routes between them were often used, perhaps in fog or snow. One day maybe the soil will yield up clues by which we may discover some, or all.

We cannot drive through the Bwlch today, though coaches went through long after the start of the nineteenth-century, and within the memory of many alive now, farmers with traps went through, most particularly at the times of rounding up of sheep, but also quite regularly to inspect the flocks. Nowadays if a vehicle is seen, it will most likely be a Land-rover or a similar type.

Here at the top of the pass, we can see back to the Denbigh Moors, over the whole width of the Conwy valley, and forward across the sea, across Anglesey, provided it is clear, and feel that the world is at our feet. How many travellers, through how many ages, have stood at this same spot, to breathe the same clear air, listen to the ancestors of the birds we hear, and watch those of the ones that fly above our heads? Here, surely, is one of the few places within these islands where there is yet the all-pervasive surety that behind all living is a power omnipotent, a God. Is there any wonder that our ancestors chose this area for their homes, for their places of religious fervour, their stones and cairns and mounds and later their churches, of whatever age, for what ceremonial aim? Here, except for the clamorous passage of low-flying plane from the RAF. Station at Valley on the Isle of Anglesey, past and nearly out of sight before its sound comes following on, all is as it must have been through countless ages. There would be no surprise if around the edge of rising ground there came a funeral cortege from the days of the axe-men, or a medieval farmer with his shepherd and his sheep. Here we can sit and dream, and time stands still.

But we must return, along the road by which we came as far as the junction of the ancient ways near the ruin of Tan-y-braich. Beyond that we will walk on foot along the road other than that by which we came — for now it is no longer kept fit for vehicles. The Roman road came this way, to places far away, but not along the exact line of the road on which we walk; their road was for a long way on a terrace on our left above the present line; that terrace is still there, and in part the old paving which they so laboriously laid can still be seen. How much of what was there disappeared to build the very walls beside the road on which we go? We pass an older burial chamber, then on the opposite side is Rhiw, a farm of the past, but now a Youth Hostel. From here the road drops very steeply into the village now called Ro-wen, and on the hillside as we go we pass again an area of ancient field systems, the works of one age mixed with those of another, as we saw near Pen-y-gaer.

To get our car to Ro-wen village, we must travel back along the road on which we came from Llanbedr-y-cennin, but for only half a mile to where the road on the left leads steeply to the village.

In the days of the coaches, before the descent there would be a halt on the older road past Rhiw. All but the first class passengers would have to alight, and the guard would unhitch an iron skid one side of the vehicle, to slide it under a rear wheel, still held by an anchor chain. The coach would move slowly with one wheel sliding on the skid until the slope increased, when the guard would produce a second for the other side; but now the coach would veer, the back to slide into the ditch unless restrained, and second class passengers must needs hold ropes, to heave and tug, to keep it on its proper course, to help to hold it back from rushing headlong, to topple and roll to the foot of the hill. On a wet and muddy road, on a cold winter night, the task was hard, and welcome would be a quenching draught at one of the beer-houses or inns within the village. The tankards would be ready on the tables, the ale or beer in jugs and water for the horses, for the noise of the shouting as the coach was held on course would have echoed to Bryn Piogod [126] and back again. But more than that, the coachman would have blown loud and clear upon his horn, and blown again, before descent was started, to ensure no coach on the upward trip should go; if two were to meet on that terrible hill, all night would go in getting them past. The horses, too, would get their reward, for they were not neglected — good coach operators never worked their horses more than one hour in twenty-four, while a coachman drove a dozen hours or sixteen or more, and the guard who left Holyhead with the mail was the same who arrived with it in London. [127]

Think on, as a man from Yorkshire would say, all you, all we, who undertake a journey by road in these days of cars, by day or night, on modern roads, with heaters and our radios.

Roewen, or Rowen or Ro-wen, the modern maps and signposts call this village, according to which map you have, or along which road you approach. But all are wrong — the name of the past, the name on the maps of old, even into the first half of this century, have none of them. The name they use is just Y Ro; that means "The Pebbles" or "The Gravel", though Ro-wen appears in the Religious Census of 1851.[128] Were the pebbles in the river, or was the gravel on the fearsome hill, making it a place to slip and slide in dry weather as well as wet? We may never know. We may also wonder when and why the "wen" appeared, and was it white, or was it holy? We may also ponder again on the name of the little river which glints and glistens its way over rocks behind the houses, but once in a time gone by turned into a torrent, and swept through the valley to lay all before it, taking houses and part of one of the inns, and trees and rocks. In the lower valley, where for ages before, if not for always, it had flowed north, to Henryd and Gyffin, when daylight came it was found to flow south, to join the now much lesser streams which come down the mountainside by Gorswen, and on to Farchwel, and the Conwy near Porth Allt Goch.

The mill at the farm still known as Llannerch-y-felin was high and dry, but the Bulkeley Mill was well provided. The flood had formed a lake in the valley bottom, but the owner of the land reformed the bund or bank of the old mill leet as it is today, to take all the waters to the south, to Bulkeley and Pontwgan mills. The stream from Gorswen is now only a trickle, for the catchment canals which we saw before have taken most of its headwaters.

Old Ro-wen

Here is a village which has seen all of history. The pack trains of the stone-age men came through, and those of the Iberians and Celts with copper from the mines of Anglesey. Suetonius Paulinus forced his army with all its baggage and its engines of war over the top to Aber. At the time of Agricola, before his armies came here under Ostorius, no doubt of a night Brython and Iberian sat in inns, round smoking fires, beguiled by the serving wenches as well as by the stories of news and fable retailed by passing packmen and drovers and travellers of many kinds. In the years to come they would be joined by Celtic and Iberian soldiers from Gaul and Spain, garrisoned at the fort at Caerhun, by servants and clerks from the settlement growing at Canovium.

When the Empire broke up, and the princes of Gwynedd took over from the Roman administrators, the travellers still came, with Christian missionaries from Ireland and trading Danes from the Isle of Man, from Scotland, with Brythons from Cornwall and the coasts of Brittany. Through all the middle ages and into the last of the Georgian era the scene would be the like. The raptorial men of Cromwell's army no doubt rested on their destructive way to Caernarfon. The clothes would change, but the talk would be the same, of wars and pestilences, births of princes and deaths of kings, of crops and stock, of the terrors of the Bwlch already encountered, or feared to come, the Lafan Sands or the Denbigh Moors.

That was the Ro-wen of the past, so important that it had three mills and many ale and porter houses, and inns as well. It even had a pandy, so woollen cloth must have been made nearby. Two of its mills are now just houses, and one has gone and no trace remains. Of the ale houses there are none, and of the inns but one — Tŷ Gwyn — which should be visited. A lovely building, preserved more or less as it was, the talk is still of sheep and cows, of births and deaths, of the affairs of kings and countries, and a fire burns in winter in the hearth of old. Here later in the day we may return to spend the night — or there are other hotels of modern kind, farms and houses where welcome is extended.

Many of the old houses are still here, though some were lost in the great flood and replaced with new, and some have gone of recent years. The street is now well paved with tarmacadam, where photographs of but sixty years ago and less show gravel bound with water. There are now great glaring street lights, where till not long ago the monthly parish lantern[129] had to serve, and that was often hidden by the clouds.

After Suetonius Paulinus and the forces of Agricola came the armies of the Princes of Wales and those of invading John and Henry III and Edward I, and last of all those of Cromwell in a later time; travelling Irish saints,

Lords Lieutenant of Ireland, civil servants and officers, traders and trippers, all have come in the wake of the trains of pack-horses which traded the axe-heads of five thousand years ago. Now so quiet and sleepy and off the map, this has been a most important place.

Here in 1784 John Williams "kept school". He was not a local man, and his importance to Ro-wen is only that his record shows that there was a school here two centuries and more ago. Known as "Sion Singer", he moved on to Glascoed at Llanrwst, and there he founded a Baptist Church before Soar Chapel there was built in 1816 with space for 450 souls. After that he left the district, his only other connection with the Valley being that he published, probably at Trefriw, the first book in Welsh to teach the elements of music.

The Inn, Ro-wen

118. *Ffynnon Bedr, house and well, belonged to Maenan Abbey in the 14th and 15th centuries—see also footnote 122 below. The house was re-roofed in the 18th century.*

119. *See footnote 23 on page 44.*

120. *This was a substantial fort, with a blast furnace. Only in two places in Scotland and two in Ireland have such comprehensive defence works been found.*

121. *It is equally likely that it was manned by "Romanised" Celts.*

122. *It was even said that the tunnel extended to Maenan Abbey. If so, it was probably for water supply.*

123. *Originally the Fair was held when the last crops were brought in, but in the nineteenth century a fixed date, October 3rd, was adopted.*

124. *See page 195.*

125. *In Welsh Traeth Lafan, itself a corruption of Traeth Llefain, the weeping sands. Whether that referred to the weeping following the great inundation of the sea over the lands of Helig ap Glanawg (see page 10), or to the weeping of relatives of people trying to cross to or from Anglesey who were caught by the tides and lost, or whether it just refers to the weeping sound which can be heard from beneath the sands, is a matter for speculation.*

126. *The hill on the east of the valley.*

127. *The Holyhead to London coach never used this particular route regularly, only diverting to it when the weather was too bad to use the coast road, or the Conwy Ferry, or if that route was blocked.*

128. *The Registers of Conwy up to 1793 used "Roe".*

129. *Parish lantern — the moon.*

It is now evident that the Celts had a fort at
Caerhun before the Romans came — that
the name was derived from Caer Hen, the
Old Fort, and that the alteration to Caer
Rhun came in the sixth century when Rhun
the son of Maelgwn Gwynedd came to live
here, perhaps occupying one of the great Roman or Celtic villas which
must still have existed. He succeeded his father as ruler of western
Gwynedd, but before that is reputed to have led his father's army when it
advanced to the River Forth in 547 to punish the Danish Hael for a raid by
sea on Arfon.

At Bryn-y-castell (Tal-y-cafn), at Pen-y-gaer (Llanbedr-y-cennin) and Caer
Oleu (above Maenan) there were surrounding fortified camps, all so located that the smoke or light of fires could be seen from the others and
from Caerhun, to give warning of approaching enemy. They were so placed
that they could cover all lines of approach except that through
Llangelynnin, where there may have been a look-out post of which we
have no record so far.[130] They were all part of a defensive system which
included Braich-y-ddinas and Caer Leion, the Great Orme and Dinerth on
Bryn Euryn.

The river communications, the pack trail crossing the Conwy, the pearl
beds, all point to the importance of this place being such in those days as
to justify such a camp, and the field systems, huts and enclosures, camps
and forts, in the surrounding areas are evidence of a populous district.
The camp could well have been, in early Celtic times, as it was in Roman
times and later, a place for storage of supplies of grain.

It would be logical for the Romans to make use of an existing fortified
site for a camp, and there are good reasons to believe that they did take
over an Ordovicean fortification somewhere hereabouts. The land would

be already raised, and the site was well located
in relation to surrounding look-out posts.

That happened in A.D.78, for the first Roman
fort built by Paulinus after the Celts had destroyed their own in the face of his advance was
a staging post only, and was probably razed to
the ground when the army advanced over the
mountains, or at any rate when it retreated.

Top inset: St Mary's Church, Caerhun. Bottom inset: Lych Gate, Caerhun

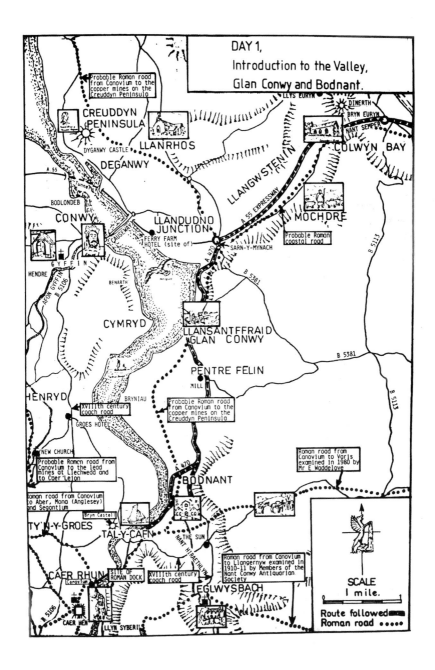

When Agricola's armies took it over, most likely by agreement, they built first a wooden fort on the Roman pattern, which they replaced a few years later with a stone-built fort which was to stand for centuries. The supposition that its purpose was to suppress the local population is unlikely to be founded on any fact — although naturally the Romans had always to consider the possibility of what they would regard as a local revolt. But when Agricola came in the days of the Emperor Vespasian, Roman policy was to harass only the recalcitrant within what they considered Roman domain, but to hold out the hand of friendship and peace to all those who could be persuaded to see and accept the advantages of being in or with the Empire. It was a policy in which Agricola himself believed.

In northern Wales the advantages would be most clear — there would be trade in the ores and pearls and wool, and a common defence against the raids from the Irish sea — raids by the Scots and the Danes from Ireland and from the Isle of Man, and raids by the Picts and the Brigantes from the mainland of northern Britain, any of whom could muster strength enough to menace Roman and Celt alike, to threaten trade as well as lives. Against them a fort and garrison would be a need.

And so Canovium developed out of Caerhun, not as a beleaguered fort, but as a garrison town, a minor naval base, a port and centre of trade, a confluence of roads and a travellers' staging post. These functions it fulfilled for centuries, the fort becoming of less importance than the town, then later both declining as the castle of Deganwy grew. By the twelfth century what remained was a house at Caerhun and a church, and separate villages at Tal-y-cafn, Ro-wen and Llanbedr-y-cennin, some isolated houses between the three, and the Cantref town and centre of Trefriw not far away.

The great house of Caerhun was rebuilt in the days of King Stephen, between 1135 and 1154, and was the home of Welsh families until the times of the Davies and the Griffiths in the eighteenth and nineteenth centuries. It was then pulled down by an immigrant whose family origins were Welsh, but long settled in Ireland — General Gough, who was nephew of the General Sir Hugh Gough who commanded the forces in India which quelled the Sikh rebellion, and also was cousin of the General Sir Hubert Gough who played a major role in the East African campaigns of the 19th century. General Gough then built the present house in 1895, but after the early part of the century the family let the house on lease to various occupants for more time than they occupied it themselves, eventually selling it to a Dr Kendrick, whose main importance seems to have been that he professed to be totally anti-Welsh. It is now in use as an accountancy college —

what a change from the mighty Roman fort and town!

The history of this part of Wales in Roman times is very vague, perhaps because the historians Tacitus and Paulinus emphasized campaigns and battles rather than peaceful co-existence and development. It is probable that about the times of the governors Quintus Petillius Cerialis and Sextus Julius Frontinus, between A.D.71 and A.D.78 the Romans first infiltrated the northern Wales lands of the Ordovices, and established friendly trading bases, and maybe small camps and forts,[131] as they often did in the areas of "friendly barbarians".

After the defeat of Caratacus in A.D.49 no more campaigns are heard of involving the Ordovices, except Paulinus' disastrous campaign, until about A.D.78 when a disruptive element among the tribe slaughtered a cohort of Roman cavalry, probably somewhere near Wroxeter. As likely as not this was as much a revolt against the tribal leaders as it was against the Romans.

Gnaeus Julius Agricola, back in Britain for the third time, but now as Governor, moved in the XXth Valeria Victrix Legion from Wroxeter — a good choice, since they were mainly Iberians and Celts from Spain and Gaul who spoke a language similar to that of the Ordovices, and had cultural affinities. Tacitus seemingly reported that this force under Ostorius,[132] wiped out the Ordovices, but either we misunderstand what he intended to say, or he misremembered what he had been told by Agricola, or misread the records from which he was working. It is known, for instance, that the Celts continued as before to take their part in the defence of the area, manning such important forts as Braich-y-ddinas. In fact, Ostorius destroyed the rebellious forces. He did also, of course, man the fort at Caerhun and that at Segontium, and then he crossed into Anglesey and drove out the Irish Gangani who had established themselves there in Ordovicean territory. The navy bases at Caergybi (Holyhead), Aberffraw and Segontium were set up to keep them and other raiders out.

It is probable that the XXth Legion was followed at Caerhun and Segontium by the Xth Antonian Augustian Legion (that which at an earlier time had seen the Crucifixion of Christ at Calvary). It is true that records do not show the presence of Xth Legion in Britain after the times of Caesar, but that only provides further example of the lack of recorded history of this part, and of some other parts of the British Province. Even the Segontientes Legion, formed in this area, does not appear in records until it turns up in the Balkans in the second half of the fourth century.

As this period of history is increasingly examined, as more is found locally of roads and forts and buildings, coins and artefacts, from Chester to the western coast, it is becoming clear that Celtic life went on peacefully alongside Roman life and that as intermarriages and education in the Roman language increased, Caerhun became Canovium, the Roman garrisons gave way to Welsh, Romano-Celts, and Gwynedd started in its infancy.

The town of Canovium grew up around the fort, and since the houses so far found were very close to the fortification walls where they would have hampered defence, it is evident that it was a garrison town rather than defensive post. In A.D.119 the Emperor Hadrian must have visited it, for a milestone was erected 7^1/2 miles (8 Roman miles) out on the way across the Bwlch-y-ddeufaen, not far from Aber, which was inscribed:

IMP . CAES . TRAI
ANVS . HADRIANVS
AVG .P:M. TR. P. V
P. P. COS . III
A. KANOVIO
M. P. VIII

The translation being:
Imperator Caesar
Trajanus Hadrianus
Augustus, Pontifex Maximus
Tribuncia Potestate
Pater patriae, Consul III
A KANOVIO
Mille Passuum VIII

Only fifty such milestones have been found in the whole of Roman Britain, and this, like the others, recorded a visit — the visit of an important person to a place that was important.

It may be that it was about this time that the name Gwynedd started to appear, in the form of the lands of the Genouni. The great tribe of the Brigantes occupied the north and west of "England", from Cheshire to the Scottish Lowlands, and in about A.D.144 or thereabouts they started to overrun surrounding territories, including the lands of the Genouni. It has long been taken for granted that the lands of the Genouni must have been in the north-east, because when the Emperor Marcus Aurelius (who adopted the name of Marcus Aurelius Antoninus Pius, after his adoptive father) sent replacement troops to Britain, the new Governor, Julius Verus, took them to the Tyne, where he took over from Gnaeus Papirius Aelinus.

However, in 1820 a stone was found at Caerhun Farm, Tŷ Coch, which bears the inscription —

NVMC.
IMP. CAESAR M...
AVREL ANTONINVS
PIVS. TI. IX AVG. ARAB IX.

and it has been determined that it was erected by the Ninth (Arabic) Legion to record the driving of the Brigantes out of this area, Canovium having been its base during the time of the campaign. The year, the ninth of the Emperor Antoninus Pius, A.D.147-8, matches that of the references to the Genouni in Pausanias' historical record. It now seems that perhaps the people of Gwynedd were the Genouni.

Another milestone was found not far from the first, but its original siting is not precisely known, for it was broken off, so that part only of its inscription remains which reads:

IMPP. CAES
L. SEP . SEVERVS
PP.ET.M.AVR
ANTONINVS
AVGG.ET.P...

Imperatores Caesares
Lucius Septimius Severus
Pius pertinax et M. Aurelius
Antoninus
Augusti et P (Septimius Geta).

Lucius Septimius Severus became Emperor of Rome in A.D. 193. He had two sons, Marcus Aurelius Antoninus and Publius Septimius Geta who were always quarrelling. Marcus Aurelius Antoninus was not raised to the rank of Augustus until A.D. 198 and the stone must therefore date from later than that. In A.D.208 the three of them with Septimius Severus' wife Domna came to Britain. Geta and his mother were left at either London or York in charge of the administration of the country, while Septimius Severus and the other son toured the Province and conducted an unsuccessful campaign against the tribes of Scotland. Geta was raised to the rank of Augustus in A.D.209, and it was arranged that the two brothers would succeed their father in joint Emperorship, but when Septimius Severus died at York in A.D.211 the quarrelling between the brothers came

217

to a head. They did succeed to joint Emperorship, Marcus Aurelius Antoninus adopting the name of Caracalla, a nickname given to him because of the cloaks he wore, but within a year Geta was murdered at Caracalla's command, or maybe even by him.

This stone no doubt marked a visit of Septimius Severus and Marcus Aurelius to Canovium about A.D.210. There are two possible explanations about what happened to the inscription, and how the stone came to be broken. The first is that when Caracalla, after Geta was murdered, ordered the removal of his name from all records, the stone was broken in the process of deleting Geta's name: but it is equally likely that the stone was prepared before Septimius arrived, and when it was found that Geta had not come with him, the attempt to remove the name was made then.

We can only surmise the order in which the Romans constructed and paved the many roads which converged on the town. No doubt they did not all come at once. Maybe first would be that from Chester via the coast to Mochdre, then up the eastern side of the river over Bryniau to Caerhun ford (Caer Hen ford it would then have been). From there it went south of the fort, through Ro-wen and over the Bwlch-y-ddeufaen along the old pack trail to Aber, then along the coast to Segontium. After that we may assume there would be the paving of the road from Varis, the old pack route from the east, and the other old pack route through the cultivated areas of the Ardda uplands, past Llyn Cowlyd to Bryn Gefeiliau and on to Beddgelert and the western coast, with another road from Bryn Gefeiliau to Tomen-y-mur. Next no doubt came the road through the Valley to Bryn Gefeiliau by way of Llanrhychwyn and the mines, to Trefriw and the Pearl Beds and the Mineral Springs. Probably the last to be constructed would be that from Denbigh and Llangernyw through Eglwys-bach to pass south of the fort, through Llanbedr-y-cennin to the Bwlch-y-ddeufaen, which in the process passed through the southern part of the centre of Canovium the town. At some stage there was also a road from Conwy Mountain (Caer Leion) and the Henryd Mines, and another from Pentrefoelas through Llanrwst and down the east side of the river. All these have been identified by various learned and sound authorities at different times. In all nine roads converged on Canovium, not, it will be noted, directly onto the tiny area of the original fort, but onto a much larger area, which indicates that it was to a town they came.

The original fort covered about five acres within its walls, and that is almost all of Canovium that has been traced so far. Our knowledge of it derives from some small excavations carried out in 1801 and ensuing years by the then owner, the Rev. Hugh Davies Griffith and a friend, Mr Samuel Lysons. They put on record that much had been found in the area in the previous century, but had then been destroyed or lost. What they excavated in the way of foundations they left open, and time and weather have seriously damaged them — no doubt they have been pillaged as well. Their findings of artefacts became widely dispersed.[133] There was some more systematic work between 1926 and 1929, but it was limited to the fort area and immediate surrounds, and the gardens of Caerhun Hall and the churchyard had to be left untouched; it added little to what was already known. In some respects the conclusions of both have been overtaken by time. For example, it was decided then that the fort ceased to be used about A.D.180, and that the garrison was then removed. That now seems unlikely, not only because of the date of the Septimius Severus milestone, but also because many coins, some in hoards of up to 135 and some in single finds in the locality, date from the second century B.C. (suggesting trading long before occupation) to the fifth century A.D., the times of Macsen Wledig, Maximus Magnus, when the last of the Roman Legions were withdrawn from Britain, and almost as late as any coins found anywhere in Britain.[134] The renaming of the fort to Caerhun indicates that as late as the middle of the sixth century it was still in such state as to justify occupation by Rhun ap Maelgwn.

We have already seen that it is becoming increasingly evident that the men who came to Britain as soldiers, administrators and traders brought with them their wives and families, and that they had a normal social life. One lady, Flavia Severa, was at an isolated fort on the Scottish border before even Hadrian's Wall was built, sometime between A.D.100 and A.D.117, and she wrote a letter which has recently come to light (referred to on page 176 - footnote 109, *"Fla via Severa sends greetings to Lepidina. Please come to my party on the (tenth September). It will make me particularly happy. I include greetings from my husband Aelius and my son"*.[135] Reference to a party would indicate that there were other women as well as Flavia Severa and Lepidina, and since Flavia Severa had her son with her, there would be others with families.

Canovium would be unlikely to be more backward than an isolated northern fort, and must quickly have become more than just a military camp. As well as providing guards for the coast and for the mines which spread from the Great Orme to Trefriw and Llanrhychwyn and into the Llugwy Valley, it had to provide protection at sea for the trading ships of the Conwy Estuary, the Orme, and maybe on the seas as far as Anglesey, for the nearest other navy bases seem to have been at Segontium, Caergybi (Holyhead) and Deva (Chester). It would be the administrative centre for law and order and the inevitable taxation. It was the trading centre for the export of ores and timber, sulphur and slate, woollen cloths, pearls and

Celtic jewellery, and for the import of silks and spices and the products of the Mediterranean lands, controlling the shipping from the Orme, Tal-y-cafn, Trefriw and maybe even Llanrwst.

All these would bring military and civilian staff, with their families, and demands for services to provide which more would come — scribes and servants, dressmakers and tailors, shoemakers and farriers. There would be a market for food, for meat and fruit and vegetables, and shops for furniture and pottery and goods for household use. As the community grew, its needs would grow, but Celts and Romano-Celts, the Welsh of the years to come, would gradually replace the Romans as the years went by. The development must have spread over a wide area, from Trefriw and Llanbedr-y-cennin to Deganwy, from Ro-wen to Eglwys-bach. The Mineral Springs at Trefriw would bring visitors from Chester and Segontium, and maybe further afield, and there would be hostelries for them and for those on passage on the highways. According to Richard of Cirencester (1335-1401) the town still existed after the middle of the fifth century.[136]

But so far all we know with the certainty which comes from finding the remains of buildings is that the fort itself at Caerhun covered some five acres on the standard pattern, square, with gates in each side and protective towers. Inside was accommodation for a garrison of about 500 men and horses, with granaries and all provisions for at least a year. Between that fort and the river was a large building which contained baths and maybe a pottery. A short distance to the north-east was a dock, and alongside it a sloping ramp to the river's edge. Outside the south wall there was some civilian housing. Several burials and cremation burials have also been found. Further afield, there have of course been finds at Henryd, Llanrhychwyn, the Great and Little Ormes, and on the Carneddau, some of which have been referred to. Samian and the other pottery and coins have been found, as well as shields and ornaments. No doubt there have been other finds not disclosed because of the nature of our laws relating to treasure trove.

The Romans used materials to hand for building, importing only when essential for special work, or just for vanity. In this area there was plenty of local stone from nearby quarries, even in many places lying on the surface, which when in later years the buildings fell into disuse would be used again with nothing to identify their previous Roman use. Where flooring and roofing have been found, they have been of local slate, which likewise would be used again. Timber was in great supply, and the local Celts were craftsmen in its use — no doubt the Romans used it locally as well as exporting it. Of all these materials, much no doubt was used and perhaps again reused at later dates, in the building of the medieval township of Trefriw, the villages of Ro-wen, Llanbedr-y-cennin and Tal-y-cafn, the many isolated farms and their farm buildings, and the walls which cross and criss-cross the countryside — maybe some are even in the churches and the chapels.

But we are still at Ro-wen, and have yet to get to the site of Caerhun. The Roman road went up the hill now beside the Groesffordd Ro Stores, by way of Bryn Piogod, to Ty'n-y-groes, and then most likely for 300 yards down the present road towards the Tal-y-cafn bridge, to continue to the line of the ford, probably somewhere just south of where Tal-y-cafn Uchaf Farm now stands, with a branch road, probably alongside the dock, to the Porta Principalis Sinistra of the fort.[137] But we cannot get to the site of the fort that way now, and will turn south from Groesffordd Ro, past Bulkeley Mill (now a house) and Pontwgan to join the B5106 opposite Caerhun Hall. Here we must turn right, to the south, and after about 200 yards we shall see Farchwel on the right, the old farm house with now a lane leading to it. It was along that way that the Roman road came to Canovium from Bryn Gefeiliau by way of Llyn Cowlyd and Llanbedr-y-cennin. The road from Trefriw may also have come to here, to join that from Llanbedr, but maybe it came nearer the river, direct from Tal-y-bont to the Porta Principalis Dextra.

Much of what might have been found hereabouts must have been lost in centuries of cultivation of land, of robbing to build walls, in the construction in 1777 of the toll road, and even in the building of the twelfth-century Caerhun house, with its farm and farmbuildings. Some no doubt went into the building of Caerhun Church to get to which we must turn around, and go east along the lane beside the wall of Caerhun Hall — there is a direction sign pointing the way.

It may be that the earliest church was allocated a site within the fort, in the Christian days of the later Roman Empire, when Maximus Magnus was in these parts, for there would be Christians among the soldiers and their families. The official allocation of a site would have been quite normal at any time after the middle of the fourth century. No doubt there have been churches here ever since, and the present church dates from the eleventh or twelfth centuries, but has been rebuilt in stages and extended from time to time. Some details of its history are set out in a pamphlet obtainable in the church.

130. *Caer Bach, on the eastern slopes of Tal-y-fan, could possibly have served that purpose.*

131. *W.S. Hanson in "Agricola", page 5l, says "on the basis of the archaeological evidence alone almost all of the forts in North Wales could as easily be foundations of Frontinus as of Agricola. Many of the sites have not provided artefactual evidence which is sufficiently abundant or diagnostic to indicate a foundation more precise than Flavian (i.e. C.A.D. 70-95);for example the forts at Caerhun (Reynolds 1938), Tomen-y-mur (Jarrett 1964, 173) and Pen Llwyn (A. W.1983, 32), the putative fort at Rhuddlan (A. W.1983, 36)*

132. *He is often referred to as Ostorius Scapula, Governor of Britain, but that man died while Governor in A.D.52, 26 years earlier.*

133. *An informative paper on those was read to the Llandudno and District Field Club by GA. Humphries, FRIBA, in 1911. It is unfortunate that the "finds" of the various excavations have been widely distributed, and not kept assembled locally.*

134. *Vide the Report of the Royal Commission on Ancient and Historical Monuments in Wales and Monmouthshire for Caernarfonshire, and also the report in Archaeologia Cambrensis. 1925, pages 322 et seq.*

135. *Vide the Daily Telegraph, Monday, July 1st, 1986*

136. *The total disappearance of a town of such a size over a period of fifteen hundred years is not uncommon, and need be no more cause for surprise than the even more complete disappearance of the once mighty Maenan Abbey in less than a third of that time. There does not seem to have been any proper search for a town in the area which is suprising in view of the confluence of roads. Indications of previously unknown towns still come to light, as, for example, nearby Prestatyn, which may yet turn out to be Roman Varis.*

137. *The names of the gates to the fort were allocated at the time of the 1926 to 1929 excavations, and not by the Romans. The internal layout of the fort has been worked out partly from what was found at that time, and partly from the assumption that the rest of the layout would be according to the standard design for such forts. There would not be any such standard design for layout outside the walls.*

We come to the last day of our travels, and are in an area which is not famous for any particular person or place, and yet in a way may be said to have been the centre of all that has happened in the history of the Valleys, of Wales and perhaps of even wider fields. It is the Llechwedd area of Arllechwedd, which, with Rhos across the Conwy, became at many times the hub of the kingdom of Gwynedd.

Copper was mined in the Creuddyn Peninsula by the Romans, and lead at Henryd, and others have mined there before and since. Stone-age man quarried for axe heads at Graig Lwyd, and after that before the Romans came there was a fortified camp at Caer Leion (Conwy Mountain). Perhaps they took it over, as they did some other forts in the area, or perhaps this, like Braich-y-ddinas, was one which was still manned by Celts. Caer Leion and the Great Orme between them provided good look-out over the sea and the entrance to the Conwy River, and protection for the Valley from surprise attack by foreign invaders. So it was up to the time of the last of the Princes of Wales.

But at an earlier date, in A.D.45, Ostorius Scapula[138] came to Chester, and he personally tried to take over north-west Wales. Suetonius Paulinus in turn came personally in A.D.61 and failed, though he did get as far as the shores of Anglesey. At a later time, in a different manner, came the forces of Agricola under another Ostorius, as friends and allies,[139] after which virtually nothing is to be found in Roman history of wars, campaigns or even skirmishes in this area except for an attack by the Brigantes in A.D.145 or thereabouts. There are no writings of Romans and Barbarians, but only of one people, the Venedotes, then later it must seem the Genouni, and there are some records of trade, of Irish incursions into Anglesey, and Danish raids.

It took little more than two generations for the Celts and the Romans to realise that they had so much in common, and at the same time so much to learn from each other, that they settled down to live in real harmony, to fraternise, and to intermarry. Within less than 150 years the Roman Legions were withdrawn from these parts, and what remained was a local

223

Bottom inset: Llangelynnin Old Church

force, probably the Legio Segontientes, to defend against invasion from abroad, from Ireland, from Norway and from Gaul, in later years most likely under local leaders such as Endaf ap Caradawg of Arfon.

In the year 364 came the separation of the Roman Empire into two parts, the East based on Constantinople, and the West based on Rome. The Goths and the Vandals were starting on the move against the Empire, and there was internal strife. The Legions were gradually withdrawn from Britain, until the last left in A.D.410.

But half a century earlier, other forces than the Goths and the Vandals were on the move, and in the middle of the fourth century invasions of Britain were rife, these western parts suffering particularly at the hands of the Scots from Ireland, and the Danes, largely because even local forces as well as residual Roman troops had been taken from here to defend the east and north of Britain. There was an appeal to Rome for help.

The Emperor Valentinian sent forces under Magnus Clemens Maximus and Theodosius. The latter went through eastern England, and into Scotland, and for the moment is of no further interest to us. Magnus Maximus came through Wales to Caernarfon and the Conwy; this was the Macsen Wledig of the Mabinogion, and he came with a large army in A.D.368. His name and that of his wife have cropped up so many times that now seems the time to hear more of who they were, and what they did.

Probably some years after he arrived in North Wales Maximus married Elen, daughter of Endaf ap Caradawg, the Celtic Lord and probably set up his headquarters at Deganwy. When Maximus was proclaimed Emperor of the Western Empire in 383, she accompanied him to Gaul, and with him accepted the allegiance of Spain, Gaul and Britain. At Tours they met St Martin, but they were probably already Christians. Elen and her one son, Cystennin (Constantine) were very much influenced by him; it seems likely that their daughter, Severa, was not; probably she was much too young.

Maximus was accompanied to Gaul by an army of Brythonic Celts from Gwynedd and other parts of Wales, under Elen's brothers, Cynan and Gideon, and with these he crossed the Alps in 387 and defeated the armies of Valentinian II, in which process at one stage (according to *Notitia Dignitaum,* Roman Historical Record of A.D.429) the Legio Segontientes advanced as far as the Balkans. Then they proceeded to capture Rome itself.

The following year, Theodosius II (son of the Theodosius who had come to Britain), Emperor of the Eastern Empire, heavily defeated Maximus at Siscia and Poetovia, and finally cornered him at Aquileia, where he and his son by an earlier marriage, Flavius Victor, were captured and killed.

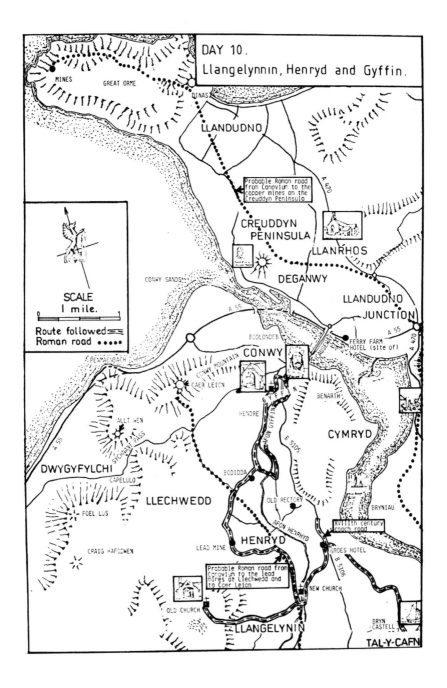

DAY 10.
Llangelynnin, Henryd and Gyffin.

SCALE
1 mile.

Route followed
Roman road

The Welsh forces had not been present at those battles, and they withdrew; Elen, Cystennin and Gideon, with part of the force, came back to Gwynedd; Cynan and the rest went to Brittany, and Breton records indicate that they settled at what is now Nantes. They were largely responsible for the start of the Breton Spirit of Celtic independence and the affinity with Wales. Our interest lies in Elen.[140]

In North Wales she set about organising the people in resistance to the Irish and other invaders who had become active again after the departure of Maximus (Macsen) and the army. She formed a combined defence force, and from this derived her name of Elen Llueddog, Helen of the Hosts. She moved rapidly all over Wales, from the Creuddyn to Caer Leon in South Wales, driving the invaders from the western coasts, the Severn and the north, and it was because of the way she and her armies used the Roman road between Canovium and Nidum (Neath) that the road became known as Sarn Helen, Elen's Causeway. She was assisted towards the turn of the century by her son Cystennin but he seems to have helped more in organising forces in the rest of Britain, although the Cystennin area of the Creuddyn is named after him, so he must have lived there.

Somewhere just after the year 400, by which time Cystennin may already have been murdered by, or at the instigation of, his brother-in-law, Vortigern,[141] who hated the Roman influence, and Elen was approaching or in her forties, another appeal was sent to Rome for help against invaders. This time the Governor of Rome, Flavius Stilicho, sent a local commander from Scotland, Cunedda Wledig, who was also a Christian. The term Gwledig meant commander or leader,[142] so it is apparent that Cunedda, like Macsen before him, held high office in the Empire. He was a contemporary of Coel, probably of similar rank. He came with his "sons" and armies. Whether they were really his sons or his army officers is open to some doubt.

Some think he came nearer A.D.440, mainly because his great grandson Maelgwn Gwynedd did not die until 547 and they say that a generation average of 34 years was high for those days. But there is clear evidence that Cunedda was sent by Stilicho, and Stilicho was murdered in 404.[143]

Cunedda and his family settled in Wales, and they intermarried with the local Celts: they themselves were Celts, or part-Celts, from Strathclyde. The sons took over control of various parts of Wales, and his grandson Meirion took over Meirionnydd, as it came to be called. Cunedda himself settled in Anglesey first, probably at Aberffraw, but later almost certainly in the Creuddyn, and welded the whole area from Cricieth to the Conwy and north to Holyhead into the one unit that was to develop into the

Gwynedd which for a thousand years was to vie for power with the rest of Wales and of England, until Henry Tudur, a son of one of its great families, was to take over the throne of England.

In this work Cunedda's son Einion Yrth [144] helped him, but does not seem to have survived to take over the control of the new state; it was his grandson, Cadwallon Lawhir, who succeeded him and who finally drove the last of the Irish out of Anglesey in a great battle at Cerrig-y-Gwyddel, near Trefdraeth, in A.D.470.[145] The Western Roman Empire had, to all intents and purposes, collapsed in 455, after that being under the control of the Vandals. The consolidation of Gwynedd was, therefore, solely the work of the Celts and the Romans who had stayed in these parts; together they became the Welsh.

Vortigern,[146], and Severa, his wife, in their dislike of anything to do with Rome, set out to take the whole of Britain back to pre-Roman, pre-Christian systems and principles — it was they who in A.D.449 invited Hengist and Horsa to the shores of eastern England. Elen and Cystennin, probably also Gideon, were staunch Christians, and the faith had strong hold in the rest of Wales, as it had in Ireland and Strathclyde. The murder of Cystennin probably had a great part in the start of the animosity between Gwynedd and the rest of Britain which was to last until the start of the Renaissance.

Cadwallon was followed by his son Maelgwn, who was the first to be known by the name of Gwynedd. Maelgwn Hir (for he was tall) became Maelgwn Gwynedd. He was the first of whom we know for sure that he held his court at Deganwy, where, however, it is fairly certain that his predecessors probably as far back as Elen had a major fort, and possibly a castle. Maelgwn rebuilt the castle. He died in 547 of the Fad Felin, thought to have been an epidemic form of jaundice, and is buried at Rhos, in the Creuddyn. That is fact, but there is a legend that the fever could be caught by just looking at someone who had it, and so Maelgwn shut himself up in Rhos Church to be safe; however, he could not resist looking out through the keyhole, and of course someone with the plague walked past, he caught it, and died.

The later princes of Gwynedd, at least until the time of Henry III, continued to have castles at Deganwy, and most likely many of them had their courts here, like their predecessors. The Creuddyn was a good place to watch out for, and defend against, Irish and other invaders along the northern coast. It was easy to send armies to the east, south and west along the Roman roads. It was along the road to the east that Cadwallon's army marched to Heathfield in 632 to destroy the power of Northumberland, and in 654 that of Cadafael set out to stop a resurgence of the power of the aggressive northerners.[147]

But the road that could help armies to advance from the heartland of Gwynedd could also be used by armies coming in from the east to speed their advance to Conwy, and many a time in history such armies came as far as Deganwy, to besiege the castle, and sometimes, as Henry III, to capture it. It became increasingly important to have a ferry from Deganwy to the western side of the estuary, to link to the Sychnant Pass and the camps and forts on the way to Aber, and the road south to Caerhun, Trefriw and Dolwyddelan.

No doubt a small community grew up at the western end of the ferry around Bodlondeb, perhaps in the Gyffin estuary, but the area remained quiet and generally secluded. For those reasons — good communications and quietude, coupled with a site of great beauty — this was an understandable place for monks from Strata Florida to set up a convent in 1172. Here they built their first Aberconwy Abbey, which they had more or less finished by 1186, two years before Archbishop Baldwin came to these parts seeking soldiers for the Crusades. With him came Giraldus Cambrensis, a grandson of Nest, whose writings have given us some knowledge of the people and ways of living of Wales and Ireland of those times.

In 1198 Llywelyn Fawr granted the Abbey a Charter. That he could do so, and that it should be recognised by Henry II and later monarchs of England, even including Edward I, and by the Popes, is indicative of the status of the princes of Gwynedd.[148] Llywelyn also granted the monks great areas of land, mostly it seems, in the cwmwd (commote) of Nant Conwy, but partly also in the cantref (hundred) of Arllechwedd. Most of those lands were in Gwynedd-uwch-Conwy, west of the Conwy river, but some, as Mochdre, were to the east, in Gwynedd-is-Conwy.[149]

With development of the Abbey, there came development of a community around, attracted by protection and trade, culture and learning. Some of the farms and houses still in the area date from those times, as Tan-y-berllan,[150] and the community of Mochdre, as indicated by their names. No doubt much was destroyed when the troops of Henry III ran amok through the area just before Michaelmas, 1245, to the extent that, contrary to all the customs of those times in Christendom, they even destroyed the ecclesiastical buildings and treasures, books and property. The crude ferocity of the Normans and their followers was seldom more clearly indicated.[151] The years that followed up to the time of Edward I were times of great upheaval, and the area never really became re-established before Edward I laid it waste again, settled English in Conwy Town, and by charter excluded Welsh from within its walls.

The Charter extended within the town and as far as the Gyffin River —

the word cyffin, mutated to gyffin, means border. A Welsh community grew up again on the south side of the river and its then wide estuary, and on both sides of the Gyffin river itself through Hendre and up to Henryd. At Gyffin the Town Mill was on the northern side, and the Welsh were prohibited from having grain ground anywhere but at that mill. In practice, however, for many generations, English rule did not extend far outside Edward's fortified towns, and it was not long before the Welsh had their own mills at Henryd, Ro-wen and Glan Conwy, because the town burgesses tried to rook them for work.

At Cymryd, a mile and a half south-east of Conwy, there was once a hazardous ford, and here in A.D.881 Anarawd ap Rhodri Mawr heavily defeated a Mercian army which, after killing his father in 878, had advanced this far into North Wales. The Mercians never returned.[152]

Such is the area into which we go from Caerhun, and we will do so by going first to Tal-y-cafn, to the western end of the bridge, and from there along the toll road of 1759 in the direction of Conwy. We will, however, leave the Conwy route at Groesynyd, where it joins the 1777 toll road from Llanrwst and Trefriw, and where we shall find an hostelry, the Groes Hotel, perhaps of fifteenth century, and therefore indicating that roads existed before the toll road was built. It was spoilt in appearance in the Georgian or early Victorian era by the rendering of its outside walls, hiding the stone which once delighted the eye; not long ago that cover was removed, to show again the lovely original stone, but after a while the owners were ordered to replace it, and the real beauty of the building has been lost again.

From the road on which we come, from here, and from a little way along the road to Conwy, are views of the Valley which are superior, perhaps, to those we have seen before, down river towards Glan Conwy, and up towards Maenan and Llanrwst. No tour of the Conwy Valley can be considered really complete until these views are seen on a sunny day, in winter or in summer, but best of all when the trees have the delicate hues of springtime green or the entrancing, but foreboding, golds and reds of later autumn.

We will not just now go on to Conwy, but will turn again south, along the Ro-wen road, and go till we come to Llangelynnin church, the "New Church", itself now a hundred and sixty five years old, almost lost among trees on our right. A notice inside the church doorway refers to "re-erection" of the building in 1839, which would indicate that there was an earlier church on the site. However, authorities who have researched the matter, including E.C. Bryan, Ll.B. (who has written a paper on the church which can be purchased from him) have not found any record of an earlier building here, and existing gravestones do not predate 1839. The Religious Census of 1851 referred to it as "erected 1839 or 1840" — it does not even mention the old church.

But some people ask why at that time a new church should be built so far from any village. A rectory was built at Henryd at about the same time, on land which in 1817 was occupied by a glebe house, and since a glebe house in earlier times was a manse, an ecclesiastical residence, that is suggested to confirm an earlier church, if not on the site of the present one, at any rate nearby. They suggest that the manse was too far away from the old church in the mountains to have served it. The Rectory, now privately owned, is no longer used as a minister's residence.

The *Topographical Dictionary of the Dominion of Wales* published in 1811, which gave the population of the parish as 259, defined it as "a discharged R. valued in the King's Books at £7", and made no reference to more than one church or chapel.

Now austere, almost plain, this church has exposed roof trusses which are really masterpieces of timber engineering of the late Georgian era, and it is well worth inspecting, although regrettably a shadow of its former self. The west doorway is an ugly red brick and alien insertion in the base of the tower, which Mr Bryan reports was put in as recently as 1949, apparently under the supervision of an architect. At an earlier date, in 1903, much more extensive alterations were made, under the guiding hand of Herbert North, the architect who did so much to churches in this area. Mr Bryan says that the application for Faculty at that time said that the pews were too cramped for people to kneel down; that was made an excuse for taking out all the pews, which extended from the west end nearly to the altar, and for removing the two pulpits which were up against the east wall, each side of the altar. There were either three or four rect-angular "family" pews. The door was on the south side, the present vestry being the porch. The room on the north side, now used as a cleaners' store, was the old vestry. There was a gallery at the west end, access being by a staircase up through the bell tower, and from the layout of the pews, and the absence of choir-stalls, it would seem that the gallery was for musicians and choir. That theory is supported by the fact that the staircase went up from the choir assembly room under the tower. By 1903 music was supplied by a harmonium, which would hardly have been the case when the church was built. There is now a very nice organ.

But it is to get to the old church that we have come this way, and to do that we must turn right 350 yards beyond where we are now, and then, to park the car, right again. From here we can walk, not along the road into which we have just turned to park the car, but continuing on the other which we left. It is a little over a mile to the old church, which lies in a small sheltered cwm between Cerrig-y-ddinas and Craig Celynnin, in a small churchyard surrounded by a wall, in the manner of the Llan of old. To get there we walk first along the lane, then on a farm track past Gwern Borter and Tyddyn Mawr, Pen-yr-allt and Cae Iol, on footpaths which not long ago were tracks for horses and for traps.

In the churchyard the rock outcrops to such degree that it has been hard throughout the centuries to find space for graves. The little stone building, according to North in his *Old Churches of Arllechwedd,* dates from the eleventh or twelfth century, and he thinks there was probably a timber, or wattle and daub, church on the same site before. That seems to be almost certain, since St Celynnin was the son of Helig ap Glanawg, and lived in the sixth century.[153] He was, according to Mr Bryan, somewhat related to Rhun, son of Maelgwn, Prince of Gwynedd, which would confirm a sixth-century dating. He was also, it seems, a brother of St Rhychwyn, which would correlate the date of this and Llanrhychwyn churches, a century later than St Grwst church, and a century and a half later than Llangystennin and Caerhun. All those datings appear to conform to the history of development of the Valley, except that of Llanrhychwyn, which would be expected to be at least a century and a half earlier. It makes one wonder if Llanrhychwyn was rededicated at some time from an earlier dedication.

These upland regions became quite well populated after the Roman era, as they had been before, but for a very different reason. From the date of the Edict of Milan, conferring Imperial favour on the Christian Church in 313, this area had become increasingly Christian — we know that Elen was Christian. The people suffered particularly from pagan raids, especially from over the sea. It was about A.D.366 that these raids became so serious that the appeal was sent to Rome for help, as a result of which Maximus Magnus came. But he left in A.D.383, when he was proclaimed Emperor. The raids from the sea resumed, and although they were quelled for some time when Elen returned, and later by Cunedda Wledig, they were to continue to be a cause of trouble for many centuries. From time to time there were raids by the Mercians and others from England, and in later times came the frequent invasions by the Normans, followed by two centuries of Norman suppression before Henry Tudur turned the tables. The population lived in the hills, away from the raids.

The old field patterns above Llanbedr-y-cennin, at Ardda and Ro-wen show signs of post-Roman use and occupation, possibly mainly as the old Welsh "gardd" refers to cultivated, ploughed land. The post-Roman Celts had the pre-Roman Celtic wheeled "ard" with coulter, to cultivate the larger unwalled areas for grain, that implement which had put them ahead of the world which used the wooden drag plough like that used in parts of Africa and the East today.

So the great upland plains and undulating lands which were good for grain crops remained so until modern farming methods made them uneconomical. They were good for summer grazing of cattle, sheep and goats. They really were the farmlands, with great numbers of farms and holdings and cottages from which the population only retreated to the valleys to escape the worst of winter. The Ordnance Survey of 1841 showed many farms and other buildings, most of which were there in 1910, but now have gone, or remain as mere shells.

But in the eighteenth century had come the industrial revolution and changes in farming methods. Although the needs of industry and of building led to the re-opening of lead mines at Llechwedd, and of slate and other quarries, the area, like many another, suffered from depopulation as people went off to work for higher wages in the industrial towns and cities and the conurbations, some even emigrated, so that by the early part of the nineteenth century it was "decided that it [154] (the church) had become too remote and difficult of access in bad weather from the more populous part of the parish which had moved to the lower more hospitable lands centred on the hamlet of Henrhyd". The parish population which was 259 in 1801, was reduced to 204 in 1851 — moreover, a Congregational church for 210 had been built in Henryd in 1822. That being the case, it may seem rather surprising that a site so far out of Henryd village was selected for the new church.

The nave is the oldest part of the building, eleventh or twelfth century, the chancel having been added in the fourteenth century and the north transept in the fifteenth — work was carried out in 1989, and the remains of a south transept are being uncovered. The dates of the alterations and extensions indicate that the population of the area was increasing during the time of the Norman invasions and the subsequent Norman suppression.

The font is very old, of octagonal shape, with a square base, and cut from one solid block of rock. On the walls are age-old texts, painted on the plaster. They once comprised the Lord's Prayer in Welsh, the Ten Commandments and the Creed, but the Lord's Prayer disappeared some years ago. What remains should, if possible, be restored by experts before that too is lost. There is an enclosure off the nave, where shepherds could put their dogs. No electricity, no central heating, have changed this church, which is much as it was many centuries ago, with the original earth floor to part of the transept.

Within a few hundred yards of the church are the remains of quite a considerable number of roundhuts and roundhouses, and many more within less than a mile, which those who know about these matters suggest were occupied for many ages.

Wandering from the cwm to the higher ground, if the day is clear we shall see across the waters to the Fylde Coast of Lancashire, the Isle of Man, and nearer Anglesey. Behind we can see to Carnedd Llywelyn and Carnedd Dafydd, across the high cynefin, the lands of lakes and sheep, or to the east across Rhos and the Perfeddwlad, the central part of Gwynedd.

To get again to the car, we must needs return the way we came, or walk for many a mile. But back at the car, we will continue north along the lane to Plas Newydd on the map, there to turn left, up meandering lanes past the old Henryd Mill, and past the lead mines which were worked into last century, but which the Romans also worked, and perhaps others before them and since. Of more recent times, they featured in the television film, *A Family at War*.

At Plastirion on the map we will take the road to Hendre, which also leads to Conwy. Here in Hendre we are in an area to which the Welsh

Groes Hotel

retreated when expelled from Conwy, where many houses are old, but many older have disappeared to be replaced by new. Along this road we come in time to St Agnes Road, and development of a very modern era, and here turn right — we have passed into the ancient Borough of Conwy. Down the hill we pass an untidy plot of level land beside the steeply sloping road — here till a few years ago was still the pool to feed the leet for the Gyffin mill, one of the two town mills. The other was near the foot of the slope from the Mill Gate, and was known as Y Felinheli, the Salt Water Mill.

Mill House below the old mill pond is of great age, perhaps of the time of the early mill itself. Here we turn right again, across the river which has been a boundary through so many ages, we come to Gyffin church. The Church of St Benedict was built, it seems, in the thirteenth century by the monks of Aberconwy Abbey. Records suggest that the Church of St Mary, which was built within and as part of Aberconwy Convent and is now the Parish Church of Conwy town, was built at almost the same time, so it would seem that Gyffin Church was for the use of the local population, the convent church being for the monks and (no doubt) their many illustrious guests. As the population grew, most particularly after the removal of the Abbey and with the exclusion by Edward I of all the Welsh from his new town, St Benedict's was extended, first in the early fifteenth century, and then again at the end of that same century or the beginning of the next. In 1858 a great deal of work was done, as in many other churches in the area, which destroyed much which had come down from the past.

In the porch is a slightly tapering memorial slab, reset at some time from somewhere else, inscribed:

HIC IA.. T LYWELY. .P IOR...

Was this, one wonders, a gravestone or slab to Llywelyn ab Iorwerth salvaged from Conwy church and brought here into Welsh safety when Conwy was peopled by Edward's Norman and English immigrants? Or perhaps it was taken from the Abbey when the third King Henry's men raided and pillaged the area, and when later found was taken to the safety of Gyffin church.

The yew trees in the churchyard may date from when the church was built. Why were yew trees grown in churchyards, so that in time they acquired a mystic significance associated with pagan as well as Christian rites? The answer, perhaps, is much more simple than most historians would have us think. A churchyard was walled or fenced, and cattle were well kept out; what better place could there be to grow the yew, needed to make the long-bow of the early and middle ages, but whose hanging branches poisoned, and often killed, cattle which browsed upon them?

Porch, Llangelynnin Old Church

Here in Gyffin on June 9th, 1790, was born John Gibson, the famous sculptor. He was the son of a market-gardener. He went to London in 1817, but shortly after he moved to Rome, where he settled. He spent most of the rest of his life in Italy, where he died on January 27th, 1866. From time to time he returned to Britain and he became a friend of Queen Victoria, of whom he carved two busts. He also carved a statue of Albert, the Prince Consort.

Nearly 300 years earlier Richard Davies was born here, the son of Dafydd ap Gronw, curate of Gyffin,[155] and his wife Jonet. He entered New Inn Hall, Oxford and became an MA and a BD Under Queen Mary he was deprived of his livings because he was a Protestant, but later he was reinstated, and in 1559 he became Bishop of St Asaph. In 1561 he became Bishop of St David's. It was he who invited William Salesbury to translate the New Testament into Welsh. He died in 1581.

Past Gyffin church, on along the road towards Henryd, in a little over a third of a mile on the left, beside the Gyffin stream are the remains of the old candle factory, a two-storey building whose age-old product went out of demand with the coming of electricity. The last owner, it seems, was Hugh Williams, whom some people can still remember seeing in his pony-cart collecting his raw material from slaughter-house and butcher, or delivering his finished wares to local shops, but that was at the time of the First World War, in the early part of the last century.

Further along the lane, just under a mile from Gyffin Church, is a turning on the right, and along that road quite shortly is another to the left, and here is Bodidda, a house built in the middle of the sixteenth century by Hugh Stodart or his son John. John Stodart was buried at Gyffin Church in 1627, and the house must have passed into the hands of the Owen family within relatively few years — Hugh Owen's tomb in Gyffin Church is dated 1668, and records that he lived at Bodidda. His widow was buried with him — she lived well into the eighteenth century.

If, as the final part of our journey, we walk from Gyffin towards the Conwy River and the castle of Conwy Town, beside the Gyffin River now tightly enclosed between banks of filling from the time when the railway was built and later, we may try to imagine when this was tidal reach, and when the Gyffin carried the waters of the Afon Ro.

235

In the days before the railway was constructed, the rock face below the southern wall of the town fell sheer to the banks of the Gyffin estuary, with only a steep path down from the Mill Gate to a quite narrow strip of land along the river bank, to boats and to the mill. The Gyffin estuary was quite wide in those days, and provided port facility for sea and river boats,

Inside Llangelynnin Old Church

mainly, no doubt, for the Welsh community, for the English town had moorings and later quays between the town and the Conwy itself, the town and castle walls being carried down to the water's edge for protection as can still be seen. There until well into the 19th century was a busy little port. There were many fishing trawlers where but two or three now moor, and little coastal trading vessels, of which some like Coast Lines would regularly schedule to circumnavigate the whole of Britain. Sailing boats and steamers mixed with the river boats from Trefriw, some even from Llanrwst, to exchange cargoes for the English and Irish ports, for Anglesey and the coasts of Wales, or to bring the imports in, timber, coal and fertiliser, groceries and wines.

If we go further, under the railway, we can, if we wish, enter Conwy; if we do that we shall leave those parts which have always been the Wales of the Celts and the Welsh, and enter into that which was for two sad centuries made by Edward I into a bastion of Norman and English occupation, which although taken over again by the Welsh by force of arms and by simple infiltration, has always remained more English than the Valley.

138. *Publius Ostorius Scapula, later Governor of Britain from A. D.47 until his death in A.D.52.*

139. *Reference 'Agricola' by W.S. Hanson and other modern works some of which are referred to in 'Bibliography'.*

140. *Writers of the middle-ages confused Elen the daughter of Eudaf with Elen reputed daughter of Coel of Colchester (see page 250) who married Constantius (later — 305 to 306 — Emperor Constantius) and who was the mother of the first Christian Emperor, Constantine — 306 to 337. From that the confusion has persisted, but the notion is quite wrong.*

141. *It is now thought that Vortigern may have taken over and adapted as his head quarter, the former Roman town of Wroxeter, which had been more or less abandoned about 100 years earlier.*

142. *Cunedda (later Kenneth) also meant leader, so Cunedda Wledig was a leader among leaders, e.g. a generalissimo.*

143. *One of the earlier sources of Historia Britonumn, (dated about 800 recognised differences in generations in those days of from 25 to 37.5 years and the likely relationship between Marchudd and Ednyfed Fychan shows the higher of those figures, while the average between Coel (contemporary of Macsen Wledig and Marchudd) is of that order.*

144. *Einion the Harsh.*

145. *The Irish leader was Serigi, but whether the Irish were settlers who rebelled, or invaders, is uncertain.*

146. *Vortigern was the King Wyrtgeorn of the Anglo Saxon Chronicles.*

147. *That was Cadwallon ap Cadfan, six generations after Cadwallon Lawhir. The king of Northumbria was Edwin, who had married Ethelburh, daughter of Ethelbert, king of Kent, and sister of Eabald of East Anglia. Ethelbert and his family had been converted to Christianity by St Augustine in 628, under Ethelburh's influence, Edwin was baptised at York, but in spite of what historians say about him, it is unlikely that he did more than pay lip-service to Christianity, or that his followers were converted, because when he was killed, his wife, Ethelburh, had to flee from the pagan north with her children and the Bishop Paulinus, to the safety of Rochester.*

Cadwallon was killed near Hexham while out on a foraging expedition on the return journey, his small troop being set upon by Oswald of Bernicia. Cadwallon's army then returned to Gwynedd, and Oswald assumed the kingship of Northumbria. He was a Christian who sought to spread Christianity by the sword in eastern England. In 643 he fell in battle against Penda, king of Mercia, and his brother Oswy, becoming king of Northumbria, proved to be more oppressive than Oswald. Hence in 654 Cadafael of Gwynedd set off with Penda of Mercia, and destroyed the power of Northumbria for ever, but Penda was killed in the process.

148. *In England, none but the greatest Marcher Lords could have granted such a charter, and then only subject to the king's ratification.*

149. *Literally uwch-Conwy means higher Conwy and is-Conwy means lower Conwy, but the sense in which the terms were used were much the same as the Scottish Highlands and Lowlands, the mountainous west, and the flatter east, now Gwynedd and Clwyd in broad terms.*

150. *Unfortunately in the recent past planning restrictions against re-occupation have led to the dereliction and later demolition of several of the most interesting.*

151. *The character of the Normans must have been very mixed. On the one hand they were capable of such acts of crude ferocity as the destruction of the Abbey, and as the treatment of Dafydd. On the other they created great beauty in the churches and cathedrals, even such castles as Conwy. Even Llywelyn Fawr could fight them one year, and marry himself and his children into their families the next.*

152. *Many a skirmishing force and army advanced from the England of the Dark Ages, from Powys, and later from the lands of the Marcher Lords, as far as the Conwy River, and no doubt many a minor battle took place on the banks of one side or the other of the river throughout the ages from the days of the Mabinogion to those of the later Normans.*

153. *The legendary submerged lands to the north were said to have belonged to Helig ap Glanawg, and the inundation is therefore dated at sixth century. But as said before, the lands must have been submerged before Paulinus came. Presumably, therefore, there must have been two men of the same name, six or seven centuries apart — not unusual.*

154. *Application for Faculty to build new church.*

155. *Gyffin Church was perpetual curacy.*

Farewell

Ten days have been spent in exploring a valley so small that it is not marked on many a map of Britain, which can be traversed from corner to corner in less than half a day in a car, or from end to end in less than five minutes in one of the jet aircraft which use it for training — but it is a valley whose importance in history has been immense through many millennia.

It was the geographical centre of the kingdom of Gwynedd, which had been Christian for about 250 years before Augustine came to England in the year 597. Half a century before that visit, Maelgwn Gwynedd had been sheltering in one of its churches when he caught the Fad Felen — a church which stood on a site where a church still stands, and his son, Rhun ap Maelgwn, was living at Caerhun in a house or a fort which the Romans had built 450 years before.

The roads through the valley were old when the Romans came, and even the Celts who built some of them half a millennium earlier still were using only routes which the Iberians had followed after the stone-age men. The Celts developed roads, in some cases with surfaces of wood, to speed their wagons and chariots of peace and war, and they constructed buildings of size and magnificence, though not, it seems, the enduring stone temples and public buildings for which the Roman Empire was famed.

It is increasingly evident that the legions of Rome found here an area which was civilised and rich in the history of six or more centuries of Celtic settlement, and millennia of previous history, civilisation and trading with the nations of the Celtic Seas and the far-off Mediterranean, culminating in the era of the Iberians.

Throughout our journey we have been finding that by the time the Romans left, long after the last men of the legions had been withdrawn from this part of the British Isles, the people of north-west Wales had developed a high stage of civilisation, like that of the Brythonic Celts of Strathclyde (the Scots lived in Ireland!), well in advance of most of western and northern Europe, and for a number of reasons this was to continue to be the case for many centuries. This fact is obscured and often doubted because neither the Romans nor the Celts erected great buildings of enduring stone which we have found.

239

It has been customary for history books to give the impression that the Britain to which Julius Caesar came was a land of backward barbarians, mainly, no doubt, because Caesar said so. But that was not the case. The towns like London had, it seems, buildings that were several storeys high, but finely built of wood. The roads were good. The reason why he did not stay to conquer and settle was that the forces against him were better armed, with war chariots that decimated his troops, good armour and other engines of war. Once he got away from the coast, he found that when they wanted to move stores and equipment, they had carts that were more manoeuvreable than his. Had he tried to stay, he would no doubt have been cut off without supplies, as might Suetonius Paulinus had circumstances not made him retreat from Anglesey in the following century. Caesar was glad to get out alive. When the Celts of southern England offered to pay him to go, he was only too thankful to accept, and it was to be a hundred years before any Romans were to try again, and that was only when they were invited by some of the factions fighting for power on the death of Cunobel in A.D.43.[156]

The Emperor Claudius was glad to accept the invitation, and sent a large force to Britain, but even with the co-operation of many of the tribes of the south and east, it was to be eighteen years before Paulinus came with the XIVth and the XXth Legions to the Conwy Valley, Aber and Anglesey, and he stayed but weeks. It was another seventeen years before the XXth Legion came in the times of Agricola.

Who and what were the people Paulinus found? Like those of southern, eastern and central England, they were Celtic. But those of south east, central and eastern England were of Belgic origin, and by travel, trade and intermarrying, they kept the Belgic, or Goedel, characteristics, customs and cultures. Those who were in Roman times in Strathclyde, Wales, Cornwall and Brittany, had originated in northern Europe, and were culturally, technically and militarily more advanced, but also more settled, pastoral people, generally known now as Brythonic Celts.

Modern historians and researchers tell us that these Celts loved music, fine clothes, good living, debate and oratory, and they believed in life after death. They were educated and wrote in Greek, though they did not keep their records in writing, unless either they were deliberately destroyed at a later date (maybe by Edward I) or the material on which they wrote did not survive. The Romans must have written much while they were here, yet only a few of their records and letters on wafer-thin wood have so far been found.

The Druids who have been so maligned were not at all as history books would have us believe. It has now been found that what Tacitus wrote of

Druids was of those in Germany and Belgium among the Goedels, and even of them he had no direct or personal knowledge. Research has proved that his words, his descriptions of them, were copied directly from the works of his friend, the writer Gaius Plinius, and that he in turn had copied from Greek works of the time of Julius Caesar. But those Greeks were far removed from the Goedel lands, and it seems that they admitted to writing based on none but hearsay, and even Julius Caesar admits to hearsay on the subject.

Where Tacitus based his writings on more direct information, reports from Suetonius Paulinus whom he had known, and from his father-in-law Agricola, who came to Britain with Paulinus as well as at a later time and again as Governor, all he could say was that before the battle at the Menai Strait they "uttered prayers and curses and flung their arms towards the sky". Was that a very dreadful act for people faced with an army of the worst barbarians in all of Europe, mercenary legionaries from Germany and the Rhine, who Tacitus said "threw alive Brythonic women and children, Druids and those who fought as soldiers, into the flames of great camp fires". All he could say of Anglesey itself was that it was "a source of strength to the rebels" (Agricola), and "heavily populated and a sanctuary for fugitives" (Annals). His reticence is most particularly notable because, like modern propagandists, he classed all who opposed the oppressive Roman armies as barbaric rebels.

The Druids, the modern writers tell us, were men of education who had a status among the Celts which largely was judiciary; as such they were required to attend at executions, of which the Celts had neither more nor less than any other people. There is no evidence that they indulged in any human sacrifice, and they most certainly did not take part in public slaughters of the kind so popular with the Romans, so often in their arenas as public "games". They sought to settle disputes by arbitration, and if they stood between opposing forces or contestant individuals, no fighting could take place. Maybe that was what they sought to do at the Menai Strait.

This picture of these Celts that now builds up, so different from that portrayed before, accounts for much in the subsequent history of the truly Brythonic areas, the fact that they were quiet, free from recorded disturbances in the Roman era, and that they developed so fast in the centuries that followed, in Christianity and in the arts.

These pre-Roman Celts were very wealthy with their mining, pearls and cloth, their craftsmanship in bronze and silver, gold and wood. Only such wealth would make the Roman Senate risk two legions and a navy on a mountain expedition beyond the fringes of the Empire, if they in fact gave the instructions for the campaign: if Paulinus came, as Tacitus said, to gather glory equal to that of Corbulo, who had reconquered Armenia, then he must have considered them a worthy and a wealthy foe.[157]

The Romans who came at later time, the reformed XXth Legion sent by Agricola, were different from those who came with Paulinus. They were a force invited, but also they were of Iberian and Celtic stock, recruited as volunteers from Spain and western Gaul, almost kinsmen of the Celts of Cornwall, Wales and Strathclyde, with whom their forebears had traded for many a century. It is no wonder that here, unlike so many other places to which the arm of Rome extended, there was no great upheaval when the Empire came. The great mining industry went on much as before, albeit with Roman supervision for a time at least. The pearl beds of the Conwy still produced their pearls, and no doubt fine jewellery was worked as it had been before. The tartan cloth still went to the markets of Rome and Athens, or made the elegant trews and plaids of the Celtic men, while fine spun wool and imported cloth still bedecked the elegant women.

The Romans mixed with the Celts and the Iberians, who shared with them the administration and defence, so that when the legions left no great change arose. Macsen Wledig, Emperor of Rome, married Elen of Arfon, and their progeny were here. Cunedda Wledig, the last of the rulers of Gwynedd appointed by Rome, was no Roman, but a Celt himself, though he hailed from Strathclyde, and he founded the dynasty that was to rule the north of Wales until the Normans came, and at times was to threaten the crowned heads of England. That dynasty carried the administrative systems and the Christian culture of latter-day Rome into the second half of the first millennium AD The Latin language and the Celtic mixed, to come to be the Welsh of later times. So grew the culture which Wales itself developed on through the times of the Normans. The servants and the princes of that dynasty were destined to produce the future kings and queens of a united Britain. From that continuity came the great importance of Gwynedd, the land of which this valley has always been the heart.

For those who may ask still what is the importance of all these matters to Britain as a whole, or to the world, the answer must lie in questions. We must ponder what may have been the influence in the world north of the Mediterranean of the early axe-heads, arrows and tools of Graig Lwyd. Equally we may wonder how the history of the Roman Empire would have been changed if the Ordovices had not allowed Suetonius Paulinus to withdraw his forces from the trap into which they had hastily marched; no doubt the Iceni would have driven the Romans out of the south. How would the history of the Empire have differed if Macsen Wledig had not advanced with the armies of Gwynedd to be declared Emperor, to go on to capture Rome, deposing and killing the upstart Gratianus? How was history affected by the partial colonisation of Brittany by Cynan and his men, setting up a kinship which was to culminate in the protection and help given to Henry Tudur nearly 1,100 years later? But in an earlier time, it was to be the Celts of Brittany and the descendants of the Cymri[158] of neighbouring northern Gaul who were to defy the power of France and Europe, as the Welsh did that of England, for nearly a thousand years.

If Christian Gwynedd had fallen beneath the yoke of pagan Northumbria, whose might would have been unleashed against the whole of Britain, would the history of Britain or the world have been the same?

But perhaps the most important of all is the question of how the history of the world would have developed if Henry Tudur, direct descendant of Ednyfed Fychan of this valley, of Llywelyn Fawr, and of Coel in the times of Macsen Wledig, had not destroyed the last relics of Norman rule in 1485, and opened up the expansive era of Tudor Britain — the development of art, of music, of exploration, and all that came with a cultured court.

It would be unwise to ignore the contributions to history of such men as William Salesbury, William Morgan, the printer John Jones Pyll, the clockmaker Watkin Owen, and even John Williams the Queen's Goldsmith, or the Doctor Owen Roberts of Eglwys-bach.

As we have passed through the villages of today, we have passed through the towns of the past, where the miner rubbed shoulders with the lord, the shepherd with the master of industry, the banker with the pauper, just as today their modern counterparts pass by. It was thus with the Georgians, with the Tudors, with those of the times of the Princes, and of the Romans and the Celts before them. In all those times have the gentry escorted their ladies in all their finery along the banks of the Conwy at Trefriw, at Llanrwst and at Betws-y-coed. Countless generations of village lads have fished from its banks, for salmon, for sparling, for trout, or just for tiddlers.

Its river, of no great length or volume, has led to the construction of five of the world's masterpieces of bridge engineering of their ages, Pont Fawr, the Beaver and Waterloo Bridges, Telford's suspension bridge at Conwy, and Stephenson's tubular bridge, and opened in the mid-1990s, a tunnel of equal pioneering status. The castle at Conwy is recognised as one of the two finest examples of medieval military engineering in the western world. Its small dam at Eigiau changed dam construction thought. Even the Mulberry Harbour was built at the river's mouth, at Conwy Morfa.

Its beauty is famed throughout the world, and pictures in watercolour

243

or oils, crayon or pencil, and on bromide printing paper, by amateurs and professionals, the famous and the unknown, hang on many house and gallery walls.

And that is the way we seek to keep it, advancing with the needs of every age, but keeping its culture and its beauty, to be a place of peace and joy for all who come to visit. And maybe in the future we shall provide another Cadwallon, Llywelyn Fawr or Henry Tudur, or our geological formations will produce more masterpieces to vie with Telford's roads and bridges, Stephenson's bridge, and the tunnel that has now been constructed.

---

156. *Recommended for reading is "Caesar's Invasion of Britain", by Peter Beresford Ellis, Orbis Publications: "It shows that the Britons were not crude, woad-painted savages but members of a complex and cultured society. It tells of the campaign plans of Caesar and the preparations of the defenders of Britain. It reveals how a set conflict soon changed to a guerrilla war, and how each side countered new military methods introduced by the enemy. Finally it shows how, by a combination of British tactical sense and good luck, the Romans were forced to abandon their invasion and leave Britain in peace for another century" — quote from the wrapper to the book. It is not often understood that Caesar had the co-operation of Commius and the Atrebates of the Hampshire region, and that their combined forces fought only against the armies of Caswallon. They never came up against the other major tribes, nor the forces of mid, north or western Britain — it was Caswallon's forces alone that made Caesar glad to retreat with some appearance of dignity with a demand for tribute which the Britons never had any intention of paying, and Caesar had no means of collecting. There is the interesting question whether he did, as he reported, lose most of his fleet in a gale, or whether it was lost to a British "navy" — many hold the latter to be the case. Also recommended for reading are "The Celts", by T. G.E. Powell, Thames and Hutton, and also the "Oxford History of England", Volume 1, "Roman Britain", inter alia.*

157. *Recommended reading, "The Druids" by Nora K. Chadwick, "The Celts" by T.G.E. Powell, "The Blood of the British" by Catherine Hills, and "Roman Britain" by Peter Salway. For details see Bibliography.*

158. *Not to be confused with Cymraeg, derived from Cymru — Wales.*

Acknowledgements

I am indebted to the following for invaluable co-operation and assistance in many ways:

Mrs H. Barling of Llanbedr-y-cennin (Heather Craigmile)
Mr E. Bryan, Ll.B., Ro-wen
Myrddin ap Dafydd of Capel Garmon
Mr D. Lloyd Griffiths, Eglwys-bach
The late Bob Owen (Pernant) of Llanrwst
Mr Ifor Owen of Maenan
Mrs Nesta Jones, Llanrwst Library
Mr Hugh Pritchard, Llandudno Library
(Reference Section)
Mr and Mrs Dafydd Parri of Trefriw
Mrs Muriel Williams, Llanrwst Library
Members of the Staff of the National Library of Wales

Publisher's Note

This comprehansive study by Kenneth Mortimer Hart remains the classic work on the Conwy Valley. We have taken the opportunity to update the book where changes have occured and taken account of recent research and thinking. For this we are indebted to our editer Mr Eryl Orwain, who freely states that the book extended his knowledge of the valley and that it was a delight to read.

Perhaps this is the best recommendation we can give you, our readers. We have also included a few more illustrations.

Bibliography

This is truly a bibliography in the dictionary definition of the term — it is just "a list of books". They have helped me by extending, confirming or correcting information garnered from a multitude of sources, some long ago forgotten, and by supporting or adjusting theories amateurishly built up. I thank the authors and the publishers, and acknowledge my debt to them. The list is also one which I recommend for further study of the matters contained in this book. In many cases, of course, a small part only of the recommended book covers matters in any way related to this small part of the world.

W.S. Hanson, *Agricola and the Conquest of the North* (B.T. Batsford Ltd, London).

Ancient Monuments in Wales—A Guide of... (Her Majesty's Stationery Office).

Michael Fitzgerald, *Ancient Monuments in Wales* (Abercastle Publications).

Anne Savage, *The Anglo-Saxon Chronicles* (William Heinemann Ltd).

Archaeologica Cambrensis — The Journal of the Cambrian Archaeological Association.

Aspects of Welsh History

Atlas of Caernarfonshire (Gwynedd Rural Council).

Catherine Hills, *Blood of the British* (George Philip and Son Ltd.)

Bristol City Records (Published by the Bristol Record Society).

William Camden 1610. *Britannia, A Survey of the British Isles.*

Caesar's *"De Bello Gallico"* — *The Invasion of Britain.*

J.P. Hall. F.S.A.. *Caer Llugwy* (Taylor. Garnett Evans and Co.)

A Calendar of Deeds and Documents, Vols 1 & 2 (The National Library of Wales).

Richard Avent, *The Castles of the Princes of Wales* (Her Majesty's Stationery Office).

John Rhys, *Celtic Folklore* (Wildwood House Ltd).

Frank Delaney. *The Celts* (Hodder and Stoughton and Book Club Associates).

T.G.E. Powell. *The Celts* (Thames and Hudson).

Chambers Twentieth Century Dictionary.

Peter E. Baughan. *The Chester and Holyhead Railway Company* (David and Charles).

Iorwerth C. Peate, *Clock and Watchmakers in Wales.*

Gilbert Askew, *The Coinage of Roman Britain* (Seaby's Numismatic Publications).

A.J. Taylor. *Conwy Castle and Town Walls* (Her Majesty's Stationery Office).

"Country Quest" Magazine.

Martha Rofheart.   *"Cry God for Harry"* (Talmy. Franklin).

Customs House Registers.

"Cymru a'r Mor", Volumes 1 to 10 (Gwynedd Archives Service,

Gwasg Gee).

Department of Archaeology Publications (National Museum of Wales).

The Dictionary of Welsh Biography (The Honourable Society of Cymrodorion, London).

K.G. Bonser. *The Drovers* (Redwood Press and Country Book Club).

Nora K. Chadwick, *The Druids* (University of Wales Press).

Gerald Morgan, "*Y Dyn a Wnaeth Argraff*" (Gwasg Carreg Gwalch).

Christopher Hibbert, *The English, A Social History 1066-1945* (Guild Publishing).

Ian Nial, *The Forester.*

The National Trust, *The Gardens at Bodnant* (Country Life Ltd).

H. Meurig Evans and W.B. Thomas, "*Y Geiriadur Mawr*" (Llyfrau'r Dryw and Gwasg Aberystwyth).

Askew Roberts and Edward Woodall, *The Gossiping Guide to Wales* (Simpkin, Marshall, Hamilton, Kent and Co.)

David Stephenson, *The Governance of Gwynedd* (University of Wales Press).

Donald Shaw, *Gwydir Forest in Snowdonia, A History* (Her Majesty's Stationery Office).

Cecelia Holland, *Hammer for Princes* (Hodder and Stoughton and Book Club)

Harmsworth's Encyclopedia (The Amalgamated Press Ltd and Thomas Nelson and Sons).

W. Bezant-Lowe, *The Heart of Northern Wales* (W.E. Owen, Caxton Press, Llanfairfechan).

A.G. Beadley, *Highways and Byways in North Wales* (MacMillan and Co. Ltd).

Dorothy Silvester, *A History of Gwynedd* (Phillimore).

S.I. Wicklen, *A History of Printers and Printing in Llanrwst* (Cader Idris Books, Conwy).

John Peddig, *Invasion — The Roman Conquest of Britain* (Guild Publishing).

Irish Ecclesiastical Records (Journal) 1920s and 1930s.

William Plomer, *Kilvert's Diary* (Penguin Books).

Piero Ventura, *The Kingfisher History of Everyday Life* (Guild Publishing).

General Editor — Antonia Fraser, *The Kings and Queens of England* (George Weidenfeld and Nicolson and Book Club Associates).

Hamlyn Publishing. *The Larouse Dictionary of Painters (Hamlyn Publishing* Group Ltd and Book Club Associates).

Llanrwst Town Guide.

Gwyn Jones and Thomas Jones. *The Mabinogion* (Dent, Everyman's Library).

The Making of the Tudor Dynasty

The Map of Roman Britain and other Maps of the Ordnance Survey Dept (Ordnance Survey Dept).

W. Humphries Jones, *My Yesteryears — From Farm to Pharmacy.*

Brothero, *Nelson's School History* (Nelson and Sons Ltd).

M.J.B. Baddeley, *North Wales, Vol. 1* (Ward Lock and Co.)

Elizabeth Beazeley and Lionel Butt. *North Wales — A Shell Guide* (Faber and

Faber Ltd).

Harold Hughes and Hubert L. North, *The Old Churches of Snowdonia* (Charter Press and Snowdonia National Park Society).

Harold Hughes and Herbert L. North, *Old Cottages of Snowdonia* (Gee and Son, Denbigh and Snowdonia National Park Society).

Our Own Country (Cassell and Company).

Meic Stephens, *The Oxford Companion to the Literature of Wales* (Oxford University Press).

The Oxford History of England (The Clarendon Press).

The Penguin Dictionary of Art and Artists (Penguin Books).

Elizabeth Hallam, *The Plantagenet Chronicles* (Guild Publishing).

"Quest" Magazine.

The Reports of the Royal Commission on Ancient Monuments (H.M.S.O.)

Ieuan Gwynedd Jones, *The Religious Census of 1851* (University of Wales Press).

P.W. Hammond and Anne E. Sutton, *Richard III* (Guild Publishing).

Wilson MacArthur, *The River Conway* (Cassell and Company Ltd).

Richard Colyer, *Roads and Trackways of Wales* (Moorland Publishing).

David R. Sear, *Roman Coins* (Seaby's Numismatic Publications).

G.A. Humphries, *The Roman Military Station, Conovium* (W.E. Owen, Caxton Press, Llanfairfechan).

John Percival, *The Roman Villa* (B.Y. Batsford Ltd).

Norman Tucker, *Saint Grwst's Church* (R.E. Jones Bros, Conwy).

R.M. Williams *Seiri Cerdd, Nanconwy* (Gwasg Carreg Gwalch).

Wynford Vaughan Thomas and Alun Llywelyn, *The Shell Guide to Wales* (Michael Joseph Ltd).

Snowdonia National Park (Her Majesty's Stationery Office).

Ralph Maddern, *Snowdonia, Ancient Trackways. Roman Roads and Packhorse Trails* (Vario Press Ltd).

Blair Worden, *Stuart England* (Guild Publishing).

"Annals" and *"Agricola"*, *Tacitus (Graeus Julius Tacitus).*

The Topographical Dictionary of the Dominion of Wales 1811.

Robin Richards, *Two Bridges over Menai* (Cyhoeddiadau Ap Dafydd Publications).

Don Hinson, *Walks in the Snowdonia Mountains* (Gwasg Carreg Gwalch).

Thomas Roscoe, *Wanderings in Wales.*

G.H. Baillie, *Watchmakers and Clockmakers of the World* Vol. 1 (N.A.G. Press Ltd).

Brian Loomes, *Watchmakers and Clockmakers of the World* Vol. 2 (N.A.G. Press Ltd).

Welch Tours 1797.

George Borrow, *Wild Wales* (Collins).

Chris Aspen, *The Woollen Industry* (Shire Publications).

J.A. Hammerton, *Wonderful Britain* (Educational Book Co. Ltd).

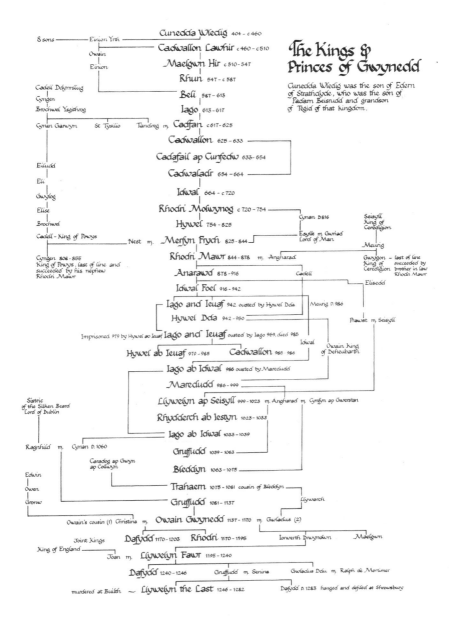

The Kings & Princes of Gwynedd

Cunedda Wledig was the son of Edern of Strathclyde, who was the son of Padarn Beisrudd and grandson of Tegid of that kingdom.

Cunedda Wledig 404 - c 460
Cadwallon Lawhir c460 - c510
Maelgwn Hir c 510 - 547
Rhun 547 - c 587
Beli 587 - 613
Iago 613 - 617
Cadfan c617 - 625
Cadwallon 625 - 633
Cadafail ap Cunfedw 633 - 654
Cadwaladr 654 - 664
Idwal 664 - c 720
Rhodri Molwynog c 720 - 754
Hywel 754 - 825
Merfyn Frych 825 - 844
Rhodri Mawr 844 - 878 m. Angharad
Anarawd 878 - 916
Idwal Foel 916 - 942
Iago and Ieuaf 942 ousted by Hywel Dda
Hywel Dda 942 - 950
Iago and Ieuaf ousted by Iago 969, died 985
Hywel ab Ieuaf 979 - 985   Cadwallon 985 - 986
Iago ab Idwal 986 ousted by Maredudd
Maredudd 986 - 999
Llywelyn ap Seisyll 999 - 1023 m. Angharad m. Cynfyn ap Gwerstan
Rhydderch ab Iestyn 1023 - 1033
Iago ab Idwal 1033 - 1039
Gruffudd 1039 - 1063
Bleddyn 1063 - 1075
Trahaern 1075 - 1081 cousin of Bleddyn
Gruffudd 1081 - 1137
Owain Gwynedd 1137 - 1170 m. Gwladus (2)
Dafydd 1170 - 1203   Rhodri 1170 - 1195
Llywelyn Fawr 1195 - 1240
Dafydd 1240 - 1246
Llywelyn the Last 1246 - 1282

249

The Lord Rhys and Nest Family Tree

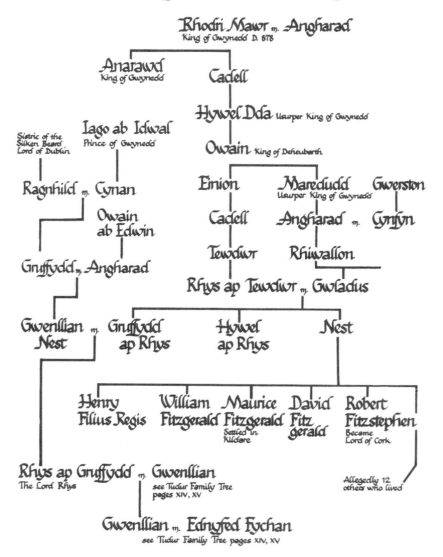

Rhodri Mawr m. Angharad
King of Gwynedd D. 878

Anarawd
King of Gwynedd

Cadell

Hywel Dda Usurper King of Gwynedd

Owain King of Deheubarth

Sistric of the Silken Beard Lord of Dublin

Iago ab Idwal Prince of Gwynedd

Einion   Maredudd   Gwerston
Usurper King of Gwynedd

Ragnhild m. Cynan

Owain ab Edwin

Cadell   Angharad m. Cynfyn

Tewdwr   Rhiwallon

Gruffydd m. Angharad

Rhys ap Tewdwr m. Gwladus

Gwenllian m. Gruffydd   Hywel   Nest
Nest   ap Rhys   ap Rhys

Henry   William   Maurice   David   Robert
Filius Regis   Fitzgerald   Fitzgerald   Fitz   Fitzstephen
                Settled in   gerald   Became
                Kildare   Lord of Cork.

Rhys ap Gruffydd m. Gwenllian
The Lord Rhys   see Tudur Family Tree
                pages XIV, XV

Allegedly 12 others who lived

Gwenllian m. Ednyfed Fychan
see Tudur Family Tree pages XIV, XV

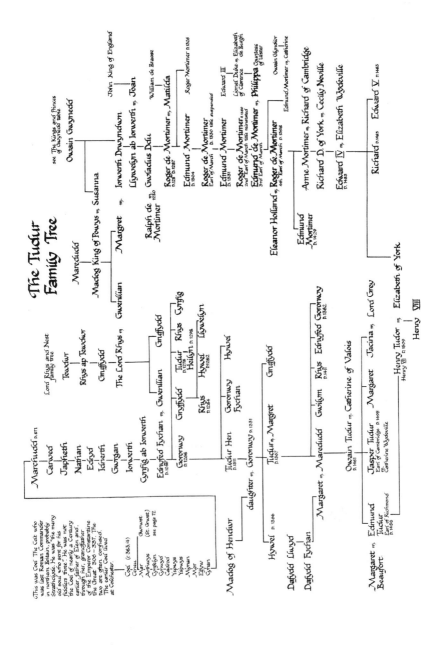

The Tudur Family Tree

From the Pindaric Ode, The Bard, by Thomas Gray

(mentioned in Author's Note - page 7)

Weave the warp and weave the woof,
The winding sheet of Edward's race:
Give ample room and verge enough
The characters of hell to trace
Mark the year, and mark the night
When Severn shall re-echo with affright,
The shrieks of death thro' Berkley's roof that ring.
Shrieks of an agonising king!

The story is that after having the Princess Llywelyn and Dafydd murdered, Edward I burnt all Welsh books that he could lay hands on. Rumour was rife at the time that he also slaughtered the Welsh poets, and it was carried down by the bards to the times of Thomas Carte, who included it in his History of England, quoting as one of his many sources of information John Parry, the Blind Harpist. Such a story, if true, would account for the paucity of written records in Wales before the Middle Ages, even perhaps those of Roman or pre-Roman times.

The prophecy was that a British (Welsh) Prince would rise up, kill the unsurper king of England, and ascend the English throne, and therby avenge the Norman, and Edward's, barbarity.

Index